ABOUT

Patrick Bond, a political eco
University of KwaZulu-Natal
Durban where he directs the Ci
ccs). He is also visiting professor at York Univ.... ,   f
Political Science in Toronto and Gyeongsang National University
Institute of Social Sciences in South Korea. He previously taught at the
University of the Witwatersrand Graduate School of Public and
Development Management, Yokohama National University Depart-
ment of Economics and the Johns Hopkins University School of Public
Health.

Bond's other recent books include *Talk Left, Walk Right: South
Africa's Frustrated Global Reforms* (published by Africa World Press
and University of KwaZulu-Natal Press, 2006); *Trouble in the Air:
Global Warming and the Privatised Atmosphere* (edited with Rehana
Dada, published by the CCS and the Transnational Institute, 2005);
Elite Transition: From Apartheid to Neoliberalism in South Africa
(University of KwaZulu-Natal Press, 2005); *Fanon's Warning: A Civil
Society Reader on the New Partnership for Africa's Development*
(Africa World Press and CCS, 2005); and *Against Global Apartheid:
South Africa Meets the World Bank, IMF and International Finance*
(Zed Books and University of Cape Town Press, 2003). He was born in
Belfast, Northern Ireland in 1961.

The Open Society Initiative for Southern Africa, who supported the publication of this book, is helping to build a region where economic growth primarily serves human development needs from food security to access to education and healthcare. OSISA's deliberate emphasis is on the importance of social and economic rights, in addition to civil and political liberties. OSISA works in nine Southern African Development Community countries: Angola, Mozambique, Botswana, Lesotho, Namibia, Swaziland, Zimbabwe, Zambia and Malawi.

OSISA supports the Publish What You Pay coalition of over 280 NGOs worldwide. This campaign aims to help citizens of resource-rich developing countries hold their governments accountable for the management of revenues from the oil, gas and mining industries. When properly managed these revenues should serve as a basis for poverty reduction, economic growth and development rather than exacerbating corruption, conflict and social divisiveness.

In addition, OSISA believes that the free flow of information is essential for the development of an open society. OSISA works to overcome the 'digital divide' between the countries of the industrialized West and the developing world, and to further Africa's participation in the information society. The Open Society Justice Initiative supports efforts not only to adopt freedom of information laws but also to implement and use disclosure tools once they are available. OSISA is pleased to support Zed Books in the wider distribution of *Looting Africa* throughout Africa, as part of this mission to further the dissemination of knowledge and ideas.

OSISA also celebrates the work of African scholars committed to economic justice. Guy Mhone (1943–2005) enjoyed a distinguished career as a development economist, both in North America and in Africa. He also worked as chief director for research at the Department of Labour in the first post-apartheid government in South Africa. He will be remembered for his books, including *The Political Economy of a Dual Labour Market in Africa* (1982) and *The Informal Sector in Southern Africa* (1997), in which he developed his theory of Africa's dysfunctional 'enclave' economies. His quiet dignity, great courage and powerful intellect are greatly missed by all those who work for a more equitable Africa.

José Negrão (1956–2005), a Mozambican, worked as a development economist and economic historian for nearly three decades in Africa and in Europe. He helped to found and coordinate the Land Campaign and the Poverty Observatory, which in 2004 published the first *Mozambique Annual Poverty Report*. He served on OSISA's board until his untimely death.

PATRICK BOND

Looting
Africa

THE ECONOMICS OF EXPLOITATION

University of KwaZulu-Natal Press
PIETERMARITZBURG

Zed Books
LONDON AND NEW YORK

Looting Africa: The Economics of Exploitation was first published in 2006.

Published in South Africa, Lesotho, Swaziland, Botswana, Namibia and
Zimbabwe by University of KwaZulu-Natal Press, Private Bag X01,
Scottsville 3209, South Africa
www.unpress.co.za

Published in the rest of the world by Zed Books Ltd, 7 Cynthia Street, London N1
9JF, UK, and Room 400, 175 Fifth Avenue, New York, NY 10010, USA
www.zedbooks.co.uk

Cover designed by Andrew Corbett
Set in 9/12.5 pt Georgia by Long House, Cumbria, UK
Printed and bound in the United Kingdom by Biddles Ltd, King's Lynn

Distributed in the USA exclusively by Palgrave Macmillan, a division of
St Martin's Press, LLC, 175 Fifth Avenue, New York, NY 10010.

A catalogue record for this book
is available from the British Library

US Cataloging-in-Publication Data
is available from the Library of Congress

ISBN 1 84277 812 9 hb (Zed Books)
ISBN 978 1 84277 812 8 hb (Zed Books)
ISBN 1 84277 811 0 pb (Zed Books)
ISBN 978 1 84277 811 1 pb (Zed Books)
ISBN 1 86914 095 8 pb (University of KwaZulu-Natal Press)

Contents

Figures and Tables

FIGURES

TABLES

Preface and Acknowledgements

What is ordinarily conveyed by the word 'looting'? On 30 August 2005 we received a vivid answer at yahoo.com, one that will serve as a metaphor for the 'common-sense' inversion of the West's economic relationship with Africa. Two photographs were momentarily on display at yahoo.com's news site, in the immediate aftermath of Hurricane Katrina. In one, Agence France-Press had snapped two New Orleans residents triumphantly wading 'through chest-deep water after finding bread and soda from a local grocery store', as the caption explained. In the other, Associated Press circulated a picture of a man walking 'through chest-deep flood water after looting a grocery store'.

The couple 'finding' were white, the man 'looting' was black.[1]

Social critic Slavoj Žižek considered stereotypes of this sort in discussing what he termed 'the subject supposed to loot and rape' in New Orleans:

> We all remember the reports on the disintegration of public order, the explosion of black violence, rape and looting. However, later inquiries demonstrated that, in the large majority of cases, these alleged orgies of violence *did not occur*: non-verified rumors were simply reported as facts by the media. For example, on September 3, the Superintendent of the New Orleans Police Department told the *New York Times* about conditions at the Convention Center: 'The tourists are walking around there, and as soon as these individuals see them, they're being preyed upon. They are beating, they are raping them in the streets.' In an interview just weeks later, he conceded that some of his most shocking statements turned out to be untrue: 'We have no official reports to document any murder. Not one official report of rape or sexual assault.'[2]

When white tourists formerly lodged at New Orleans hotels sought to escape the city, they were hustled to the front of emergency bus queues, ahead of the mainly African-American, low-income ghetto residents stuck at the wretched Convention Centre. Some such residents had indeed raided shops for water, milk and perishables, primarily as a survival mechanism, to the opprobrium of Fox News anchors and like-minded neoconservative commentators.

So who, in reality, benefited from the catastrophe? Another critical analyst, Mike Davis, observed how the Bush regime rapidly

> swung open the doors of New Orleans to corporate looters such as Halliburton, the Shaw Group and Blackwater Security, already fat from the spoils of the Tigris, [which] contrasted obscenely with the Federal Emergency Management Agency's deadly procrastination over sending water, food and buses to the multitudes trapped in the stinking hell of the Louisiana Superdome.[3]

Hence when it comes to explaining the world's growing social divides, revelations from the main port city of the world's richest country are telling. They boil down to the idea of 'looting': *not* as the logical lifestyle of imperialism's black victims, but instead as the basis for *capital accumulation* under conditions of extreme inequality.

The great African political economist Samir Amin speaks of a US strategy for Third World societies that 'aims only at looting their resources'.[4] And Princeton economist Paul Krugman, in a *New York Times* column, reminds us that 'A while back, George Akerlof, the Nobel laureate in economics, described what's happening to public policy as "a form of looting".... The Bush administration and the Republican leadership in Congress are leading the looting party.'[5]

That party – and subsequent interimperial rivalries – began many years earlier. According to Karl Marx,

> The discovery of gold and silver in America, the extirpation, enslavement and entombment in mines of the aboriginal population, the turning of Africa into a commercial warren for the hunting of black skins signalled the rosy dawn of the era of capitalist production. These idyllic proceedings are the chief momenta of primitive accumulation. On their heels treads the commercial war of the European nations, with the globe for a theatre.[6]

By 1913, Rosa Luxemburg had developed a fully fledged theory of imperialism from these insights:

Force, fraud, oppression, looting are openly displayed without any attempt at concealment, and it requires an effort to discover within this tangle of political violence and contests of power the stern laws of the economic process. Bourgeois liberal theory takes into account only ... 'the realm of peaceful competition', the marvels of technology and pure commodity exchange; it separates it strictly from the other aspect: the realm of capital's blustering violence which is regarded as more or less incidental to foreign policy and quite independent of the economic sphere of capital.

In reality, political power is nothing but a vehicle for the economic process. The conditions for the reproduction of capital provide the organic link between these two aspects of the accumulation of capital. The historical career of capitalism can only be appreciated by taking them together. 'Sweating blood and filth with every pore from head to toe' characterizes not only the birth of capital but also its progress in the world at every step, and thus capitalism prepares its own downfall under ever more violent contortions and convulsions ....

Militarism fulfils a quite definite function in the history of capital, accompanying as it does every historical phase of accumulation. It plays a decisive part in the first stages of European capitalism, in the period of the so-called 'primitive accumulation', as a means of conquering the New World and the spice-producing countries of India. Later, it is employed to subject the modern colonies, to destroy the social organizations of primitive societies so that their means of production may be appropriated, forcibly to introduce commodity trade in countries where the social structure had been unfavourable to it, and to turn the natives into a proletariat by compelling them to work for wages in the colonies. It is responsible for the creation and expansion of spheres of interest for European capital in non-European regions, for extorting railway concessions in backward countries, and for enforcing the claims of European capital as international lender. Finally, militarism is a weapon in the competitive struggle between capitalist countries for areas of non-capitalist civilization.[7]

The wealth of capitalism – based in no small measure upon looting Africa – is regularly revealed by critical scholars, among whom Walter Rodney looms large for his 1972 book *How Europe Underdeveloped Africa*, followed by Paul Zeleza's formidable *A Modern Economic History of Africa*, first published by the African research institution CODESRIA in 1993. Notwithstanding such efforts, however, thanks to politicians and bureaucrats in Washington and London, IMF and World Bank mandarins, Geneva trade hucksters, pliant NGOs, banal celebrities and the mass media, the legacy and ongoing exploitation of Africa have been ensnared in ideological confusion.

To illustrate, consider all the attention Africa received during 2005, through efforts to 'make poverty history', to provide relief from crushing debt loads, to double aid and to establish a 'development round' of trade. At best, partial critiques of imperial power emerged amidst the cacophony of all-white rock concerts and political grandstanding. At worst, polite public discourse tactfully avoided capital's blustering violence, from Nigeria's oil-soaked Delta to north-eastern Congo's gold mines, from diamond finds in Botswana to the killing fields of Sudan. Most of the London charity NGO strategies ensured that core issue areas – debt, aid, trade and investment – would be addressed in only the most superficial ways.

Perhaps this was not surprising. Mass media images of Africans themselves were nearly uniformly negative during the recent period, which plays conveniently into the hands of elites. As Giles Mohan and Tunde Zack-Williams observed, 'Africa's underdevelopment has for long been blamed on local culture and the lack of "proper" values. Such discourses designed to let imperialism off the hook have reared their ugly head again in various guises.'[8] It was from West Africa that the neoconservative US writer Robert Kaplan described a future defined in terms of 'disease, overpopulation, unprovoked crime, scarcity of resources, refugee migrations, the increasing erosion of nation-states and international borders, and the empowerment of private armies, security firms, and international drug cartels'.[9] From such a frightened worldview, it is not a distant leap for Tony Blair's adviser Robert Cooper to declare that 'when dealing with more old-fashioned kinds of states ... we need to revert to rougher methods of an earlier age: force, pre-emptive attack, deception, whatever is necessary to deal with those who still live in the nineteenth-century world of "every state for itself"', hence generating 'a new kind of imperialism ... to bring order and organization'.[10] Of such sentiments, Tim Jacoby concludes: 'In order to obscure Western complicity in, or in some cases responsibility for, the defects of states in the South, policy makers have been influenced by, and contributed to, a rise to prominence of cultural explanations for social phenomena.'[11]

As the 'dark continent', Africa has typically been painted with broad-brush strokes, as a place of heathen and uncivilized people, as savage and superstitious, as tribalistic and nepotistic. As David Wiley has shown, Western media coverage is crisis-driven, based upon parachute journalism, amplified by an entertainment industry which 'perpetuates negative images of helpless primitives, happy-go-lucky buffoons, evil pagans. The media glorify colonialism/European intervention. Currently, Africa is represented as a place of endemic violence and brutal but ignorant dictators.' Add to this the 'animalization of Africa via a legion of nature shows that present Africa as being devoid of humans', enhanced by an 'advertising industry that has built and exploited (and thereby perpetuated) simplistic stereotypes of Africa'.[12] Thus it was disgusting but logical, perhaps, that African people were settled into a theme village at an Austrian zoo in June 2005, their huts placed next to monkey cages in scenes reminiscent of nineteenth-century exhibitions. In an explanatory letter, zoo director Barbara Jantschke denied that this was 'a mistake' because 'I think the Augsburg zoo is exactly the right place to communicate an atmosphere of the exotic.'[13]

In this context, the difficulty of advancing *structural* critique to link political and economic problems, and race, class and gender, became clearer to me when, in the immediate wake of the Gleneagles G8 hoopla in July 2005, a friend emailed me a column from that day's *International Herald Tribune* authored by Daniel Altman, the paper's 'global economics correspondent'. Altman, who did not identify himself or offer conversation, was positioned next to me on a JFK–Heathrow redeye flight and made some notes while glancing surreptitiously at my computer screen. His column began as follows:

> Not long ago, Patrick Bond, an author and professor at the University of KwaZulu-Natal in South Africa, was sitting on an airplane, working on a presentation he was soon to make at Oxford. For one particular slide, he spent several minutes rearranging pictures of American troops' flag-draped caskets aboard a cargo plane and of the World Bank president, Paul Wolfowitz, dressed as an astronaut. Never mind that this was a presentation about water commodification in South Africa – to opponents of 'neoliberalism' like Bond, the supposed evils of free markets and expansionist foreign policy are one and the same.[14]

I confess: what I'd groggily asked at the next day's seminar was whether the World Bank's drive to commodify everything under the sun, including water and even the air,[15] would be modified or strengthened by Wolfowitz's unilateralist, petro-militarist record and orientation. The first slide of those three posed a couple of queries: 'Will the Wolfowitz World Bank revert to neoliberalism? What is his long-term agenda?'

My answer – which no one challenged – was that although the looting of Iraq explicitly combined neoliberalism (Paul Bremer's far-reaching privatization agenda) with military occupation, this strategic combination would be difficult to maintain in applications elsewhere. First, growing economic contradictions associated with liberalized trade, investment and especially financial markets appear insurmountable. Second, the coffins demonstrated that US militarism applied to Iraq – and maybe Syria, Iran, North Korea and Venezuela, for example – may also be untenable. Yet Wolfowitz would, I predicted, continue attempting to fuse the economic and territorial imperatives of imperialism. An uncomprehending Altman complained: 'To its enemies, neoliberalism apparently refers to an American-born urge to create unrestrained markets for everything, everywhere, even if it means overthrowing a government.' *Precisely*. Sometimes the elites cannot – or will not – see beyond their noses. In contrast, a venerable and extremely popular US radio commentator, Paul Harvey, had just a few days earlier expressed his country's basic urges more openly, in an appeal for Bush to deploy weapons of mass destruction aggressively:

> We sent men with rifles into Afghanistan and Iraq, and we kept our best weapons in our silos. Even now we're standing there dying, daring to do nothing decisive, because we've declared ourselves to be better than our terrorist enemies – more moral, more civilized. Our image is at stake, we insist.
>
> But we didn't come this far because we're made of sugar candy. Once upon a time, we elbowed our way onto and into this continent by giving small pox infected blankets to native Americans. Yes, that was biological warfare! And we used every other weapon we could get our hands on to grab this land from whomever. And we grew prosperous. And, yes, we greased the skids with the sweat of slaves.
>
> And so it goes with most nation states, which, feeling guilty about their savage pasts, eventually civilize themselves out of business and wind up invaded, and ultimately dominated by the lean, hungry and up and coming who are not made of sugar candy.[16]

When the grabbing of land or markets must be defended, there are too many proud Americans – and not just talk-show schlock-jocks like Paul Harvey or Rush Limbaugh – who shamelessly stand in favour of looting. As the suave *New York Times* columnist Thomas Friedman famously remarked, 'The hidden hand of the market will never work without the hidden fist – McDonald's cannot flourish without

McDonnell Douglas, the designer of the F-15. And the hidden fist that keeps the world safe for Silicon Valley's technologies is called the United States Army, Air Force, Navy and Marine Corps.'[17]

In short, contemporary 'looting' is not best understood through the populist, surface-level imagery epitomized by the Associated Press caption with which I began. Looting is a system driven from *capitalist* institutions in Washington, London and other Northern centres, and accommodated by junior partners across the Third World, including African capitals, especially Pretoria. This, anyway, is the argument I will defend in the pages that follow.

ACKNOWLEDGEMENTS

As always, I am grateful to a community of comradely critics who reinforce where appropriate and correct me a great deal. During a 2003–4 sabbatical year at York University's Department of Political Science, for example, my hosts were Leo Panitch and Sam Gindin, two great scholar-activists with enormous capacities to interpret and critique the strengths of US empire. Their forthcoming book will stand with – and sometimes against – other recent English-language studies grounded in the tradition of Marxist political economy which I have found invaluable, by authors including Walden Bello (*Dilemmas of Domination*), Robert Brenner (*The Boom and the Bubble* and *The Economics of Global Turbulence*), Gérard Duménil and Dominique Lévy (*Capital Resurgent*), David Harvey (*The New Imperialism, Spaces of Neoliberalization* and *A Brief History of Neoliberalism*) and Ellen Wood (*Empire of Capital*). As for documenting the overall process of resource drains from the Third World, I'm indebted to other researchers including Joan Martinez-Alier, Gernot Koehler, Eric Toussaint and Mark Weisbrot, among others, who have all been very encouraging and generous with their data.

In Africa, it is impossible not to acknowledge inspiring work by so many intellectuals who have shaped our understanding of imperialism from within similar traditions. Over the last few decades, research and polemics by African scholars and political leaders – and their international allies – unveiled many of these global/local relations of poverty, inequality and uneven development. A partial list of influential Africans from the immediate past and present who blazed trails of critical analysis I am following would include Tajudeen Abdul Raheem, Charles Abugre, Adebayo Adedeji, Jimi Adesina, Claude Ake, Neville Alexander, Samir Amin, Peter Anyang'Nyong'o, A. M. Babu, Ahmed Ben Bella, Steve Biko, Dennis Brutus, Amilcar Cabral, Fantu Cheru, John Daniel, Jacques Delpechin, Demba Dembele, Ashwin Desai, Yasmine Fall, Frantz Fanon, Ruth First, M. P. Giyose, Yao Graham, Pauline Hountondji, Eboe Hutchful, Khafra Kambon, Dot Keet, Rene Loewenson, Sara Longwe, Patrice Lumumba, Samora Machel, Archie Mafeje, Ben Magubane, Amina Mama, Mahmood Mamdani, Achille Mbembe, Henning Melber, Guy Mhone, Darlene Miller, Thandika Mkandawire, Dani Nabudere, Léonce Ndikumana, Trevor Ngwane, Njoki Njehu, Kwame Nkrumah, Julius Nyerere, Georges Nzongola-Ntalaja, Oginga Odinga, Adebayo Olukoshi, Oduor Ongwen, Bade Onimode, Haroub Othman, Mohau Pheko, Kwesi Prah, Brian Raftopoulos, Thomas Sankara, Issa Shivji, Yash Tandon, Riaz Tayob, Aminata Traoré, Dodzi Tsikata, Kwame Ture, Ngugi Wa Thiong'o, Ernest Wamba dia Wamba, Harold Wolpe, Tunde Zack-Williams and Paul Zeleza. For an Internet-based guide to the toughest contemporary arguments against imperial power emanating from the continent, there is no better web resource than fahamu.org's 'Pambazuka' weekly news and analytical service, where, thanks to Firoze Manji and Patrick Burnett, some of these authors can regularly be found. At Africa World Press, Kassahun Checole puts many of these radical writers into print – as do Zed Books, the University of KwaZulu-Natal, the Southern African Political Economic Series in Harare and of course CODESRIA in Dakar, amongst others.

Allies from beyond the continent include stalwart intellectual analysts and political activists who devoted their careers to fighting the capitalist exploitation of Africa (for example, Hans Abrahamsson, Soren Ambrose, Michael Barratt-Brown, Salih Booker, Sarah Bracking, Victoria Brittain, Jan Burgess, Ray Bush, George Caffentzis, Horace Campbell, Lionel Cliffe, Carole Collins, Dan Connell, Fred Cooper, Imani Countess, Basil Davidson, Jennifer Davis, Silvia Federici, James Ferguson, Bill Fletcher, Reginald Green, Branwen Gruffydd Jones, Joe Hanlon, Colin Leys, Bill Martin, Bill Minter, Giles Mohan, Jane Parpart, Walter Rodney, John S. Saul, Ann Seidman, Tim Shaw, Vladimir Shubin, Colin Stoneman, Carol Thompson, Meredith

Turshen, David Wiley, Gavin Williams and many others). Aside from solidarity activism, they work through radical academic associations (such as the Association of Concerned African Scholars and the Committee for Academic Freedom in Africa), journals (such as the *Review of African Political Economy*) and solidarity groups (the Toronto Committee for the Liberation of Southern Africa was exemplary in its time, as is Africa Action today). All offered ways to understand and fight the looting of Africa, and the pages that follow merely update their arguments. (Soren Ambrose gave particular advice on the text, for which I'm extremely grateful.)

As the ideas in this book came together, I was given a great deal of helpful feedback at lectures and stimulating seminars and conferences.[18] In particular, several editors and sponsoring agencies supported earlier versions of the work.[19] Others provided me with space in websites and magazines through which the international Left often shares information.[20] I have also had the great fortune of working with friends, comrades, excellent students and academic colleagues,[21] of whom the late Guy Mhone was a universally beloved role model.

Most important, from Toronto to South Africa and at many sites in between and beyond, dedicated groups of campaigners teach the academics. Many must contend not only with capital, states and the interstate system. They also confront distractions from mainly international NGOs whose proposed reforms *strengthen the system*, instead of providing the basis for its dismantling. In contrast, in South Africa many of us gain knowledge through 'praxis': closely observing challenges to the state and capital so as to understand where power makes concessions, where it co-opts grassroots critics, where it turns to repression, where it stabilizes crises, and where the next round of contradictions might emerge. This is partly as a result of an average of 16 protests by South African activists every day (of which 13 per cent are recorded by police as 'illegal'), largely against inadequate municipal service delivery and other local grievances, according to the Minister of Safety and Security.[22]

More systemically, though, organizational challenges to Pretoria's power are made repeatedly by social movements and related organizations dedicated to more radical change (what might be called 'non-reformist reforms').[23] To be sure, a great many of the organizations that make up South Africa's independent Left are in profound internal crisis as I write, yet their examples have regularly been inspiring.

One key question concerns the extent to which these and other groups – and perhaps in future more radical, mass-based political parties than are now on offer – can continue moving back and forth from local to global scales. If so, they would perhaps follow examples associated with South African popular solidarity for oppressed people in Palestine, Burma and Zimbabwe, and would offer increasing resistance (perhaps through the Southern African Social Forum and African Social Forum) to the many ways in which South Africa loots Africa. As for countervailing forces at the global scale, the final chapter provides sources for optimism. Notable amongst these are, in my view, work by Dennis Brutus, M. P. Giyose and others advocating Northern *reparations* that are long overdue to victims of imperialism; related efforts to end the regime of neoliberalism most forcefully imposed through the World Bank and IMF domination; the growing networks of solidarity within and between Africa and the North; the possibility of a more progressive programmatic orientation (and less 'trade fair of ideas' mentality) in the World Social Forum and its affiliates; and (albeit distant) prospects for a revitalized, democratized state as one of the crucial units of resistance. But on these matters you the reader – and especially African activists – will have to provide a more durable judgement.

Patrick Bond
Durban

Notes

1 <http://www.flickr.com/photos/firewall/38725768/>.

2 Žižek, S. (2005), 'The Subject Supposed to Loot and Rape: Reality and Fantasy in New Orleans', *In These Times*, 20 October.

3 Davis, M. (2005), 'Catastrophic Economics: the Predators of New Orleans', *Le Monde Diplomatique*, 2 October.

4 Amin, S. (2003), 'Confronting the Empire', presented to the conference on 'The Work of Karl Marx and the Challenges of the Twenty-first Century', Institute of Philosophy of the Ministry of Science, Technology and the Environment, the National Association of Economists of Cuba, the Cuban Trade Union Federation and the Centre for the Study of Economy and Planning, Havana, 5–8 May.

5 Krugman, P. (2003), 'Looting the Future', *New York Times*, 5 December.

6 Marx, K. (1867)[2005], *Das Kapital*, Part VIII, Chapter 31, available at <http://www.marxists.org/archive/marx/works/1867-c1/ch31.htm>.

7 Luxemburg, R. (1968)[1923], *The Accumulation of Capital*, New York, Monthly

Review Press. See <www.marxists.org/archive/luxemburg/1913/accumulation-capital/>, from which these citations are drawn.

8 Mohan, G. and T. Zack-Williams (2005), 'Oiling the Wheels of Imperialism', *Review of African Political Economy*, 104/105, p. 214.

9 Kaplan, R. (1994), 'The Coming Anarchy', *Atlantic Monthly*, 273, p. 46.

10 Cooper, R. (2002), 'The Post-Modern State', in M. Leonard (ed.), *Re-Ordering the World: the Long-Term Implications of September 11*, London, The Foreign Policy Centre, pp. 16–17.

11 Jacoby, T. (2005), 'Cultural Determinism, Western Hegemony and the Efficacy of Defective States', *Review of African Political Economy*, 104/105, p. 228.

12 <http://exploringafrica.matrix.msu.edu/curriculum/lm1/1/lm1_teachers. html>.

13 Hawley, C. (2005), 'African Village Accused of Putting Humans on Display', *Spiegel Online*, 9 June, <http://service.spiegel.de/cache/international/0,1518, 359799,00.html>.

14 Altman, D. (2005), 'Neoliberalism? It Doesn't Exist', *International Herald Tribune*, 16 July.

15 Bond, P. and R. Dada (eds) (2005), *Trouble in the Air: Global Warming and the Privatised Atmosphere*, Durban, University of KwaZulu-Natal Centre for Civil Society.

16 Cited in Zorn, E. (2005), 'Paul Harvey: Ah, Genocide and Slavery, Now That's a Good Day!', *Chicago Tribune*, 24 June.

17 Friedman, T. (1999), 'A Manifesto for the Fast World', *New York Times Magazine*, 28 March.

18 Greatest appreciation is due to organizers and seminar participants at the following sites where I presented this book's arguments during 2005: the Intercontinental Network for Promoting the Social Solidarity Economy in Dakar; Columbia University's School of International and Public Affairs; the Institute for Policy Studies, Africa Action, Center for Economic and Policy Research and Jubilee USA in Washington; Duke University's Colloquium on Southern Africa; the University of KwaZulu-Natal's African History Seminar; a Johannesburg ecological debt conference hosted by the South African Council of Churches Economic Justice Network and the World Council of Churches; the Southern African Social Forum in Harare; the SA Association of Political Science annual colloquium in Pietermaritzburg; groundWork's conference 'Another Energy Future is Possible', held in Johannesburg to counteract the World Petroleum Congress; the International Social Science Council social movements workshop in Buenos Aires; the University of KwaZulu-Natal School of Development Studies seminar; a conference of *Capitalism, Nature, Socialism* on 'Ecology, Imperialism and the Contradictions of Capitalism' at York University in Toronto; the Central European University's 'Summer School on Transnational Flows, Structures, Agents and the Idea of Development' in Budapest; a Globalise Resistance London conference and G8 Alternatives public meeting in Glasgow prior to the Gleneagles G8 summit; an Oxford University

School of Geography seminar; the Brecht Forum evening I shared with Dennis
Brutus on 'Imperialism, Subimperialism and Popular Resistance in South
Africa' in New York; a symposium of the University of California/Los Angeles
Center on Globalization (Africa); and the Africa Dialogue Lecture Series at the
University of Pretoria's Centre for International Political Studies.

During 2004, thanks are due to those who arranged and took part in events
at these venues: an Addis Ababa conference of the International Development
Economics Associates, Ethiopian Economic Association and the Council for the
Development of Social Science Research in Africa (CODESRIA); a session of the
York University Department of Political Science 'Empire Seminar' in Toronto;
the Dag Hammarskjöld Foundation's workshop 'What's Next in Economics?' at
Hazel Henderson's institute in St Augustine; an Africa University Institute for
Peace Leadership and Governance political economy course in Mutare,
Zimbabwe; the *Review of African Political Economy* and CODESRIA 30th
Anniversary Conference in Sheffield; Gothenburg University's Department of
Peace and Development Research; the Oslo Institute for Globalization
Networking, Information and Studies and Norwegian Drop the Debt Campaign;
a conference on the Latin American Left at the University of Wisconsin Havens
Center; the Equator School's Post-Graduate Course in Advanced Development
Economics and Policy Making in Entebbe, Uganda; a McGill University Medical
School conference on Achieving Global Health Equality; an International
Studies Association panel on Reconfiguring Power through the International
Aid Regime in Montreal; the New York Socialist Scholars Conference; the
Ryerson University Phyllis Clarke Memorial Lecture in Toronto; and a Bing-
hamton University Department of Sociology and Braudel Center seminar.

19 I especially thank Rene Loewenson and the board of Equinet and Charles
Mutasa of Afrodad for sponsoring different components of the research
presented in Chapters 3 and 4, and the SA National Research Foundation and
the Research Council of Norway for financing student researchers and visiting
scholars carrying out related projects. For giving sections of later chapters an
airing, I thank Joel Kovel of *Capitalism Nature Socialism* (Chapter 4), David
Held for exploring strategic disputes on global reform in *Debating
Globalization* (Chapter 5), Leo Panitch and Colin Leys of the *Socialist Register
2005: The Empire Re-loaded* (Chapter 6), Jan Burgess of the *Review of African
Political Economy* (Chapter 6), and Shahid Qadir of *Third World Quarterly* and
Roger Keil of the *International Journal of Urban and Regional Research*
(Chapter 7).

20 Kind editors at the following periodicals and e-zines allowed me, during
2004–5, to try out some of the arguments: *Counterpunch, debate, Foreign
Policy in Focus, Global Dialogue, Open Democracy, Pambazuka, Red Pepper,
Socialist Review, Socialist Worker, Sunday Tribune* and *ZNet Commentary*.

21 Space simply does not permit naming the many valued people who have given
me support these past two years, including colleagues and students at York
Faculty of Environmental Sciences and Department of Politics, the University of

the Witwatersrand Graduate School of Public and Development Management, the Africa University Institute for Peace Leadership and Governance, the Central European University Summer School and the University of KwaZulu-Natal School of Development Studies and Centre for Civil Society. And on a personal level, my gratitude is enormous to Jan and to Zoë, for continual inspiration.

22 Madlala, B. (2005), 'Frustration Boils over in Protests: Community Angered at Snail Pace Service Delivery', *The Mercury*, 14 October.

23 As of early 2006, these included the Abahlali-based Mjondolo shackdwellers movement of Durban (as well as other community groups from oppressed areas of Durban), the Anti-Privatization Forum of greater Johannesburg, the Education Rights Project, the Environmental Justice Networking Forum, Fisherfolk, Jubilee South Africa, the Landless People's Movement, the Rural Women's Movement, Social Movements Indaba, the Soweto Electricity Crisis Committee, the Treatment Action Campaign and the Western Cape Anti-Eviction Campaign, with corresponding analysis and strategic workshopping often provided by the Alternative Information and Development Centre, Centre for Civil Society, Freedom of Expression Institute, groundWork, International Labour Research and Information Group, Khanya College and Southern African Centre for Economic Justice. In future years it is likely that more radical challenges to power will emerge from the Congress of South African Trade Unions and SA Communist Party, once the increasingly dysfunctional alliance with the African National Congress ceases.

1

Poor Africa

Two views

Africa is poor, ultimately, because its economy has not grown. The public and private sectors need to work together to create a climate which unleashes the entrepreneurship of the peoples of Africa, generates employment and encourages individuals and firms, domestic and foreign, to invest. Changes in governance are needed to make the investment climate stronger. The developed world must support the African Union's New Partnership for Africa's Development (NEPAD) programme to build public/private partnerships in order to create a stronger climate for growth, investment and jobs.[1]

These sentences – from the report presented in March 2005 by Tony Blair's Commission for Africa – distil the misperceptions of conventional wisdom regarding the continent's underdevelopment. In the same year Blair hosted the G8 and the European Union leaders' summits, and his Chancellor of the Exchequer Gordon Brown advanced several initiatives on debt, aid and trade, deploying 'Marshall Plan for Africa' rhetoric. Below, we consider the way the Africa Commission coopted key African elites into a modified neoliberal – free-market – project. But to set the tone on this first page, it would be more logical to reverse all of the above admonitions, and reconstruct the paragraph as follows.

Africa is poor, ultimately, because its economy and society have been ravaged by international capital as well as by local elites who are often propped up by foreign powers. The public and private sectors have worked together to drain the continent of resources which otherwise – if harnessed and shared fairly – should meet the needs of the peoples of Africa. Changes in 'governance' – revolutions, for example – are desperately needed for social progress, and these entail not only the empowerment of 'civil society' but also the strengthening of those agencies within African states which can deliver welfare and basic infrastructure. The rich world must decide whether to support the African Union's NEPAD programme, which will worsen the resource drain because of its pro-corporate orientation, or instead to give Africa space for societies to build public/people partnerships in order to satisfy unmet basic needs.

One reason to make this argument forcefully at the outset is to remind ourselves of the historical legacy of a continent *looted*: trade by force dating back centuries; slavery that uprooted and dispossessed around 12 million Africans; land grabs; vicious taxation schemes; precious metals spirited away; the appropriation of antiquities to the British Museum and other trophy rooms; the nineteenth-century emergence of racist ideologies to justify colonialism; the 1884–5 carve-up of Africa, in a Berlin negotiating room, into dysfunctional territories; the construction of settler-colonial and extractive-colonial systems – of which apartheid, the German occupation of Namibia, the Portuguese colonies and King Leopold's Belgian Congo were perhaps only the most blatant – often based upon tearing black migrant workers from rural areas (leaving women with vastly increased responsibilities as a consequence); Cold War battlegrounds – proxies for US/USSR conflicts – filled with millions of corpses; other wars catalysed by mineral searches and offshoot violence such as witnessed in blood diamonds and coltan (colombo-tantelite, a crucial component of cell phones and computer chips); poacher-stripped swathes of East, Central and Southern Africa now devoid of rhinos and elephants whose ivory became ornamental material or aphrodisiac in the Middle East and East Asia; societies used as guinea pigs in the latest corporate pharmaceutical test ... and the list could continue.

Today, Africa is still getting progressively poorer, with *per capita* incomes in many countries below those of the 1950s–60s era of independence. If we consider even the most banal measure of poverty, most sub-Saharan African countries suffered an increase in the percentage of people with income of less than US$1/day during the 1980s and 1990s, the World Bank itself concedes.[2] Later we consider even more worrying evidence (also from the Bank) regarding the depletion of Africa's raw materials, and the implications for the continent's declining net national income and savings.

Yet the worsening statistics led to different kinds of spin.

Emblematic of the power-elite view (even if published in the ostensibly progressive US magazine *The Nation*), was Andrew Rice's review of new books on Africa by Martin Meredith, Robert Guest and Jeffrey Sachs:

> How can one continent be so out of step with humankind's march of progress? Everyone agrees that Africans are desperately poor and typically endure governments that are, to varying degrees, corrupt and capricious. The dispute is about causes and consequences. One group – call it the poverty-first camp – believes African governments are so lousy precisely because their countries are so poor. The other group – the governance-first camp – holds that Africans are impoverished because their rulers keep them that way.[3]

Sachs isn't actually so crude, since 'Little surpasses the Western world in the cruelty and depredations that it has long imposed on Africa.' But he presumes that the critique of corrupt dictators is a 'political story line' of the 'right', instead of giving credence to progressive, organic African anti-corruption campaigning. From there, Sachs proceeds to rehearse well-known accounts of malaria, AIDS, landlocked countries and other forms of geographically determinist analysis, and then reconciles these explanations with garden-variety policy advice: adopting good governance plus 'implementing traditional market reforms, especially regarding export promotion'. For Sachs, virtually none of the critical structural analyses in this book are worthy of more than a paragraph's lip service.[4]

There will be time later to question the supposed 'march of progress' (in Chapter 2), and the merits of 'traditional market reforms' (in Chapters 3–4). But another view entirely – namely, that African rulers keep their people poor *because* they are tied into a system of global power, accumulation and class struggle – is what seems to have gone missing, especially when well-meaning NGOs and charity proponents seek yet more African integration into imperial circuits of trade, aid, finance and investment, citing state corruption as the major impediment to this cure-all.[5] Northern academics provide a more sophisticated version of the argument, known as the theory of African patrimonialism, namely rule through personal patronage rather than ideology or law, based upon relationships of loyalty and dependence with a blurred distinction between private and public interests.[6]

In fact, the deeper global power relations that keep Africa down (and, simultaneously, African elites buoyed up) should have been obvious to the world in 2005, a year during which numerous events were lined up ostensibly to help liberate Africa from poverty and powerlessness:

- the mobilization of NGO-driven citizens' campaigns like Britain's Make Poverty History and the Johannesburg-based Global Call to Action against Poverty (throughout 2005);
- Tony Blair's Commission for Africa (February);
- the main creditor countries' debt relief proposal (June);
- a tour of Africa by the new World Bank president Paul Wolfowitz (June);
- the G8 Gleneagles debt and aid commitments (July);
- the Live 8 consciouness-raising concerts (July);
- the UN Millennium Development Goals review (September);
- the return to Nigeria of monies looted by Sani Abacha and deposited in Swiss bank accounts (September);
- the IMF/World Bank annual meeting addressing debt and Third World 'voice' (September);
- a large debt relief package for Nigeria (October); and
- the deal done at the World Trade Organization's ministerial summit in Hong Kong (December).

There are many different dynamics associated with these mainly top-down processes, and in retrospect it is appropriate to ask the question: what was really accomplished? This book argues that for those seeking genuine information about Africa's situation, the events above were useful mainly in so far as they revealed global-elite hypocrisy and power relations that remained impervious to advocacy, solidarity and democratization. The events also revealed the limits of strategies aimed at intra-elite persuasion rather than pressure. Tragically, the actual conditions faced by most people on the continent continued to deteriorate.

But this is not the impression that world elites and African rulers would like to leave. In September 2005, the outgoing chair of the IMF and World Bank Development Committee (one of two crucial standing bodies of the Bretton Woods institutions), South African Finance Minister Trevor Manuel, bragged: 'Right now, the macroeconomic conditions in Africa have never been better. You have growth across the continent at 4.7 per cent. You have inflation in single digits. The bulk of countries have very strong fiscal balances as well.'[7] As for

Gleneagles, Live 8 organizer Bob Geldof was ecstatic: 'On aid, 10 out of 10. On debt, eight out of 10. On trade ... it is quite clear that this summit, uniquely, decided that enforced liberalization must no longer take place. That is a serious, excellent result on trade.'[8]

Upon closer examination, Geldof appears to have been profoundly and dangerously misguided (as many of his NGO allies warned him). Manuel's statements are true only if we take misleadingly narrow economic statistics seriously. But we don't have to: even the World Bank was compelled to confess in mid-2005 that Africa is being continually *drained* of wealth through depletion of minerals, forests and other eco-social factors ignored by Manuel and mainstream economists (a point we return to in detail below).

RACISM, INEQUALITY, PATRIARCHY, ANTHROPOMORPHISM

Many critics of North–South power relations – such as Walter Rodney in *How Europe Underdeveloped Africa* – have already identified the basic processes:

> The question as to who and what is responsible for African under-development can be answered at two levels. Firstly, the answer is that the operation of the imperialist system bears major responsibility for African economic retardation by draining African wealth and by making it impossible to develop more rapidly the resources of the continent. Secondly, one has to deal with those who manipulate the system and those who are either agents or unwitting accomplices of the said system.[9]

Rodney's research showed how sub-Saharan Africa suffered a drain of wealth along two trajectories: South–North resource flows associated with what we now term 'global apartheid', and adverse internal African class formation which reproduces global apartheid's local agents ('compradors'). In the former case, the central processes are associated with exploitative debt and finance, phantom aid, capital flight, the brain drain, unfair trade, distorted investment and the ecological debt the North owes the South, in the context of profoundly undemocratic global power relations. As Rodney put it in 1972,

> *In order to understand present economic conditions in Africa, one needs to know why it is that Africa has realized so little of its natural potential, and one also needs to know why so much of its present wealth goes to non-Africans who reside for the most part outside of the continent ....*

It is typical of underdeveloped economies that they do not (or are not allowed to) concentrate on those sectors of the economy which in turn will generate growth and raise production to a new level altogether, and there are very few ties between one sector and another so that (say) agriculture and industry could react beneficially on each other. Furthermore, whatever savings are made within the economy are mainly sent abroad or are frittered away in consumption rather than being redirected to productive purposes. Much of the national income which remains within the country goes to pay individuals who are not directly involved in producing wealth but only in rendering auxiliary services – civil servants, merchants, soldiers, entertainers, etc. What aggravates the situation is that more people are employed in those jobs than are really necessary to give efficient service; and to crown it all these people do not reinvest in agriculture or industry. They squander the wealth created by the peasants and workers by purchasing cars, whisky and perfume.[11] (Emphasis in original.)

what do these mean

Table 1.1 African inequality
(Gini coefficients by country, early 2000s)[10]

Namibia	.72	Burundi	.41
Botswana	.65	Nigeria	.41
Central African Republic	.62	Burkina Faso	.40
Swaziland	.61	Angola	.39
Lesotho	.58	Senegal	.39
South Africa	.57	Mozambique	.39
Zambia	.53	Mali	.38
Malawi	.51	Ghana	.38
The Gambia	.50	Guinea	.38
Zimbabwe	.50	Mauritania	.37
Madagascar	.46	Benin	.36
Côte d'Ivoire	.43	Tanzania	.35
Kenya	.42	Niger	.33
Uganda	.42	Ethiopia	.28
Cameroon	.41	Mauritius	.19

Source: World Bank (2005), *World Development Report 2006: Equity and Development*, Washington, World Bank, p. 39.

There are indeed African collaborators who require mention and critique (Chapter 5). Instead of an organic middle class and productive capitalist class, Africa has seen an excessively powerful comprador ruling elite whose income has been based upon financial-parasitical accumulation, which in turn is subject to vast capital flight. The case of South Africa as a national 'subimperial' site of geopolitical, military, financial, trade and investment power deserves special consideration (Chapter 6).

In turn, this means that not just poverty but also inequality must be central to the analysis, for Africa hosts some of the world's worst cases. The most common measure of income inequality is the 'Gini coefficient', a number between 0 (everyone has the same income) and 1 (one person has all the income and everyone else has nothing). The following countries exceed a 0.50 Gini score, placing them at the very top of the world's ranking: Namibia, Botswana, the Central African Republic, Swaziland, Lesotho, South Africa, Zambia, Malawi, The Gambia and Zimbabwe.

The processes discussed above are also intensely gendered. Women are the main victims of systemic poverty and inequality, whether in productive circuits of capital (increasingly subject to sweatshop conditions) or in the 'sphere of reproduction' of households and labour markets, where much primitive accumulation occurs through unequal gender power relations. This is especially evident in areas such as Southern Africa, which are characterized by more than a century of migrant labour flows. Indeed, the sphere of reproduction remains central to Northern capitalism's social power over the South, particularly in the case of migrancy. Here, the superexploitation of women in childrearing, healthcare and eldercare contrasts with wealthy countries' state-supplied (or firm-based) schooling, medical aids and pension schemes.

This is not simply a local problem, but corresponds to worsening global trends. Political scientists Isabella Bakker and Stephen Gill show how

> *Reprivatization of social reproduction* involves at least four shifts that relate to the household, the state and social institutions, and finally the basic mechanisms of livelihood, particularly in poorer countries:
> - household and caring activities are increasingly provided through the market and are thus exposed to the movement of money; ...
> - societies seem to become redefined as collections of individuals (or at best collections of families), particularly when the state retreats from universal social protection; ...
> - accumulation patterns [are] premised on connected control over wider areas of social life and thus the provisions for social reproduction; ... and

- survival and livelihood [are threatened]. For example, a large proportion of the world's population has no effective health insurance or even basic care.[12]

The denial of Africans' access to food, medicines, energy and even water is a common reflection of this last problem, as people who are surplus to capitalism's labour power requirements find that they had better fend for themselves – or simply die. In even relatively prosperous South Africa, an early death for millions was the outcome of state and employer reaction to the AIDS epidemic, with cost–benefit analyses demonstrating conclusively that keeping most of the country's five to six million HIV-positive people alive through patented medicines cost more than the people were 'worth'.[13] There are many ways, as Dzodzi Tsikata and Joanna Kerr have shown, in which mainstream economic policy 'perpetuates women's subordination'.[14]

The same principles have been applied to the environment. After all, 'I've always thought that underpopulated countries in Africa are vastly *under*-polluted, their air quality is probably vastly inefficiently low,' opined Larry Summers, then the World Bank's chief economist, later the Clinton administration's Treasury Secretary and later president of Harvard, in the wake of a similar off-the-cuff cost–benefit analysis: 'I think the economic logic behind dumping a load of toxic waste in the lowest-wage country is impeccable and we should face up to that.'[15] Though this is an extreme version, precisely such combined anthropomorphic and racist logic permeates the way Africa is treated in global political-economic circuits.

THE STRUCTURE OF THIS BOOK

How, then, do we proceed from critical analysis to a political standpoint that contributes to debates already under way about ways forward? First we might consider some of the core theoretical problems associated with the looting of Africa, specifically the debates over 'development'. Posing the argument bluntly, Branwen Gruffydd Jones insists that, 'Marx's historical materialist method and theory of capital *explains why* capital is necessarily expansionary; *why* the plunder of Africa was an integral part of the primitive accumulation of Western capital; *why* the reorganization of Africa's human and natural resources to meet the needs of Europe's developing industries required colonial occupation and domination."[16] Can a broad, non-dogmatic, political-economic theory be deployed today?

In arguing in the affirmative, we might be surprised to find that the theory of 'uneven and combined development' – formulated for political purposes by Leon Trotsky in 1906 but refined during the past thirty years – should have been (but wasn't) the basis for much of the debate, for it helps to explain both crisis tendencies and crisis-displacement mechanisms at global and local scales (Chapter 2).

It is, however, mainly in the empirical measurement of Africa's wealth and income outflows that this book offers updated, synthesized information. Several components of capital accumulation and class formation – aid and finance (Chapter 3); trade, migration and direct investment (Chapter 4); and a combination of comprador and sub-imperial relationships (Chapters 5 and 6) – remain central to Africa's ongoing underdevelopment. The more durable oppositions to the looting of Africa remain open for elaboration through social struggle (Chapter 7).

NOTES

1 Commission for Africa (CfA) (2005), *Our Common Future*, London, p. 13.

2 World Bank (2005), *World Development Report 2006: Equity and Development*, Washington, World Bank, p. 66. For a superb critique of the $/day measure, see Reddy, S. (2005), 'Counting the Poor: the Truth about World Poverty Statistics', in L. Panitch and C. Leys (eds), *Telling the Truth: Socialist Register 2006*, London, Merlin Press and New York, Monthly Review Press.

3 Rice, A. (2005), 'Why is Africa Still Poor?', *The Nation*, 24 October.

4 Sachs, J. (2005), *The End of Poverty*, London, Penguin, pp. 189–209.

5 A good example is the advice from a well-regarded NGO analyst close to the British government, Matthew Lockwood, that 'expanding trade is necessary for economic growth and poverty reduction in Africa.... It is almost self-evident that Africa will need a lot more aid to achieve sustainable growth.' To advance this agenda, he calls for more advocacy by 'the African parts of international organizations', in view of his largely negative view of the strengths of organic African civil society (Chapter 9). Lockwood, M. (2005), *The State They're In: an Agenda for International Action on Poverty in Africa*, Bourton-on-Dunsmore, ITDG Publishing, pp. 23, 45, 142.

6 Those who have built up this theory include Michael Bratton, Thomas Callaghy, Patrick Chabal, Jean-Pascal Daloz and Richard Sandbrook. Critiques include those by Mamdani, M. (1996), *Citizen and Subject: Contemporary Africa and the Legacy of State Colonialism*, Princeton, Princeton University Press and

Ahluwalia, P. (2001), *Politics and Post-Colonial Theory: African Inflections*, London, Routledge.

7 Manuel, T. (2005), 'Transcript of a Joint IMF/World Bank Town Hall with Civil Society Organizations', Washington, 22 September, <http://www.imf.org/external/np/tr/2005/tr050922a.htm>.

8 Reported in Hodkinson, S. (2005), 'Oh No, They Didn't! Bono and Geldof: "We Saved Africa!"', *Counterpunch*, 27 October, <http://www.counterpunch.org>.

9 Rodney, W. (1972), *How Europe Underdeveloped Africa*, Dar es Salaam, Tanzania Publishing House and London, Bogle L'Ouverture Publications; all citations are from this edition, available at <http://www.marxists.org/subject/africa/rodney-walter/how-europe/>.

10 World Bank staff calculated Gini coefficients from household survey data, and dates differ by data availability.

11 Rodney, *How Europe Underdeveloped Africa*.

12 Bakker, I. and S. Gill (2003), 'Ontology, Method and Hypotheses', in I. Bakker and S. Gill (eds), *Power, Production and Social Reproduction*, Basingstoke, Palgrave Macmillan, p. 36.

13 In the case of the vast Johannesburg/London conglomerate Anglo American Corporation, the cut-off for saving workers in 2001 was 12 per cent. The lowest-paid 88 per cent of employees were more cheaply dismissed once unable to work, with replacements found amongst South Africa's 42 per cent unemployed reserve army of labour, according to an internal study reported by the *Financial Times*. For more, see Bond, P. (2005), *Elite Transition: from Apartheid to Neoliberalism in South Africa*, Pietermaritzburg, University of KwaZulu-Natal Press, Afterword to the 2nd edition.

14 Tsikata, D. and J. Kerr (2002), *Demanding Dignity: Women Confronting Economic Reforms in Africa*, Ottawa, The North–South Institute and Accra, Third World Network-Africa.

15 Cited in *The Economist*, 8 February 1992; the memo is available at <http://www.whirledbank.org>.

16 Gruffydd Jones, B. (2003), 'The Civilized Horrors of Over-work: Marxism, Imperialism and the Development of Africa', *Review of African Political Economy*, 95, p. 42.

2
Uneven and Combined Development
Neoliberalism, stagnation and financial volatility

Before providing evidence of the global stagnation and financial volatility that have exacerbated Africa's plight, it may be useful to consider an appropriate theoretical framework. Together with Ashwin Desai, I have been rethinking how to formulate a theoretical approach that interrogates not only economic, but also ongoing and in many cases worsening gender, race and environmental exploitations that link Africa to the world.[1]

To sum up the argument deployed in coming pages, the idea of *uneven development* suggests that growth (accumulation) and decline (underdevelopment) happen in a systematic manner, but not one which follows either a 'modernization' path – directly along a line of under-development, 'take-off' and development[2] – or a path of permanent 'dependency'.[3] Instead, accumulation at one pole and poverty at another happen systematically, according to systems of exploitation that we must carefully analyse and document, *but that can change*, depending upon political processes.

In this formulation, *combined development* is a reference to the way capitalism uses combinations of market and non-market activities for additional profits. So-called 'primitive accumulation' is not merely the one-off event that allowed a critical mass of capital to be mobilized through theft, at the outset of capitalism in eighteenth- and nineteenth-century Europe. As Marx had it, that early extra measure of profita-bility came, in part, because 'the turning of Africa into a commercial warren for the hunting of black skins signalled the rosy dawn of the era of capitalist production'.[4] But primitive accumulation did not end, and, as Rosa Luxemburg argued in her seminal work *The Accumulation of Capital,* instead it became a permanent process of superexploitation at the world scale.[5]

Uneven and combined development is, crucially, amplified by capitalist 'crisis': not a fully-fledged breakdown, but a generalized condition of excess production, given the limited ability of the market to provide an acceptable rate of return. As symptoms of crisis conditions – such as financial volatility – are displaced to weaker territories, capital seeks ever more desperately to exploit competitive differences between locations, sectors and scales, as sites to rescue falling profits.[6] While originally a purely politicized concept in Leon Trotsky's revolutionary theory, uneven and combined development has been much more broadly conceptualized, especially during the last three decades.[7]

The contemporary context of capitalist crisis is crucial. In spite of some talk that the era of the neoliberal Washington Consensus had ended with the late 1990s East Asian crises, the basic processes and policies appear intact. To illustrate, on 11 June 2005, the world's leading finance ministers 'reaffirmed' that Third World countries should adopt, amongst other measures, 'macroeconomic stability; the increased fiscal transparency essential to tackle corruption, boost private sector development, and attract investment; a credible legal framework; and the elimination of impediments to private investment, both domestic and foreign'.[8]

Specific neoliberal policies required for macroeconomic 'stability', according to the man who coined the phrase Washington Consensus, John Williamson, are:

1 Fiscal discipline;
2 Reordering public expenditure priorities;
3 Tax reform;
4 Liberalizing interest rates;
5 A competitive exchange rate;
6 Trade liberalization;
7 Liberalization of inward foreign direct investment;
8 Privatization;
9 Deregulation; and
10 Property rights.[9]

African structural adjustment programmes followed this set of strictures quite loyally from the early 1980s, leading to systematic macroeconomic *in*stability. In 1996, the World Bank provided an added element – the Highly Indebted Poor Country (HIPC) initiative – which imposed more conditionalities under the guise of partial debt relief. In 1999, the Bank and IMF began promoting Poverty Reduction Strategy Papers. By 2001, a home-grown Washington Consensus was required due to steadily deteriorating legitimacy, and coincidentally African heads of state launched the New Partnership for Africa's Development. In 2005, Blair's Commission for Africa reworded and revitalized the neoliberal arguments, and Brown's role in the Make Poverty History campaign brought many mainstream NGOs into alignment with the proposition that further integration of Africa into the world economy would be beneficial.

Recognizing the volatility and self-destructive character of global capital, this chapter disputes that basic premise.

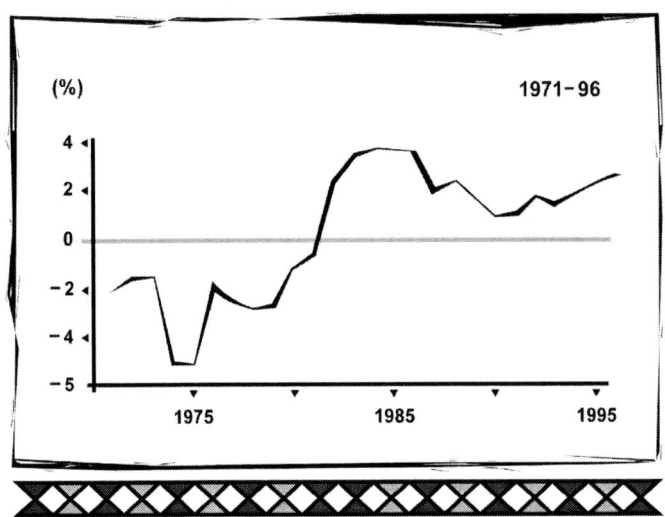

Figure 2.1 Interest rate (inflation-adjusted)
on Third World loans, 1971–96 (%)

Source: Duménil, G. and D. Lévy (2003), 'Neoliberal Dynamics, Imperial Dynamics', paper presented to the Conference on Global Regulation, University of Sussex, Brighton, 29-31 May.

GLOBAL STAGNATION, VOLATILITY AND CRISIS DISPLACEMENT

The world economy has witnessed a long slowdown in capitalist growth punctuated by extreme financial volatility. The eminent post-Keynesian economist David Felix cites 'exchange rate misalignments, excessive debt leveraging, asset price bubbles, slower and more unstable output and employment growth, and increased income concentration' in the North. In Southern countries, symptoms include 'more frequent financial crises, exacerbated by over-indebtedness that forces many of them to adopt pro-cyclical macroeconomic policies that deepen their output and employment losses'.[10]

For Africa, a decisive problem, signifying the beginning of neo-liberal dominance and financial power, was the 'Volcker shock' rise in the US interest rate in 1979, imposed by Federal Reserve chair Paul Volcker to halt US inflation and in the process discipline labour. Very rapidly, by 1982, this new monetary policy drove the Third World inexorably into debt crisis, austerity, decline and conflict.

However, an ever-deeper process, termed stagnation, was under way. The world's *per capita* annual gross domestic product (GDP)

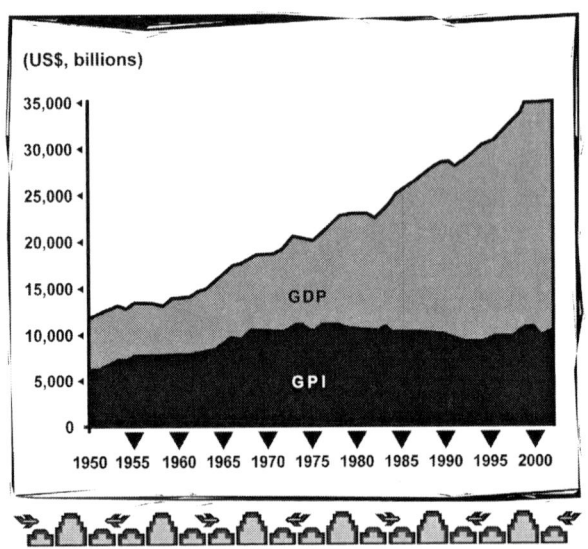

Figure 2.2 Global GDP versus a genuine progress indicator, 1950–2003

Source: <www.redefiningprogress.org>.

increase was already falling: from 3.6 per cent during the 1960s, to 2.1 per cent during the 1970s, to 1.3 per cent during the 1980s to 1.1 per cent during the 1990s and 1 per cent during the early 2000s.[11] Of course, GDP measures are notorious overestimates, especially since environmental degradation became more extreme from the mid-1970s.

At that point, a typical 'genuine progress indicator' – which incorporates much more than the GDP's annual output of goods and services – went into deficit. How would we transcend the biased, patriarchal GDP and construct an indicator of genuine progress? At the San Francisco group Redefining Progress, statisticians subtract from GDP the cost of crime and family breakdown; add household and volunteer work; correct for income distribution (rewarding equality); subtract resource depletion; subtract pollution; subtract long-term environmental damage (climate change, nuclear waste generation); add opportunities for increased leisure time; factor in lifespan of consumer durables and public infrastructure; and subtract vulnerability upon foreign assets.

The growth that occurred was concentrated much more in East Asia, the US/Canada and the European Union, with the rest of the world suffering decline in per person GDP growth.[12] With stagnation came lower demand for Third World exports, especially cash crops and minerals. Likewise, increasing competition from a few sites of manufacturing export production (Mexico, Brazil, East Asia) diminished the possibility of Africa growing through industrialization. Measures of income inequality between and within countries increased dramatically during the 1980s, according to all measures. In spite of the rise of China and India since then, even the World Bank concedes an ongoing increase in 'absolute' global income inequality, as well as sharp increases in inequality when China and India are excluded from calculations.[13]

How might this world-scale downturn and amplified uneven development be explained? There have been several powerful statements about the 'crisis' faced by global – and especially US – capital in restructuring production systems, social relations and geopolitics for the long haul of accumulation.[14] As evidence that the world economy is indeed severely threatened from within, it would be tempting to draw upon sources like Volcker, who in 2004 publicly warned of a '75 per cent chance of a financial crisis hitting the US in the next five years, if it does not change its policies'. As he told the *Financial Times*, 'I think the problem now is that there isn't a sense of crisis. Sure, you can talk about the budget deficit in America if you think it is a problem – and I think it is a big problem – but there is no sense of crisis, so no one wants to listen.'[15]

According to David Harvey, the roots of crisis are in the excess productive capacity of capital, which ultimately leaves gluts of commodities, manufactured goods, and idle workers: 'Global capitalism has experienced a chronic and enduring problem of overaccumulation since the 1970s.'[16] Robert Brenner finds evidence of this problem in so far as 'costs grow as fast or faster in non-manufacturing than in manufacturing, but the rate of profit falls in the latter rather than the former, because the price increase is much slower in manufacturing than non-manufacturing. In other words, due to international overcapacity, manufacturers cannot raise prices sufficiently to cover costs'.[17] There are important disputes amongst political economists about understanding and measuring overcapacity, of course.[18] In different ways, other political economists (Ernst Mandel, Simon Clarke, Harry Shutt, Robert Biel) argued that the 1970s–90s global capitalist slowdown can best be traced to overaccumulation.[19]

Related debates unfold over a *symptom* of capitalist crisis: declines in the corporate rate of profit. At first glance, the after-tax US corporate

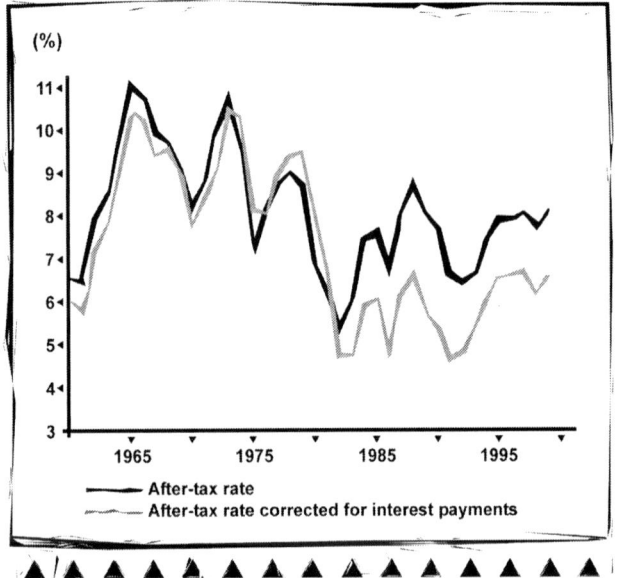

Figure 2.3 US corporate profit rates, 1960–2000[20]

Source: Duménil and Lévy, 'Neoliberal Dynamics, Imperial Dynamics'.

profit rate appeared to recover during the mid-1980s, nearly reaching 1960s–70s highs (although it must be said that tax rates were much lower in the recent period). However, interest payments remained at record high levels throughout the 1980s–90s. By subtracting real (inflation-adjusted) interest expenses we have a better sense of net revenue available to the firm for future investment and accumulation, which remained far lower than earlier periods.

Furthermore, we can trace, with the help of Gérard Duménil and Dominique Lévy, the ways that US corporations responded to declining manufacturing-sector accumulation. Manufacturing revenues were responsible for roughly half of total (before-tax) corporate profits during the quarter-century post-1945 'Golden Age', but fell to below 20 per cent by the early 2000s. In contrast, profits were soon much stronger in the financial sector (rising from the 10–20 per cent range during the 1950s–60s, to above 30 per cent by 2000) and in corporations' global operations (rising from 4–8 per cent to above 20 per cent by 2000).[21]

In addition to understanding the falling rate of profit and shifts in corporate accumulation strategies, there is another important conceptual challenge: the mix of extreme asset-price volatility and crisis displacement that together make the tracking of capital's 'valorization' and 'devalorization' terribly difficult. Harvey's analyses of 'spatio-temporal fixes' ('band aids' not solutions) captured the first phase of globalization and financial displacement of crises from the 1970s to the 1990s. These techniques have more recently been joined by mechanisms Harvey terms accumulation by dispossession or, simply, looting.[22]

Such theoretical tools help explain why 'capitalist crisis' doesn't automatically generate the sorts of payments-system breakdowns and mass core-capitalist unemployment problems witnessed during the main previous conjuncture of global overaccumulation, the Great Depression. That these systems of dispossession today more explicitly integrate the sphere of reproduction – where much primitive accumulation occurs through unequal gender power relations – make them notoriously difficult areas of political economy to measure and to correlate with accumulation.

Moreover, the context includes the overarching capacity of the US state to link the Bush regime's particular coalition constituencies – neoconservative politics and culture and petro-military-industrial accumulation – with the more general interests of capital (the Washington Consensus), as Leo Panitch and Sam Gindin have compellingly demonstrated.[23] Given US dependence on imported oil, which increased in price from $12/barrel to more than $70/barrel during 1998–2005, the implications of this scale of speculation-driven price swing are devastating to the US trade deficit, already unprecedented at more than 5 per cent of GDP. As for net international investment accounts, as recently as the early 1980s, the US held 5 per cent worth of its GDP in net foreign holdings (in other words, US claims were higher than foreign claims on the US). This figure plummeted to *negative 30 per cent* within two decades.

Another debilitating factor that pushes and pulls money in and out of presumed safe havens – especially US Treasury Bills – is stock market turmoil. From early 2000 through the first quarter of 2003, the global share index fell by nearly 40 per cent, from 1221 at the end of 2000 to 749 in early 2003. The big declines occurred not only on the Dow Jones in 2000, but also in Finland, Germany, Greece, Ireland, the Netherlands and Sweden, which in 2002 alone witnessed crashes of more than 33 per cent.[24] Taken together with 9/11, these processes resulted in large-scale funding flows of mutual funds back to US corporate funds, as the major New York investors exhibited wariness about overseas exposure.

Of course, there is an ebb and flow to capital, and it was no surprise that after the dramatic devaluations in many middle-income countries during 1995–2002, pressure from relatively lower US interest rates compelled a rethink on emerging market funds in 2005, with $345 billion anticipated in new portfolio investments (mainly funded by hedge funds, mutual funds, insurance companies and pension funds) that year alone. By late 2005, the *Washington Post's* main analyst, Paul Blustein, could predict

> the makings of future disasters, in the view of many economists, market veterans and policymakers. Having pumped large sums into emerging markets at a time of low interest rates and high prices for the commodities that many developing countries produce, investors may well bolt when conditions deteriorate, with the sudden outflow of cash devastating economies and plunging governments into default.... 'There's just a huge amount of money sloshing around looking for a place to go,' said Desmond Lachman, an economist at the American Enterprise Institute who, as a Wall Street research analyst, was one of the first to predict doom for Argentina

well before its 2001 default.... 'Even Turkeys Fly When the Winds Are Strong' is how Lachman put it in the title of an article he published recently in the magazine *International Economy*....

'So you put a little Jamaica in the fund, a little South Africa, a little Thailand,' said Christian Stracke, an analyst with CreditSights, an independent research firm. 'In a global crisis, all three will be a dog. But if you're a [hedge fund] manager, you don't care. You just want to offer as much diversification as possible, with as much yield as possible.'[25]

Finally, all of these financial dynamics must also be considered in the light of the extreme swings in the dollar's price against other currencies over the past decade.[26] In 2004, former Treasury Secretary Robert Rubin accused the Bush administration of 'playing with fire' through its policies of dollar weakening alongside continuing federal deficit spending, a combination which would generate 'serious disruptions in our financial markets'. Added C. Fred Bergsten, director of the Institute for International Economics, 'Everyone in the market knows the dollar has to come down a lot. People are starting to run for the exits.'[27]

This degree of volatility is not unprecedented in world capitalism, where empires have periodically risen and fallen in part based upon uneven development through trade. Ironically, the power of the US to manipulate the economies of other countries, and lower the value of their exports, has not changed these trade balances for the better. The US was the main beneficiary of East Asian countries' 50 per cent currency crash in 1997–8, as enormous capital flows entered the US banking system, and as imports from East Asia were acquired at much lower prices, keeping in check what might otherwise have been credit-fuelled inflation.

To be sure, this is a long-standing problem of differential power relations in trade and exchange rate deviations (together termed 'unequal exchange'), which, according to Samir Amin and Gernot Köhler, caused surplus transfers approaching $1.8 trillion per year by the late 1990s.[28] Whereas the average currency value of Second and Third World countries (that is, non-members of the Organization for Economic Cooperation and Development) in relation to First World currencies was 82 per cent in 1960, it had declined to 38 per cent by the late 1990s, according to Amin and Köhler.

Considered in another form, the importance of unequal exchange is witnessed in the difference between export volume and the value-added that goes into the exports. According to Jayati Ghosh, this is not merely a matter of primary commodity export dependence (as

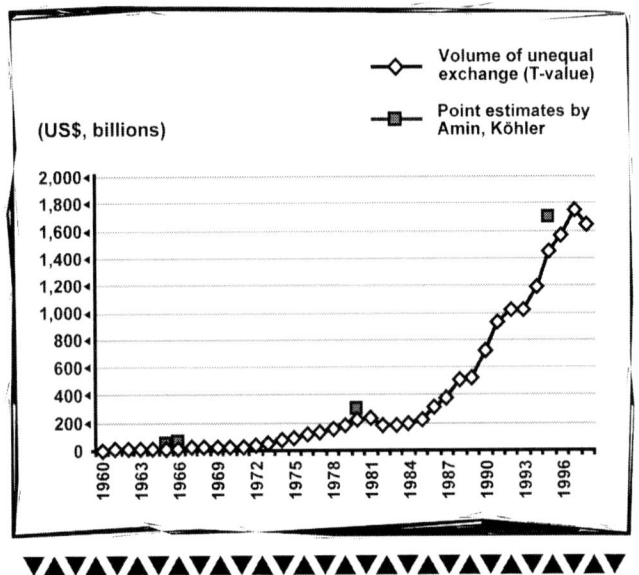

Figure 2.4 South—North 'unequal exchange' value transfers, 1960—98
(US$ billions)

Source: Köhler, G. (2003), 'Time Series of Unequal Exchange, 1960-98', in G. Köhler and E. J. Chaves
(eds), *Globalization: Critical Perspectives*, New York, Nova Press.

discussed in Chapter 4), but also of the nature of manufacturing output in the global division of labour:

> While developing countries as a group more than doubled their share of world manufacturing exports from 10.6 per cent in 1980 to 26.5 per cent in 1998, their share of manufacturing value added increased by less than half, from 16.6 per cent to 23.8 per cent. By contrast, developed countries experienced a substantial decline in share of world manufacturing exports, from 82.3 per cent to 70.9 per cent. But at the same time their share of world manufacturing value added actually increased, from 64.5 per cent to 73.3 per cent.[29]

Whether it is a function of real currency changes or of the character of what is being produced (raw materials or low-value manufactured goods), the volatile trade-related underdevelopment captured in these figures appears most important during epochs of 'globalization' such as the 1910s–20s and 1980s–90s, a point discussed further in Chapter 4.

The volatility is, of course, global in scale, as even the US current account also suffers from extreme trade/investment instability: from surpluses associated with the weak dollar in 1980 and 1991, to dramatic declines to dangerous levels in the mid-1980s (−3.5 per cent of GDP) and again since the mid-1990s (down to −5 per cent of GDP and worse). Once the Dot Com boom was finished in 2000, the US share of global foreign direct investment also fell substantially, from $321 billion in 2000 to as low as $40 billion in 2003.[30]

NEW ROUNDS OF GLOBAL FINANCIAL VOLATILITY?

The problems of a volatile world economy appear to be durable. Distortions in currencies, trade and investment accounts have been accompanied by rising financial profitability, simultaneous with relative US manufacturing decline. The past few years of massive deficit spending by the US state indicate the importance of what can be termed 'military Keynesianism'. But so too is 'consumer Keynesianism' via credit increasingly crucial to the US economy, with household debt as a percentage of disposable income rising steadily from below 70 per cent prior to 1985, to above 100 per cent fifteen years later. On the one hand, there can be no doubt that financial product innovations and especially new debt instruments associated with new information, communications and technology simply permit a greater debt load without necessarily endangering consumer finances. On the other hand, however, during the same period, US household savings rates fell from the 7–12 per cent band to below 3 per cent.

Moreover, consumers and other investors are also more vulnerable to larger financial shocks and asset price swings than at any time since 1929. Although there were indications from around 1974 that major financial institutions would be affected by the onset of structural economic problems, few predicted the dramatic series of upheavals across major credit and investment markets over the subsequent quarter century: the Third World debt crisis (early 1980s for commercial lenders, but lasting through to the present for countries and societies); energy finance shocks (mid-1980s); crashes of international stock (1987) and property (1991–3) markets; crises in nearly all the large emerging market countries (1995–2002); and even huge individual corporate bankruptcies which had powerful international ripples.

Most importantly, the US stock market was the site of an enormous bubble until 2000, perhaps culminating in the Dot Com bubble crash which wiped $8.5 trillion of paper wealth off the books from peak to trough – but, on the other hand, seemingly reinflating in 2003–5 thanks to the return of household investors and mutual fund flows, and possibly rising further in future years if Bush begins social security privatization. The market's bubble was worse even than prior episodes such as the run-up to 1929. Of course, the lost paper wealth from 2000–2 brought these ratios down, but with the subsequent rise, the markets are by no means yet down to levels that are in keeping with historical averages.

The implications of the 2000–2 crash are still important, however. Combined with the demographic trend towards baby-boomer retirement, it appears that there are some substantial pension shortfalls in the US (and also in Japan, notwithstanding the Nikkei's slow recovery). Moreover, household assets also crashed because the share bubble burst, although fast-rising housing prices kept overall asset levels at a respectable level, at least for the top 60 per cent of US households who own their homes, and at least through 2005. This particular bubble was enhanced by the 1998 drop in interest rates – the Federal Reserve Bank's response to the Asian and Long-term Capital Management crises – which spurred a dramatic increase in mortgage refinancings. As a result of the huge rise in property prices that followed, the difference between the real cost of owning and of renting soared to unprecedented levels. The fact that the housing sector has contributed to roughly a third of US GDP growth since the late 1990s makes this bubble particularly fragile.

Warnings about volatility were, by late 2005, most urgent in relation to global property markets. South Africa experienced the world's highest increase in property prices during the early 2000s, but everywhere the bubble grew to untenable heights. For 1997–2004, the cumulative increase in housing prices was of the order of 200 per cent in South Africa, 160 per cent in Ireland, 130 per cent in Britain, 120 per cent in Spain, 90 per cent in Australia, 80 per cent in Sweden, 70 per cent in France and 60 per cent in the US.[31] In April 2005, Morgan Stanley's Steven Roach offered this assessment of the dangers to the US economy:

> Should asset-dependent, saving-short, overly indebted American con-
> sumers feel at risk if the Fed assures them that there is no housing bubble

– that the asset-based underpinnings of their decision making are well grounded? A record consumption share in the US economy – 71 per cent of GDP since 2002 versus a 67 per cent norm over the 1975 to 2000 period – speaks for itself.[32]

By June 2005, the world housing boom represented 'the biggest bubble in history', according to *The Economist*, because '*never* before have real house prices risen so fast, for so long, in so many countries':

> The total value of residential property in developed economies rose by more than $30 trillion over the past five years, to over $70 trillion, an increase equivalent to 100 per cent of those countries' combined GDPs. Not only does this dwarf any previous house-price boom, it is larger than the global stockmarket bubble in the late 1990s (an increase over five years of 80 per cent of GDP) or America's stockmarket bubble in the late 1920s (55 per cent of GDP).... Japan provides a nasty warning of what can happen when boom turns to bust. Japanese property prices have dropped for 14 years in a row, by 40 per cent from their peak in 1991.[33]

Because Japanese authorities skilfully bailed out banks regularly and kept other state stimulants – such as public works programmes – going, the bubble's burst was less of a pop and more of a slow but sure deflation, like a bicycle tyre going flat over time. But flat it will eventually be: Yale economist Robert Schiller predicts a 40 per cent real decline in US real estate prices over the next generation, given the 'irrational exuberance' that pushed the market's prices so high.[34]

The big question is whether the volatility in housing will be contagious, given that 40 per cent of the two million jobs created from late 2001 through mid-2004 were directly linked to housing. Writing in the *Financial Times*, Stephen Schurr offered a sobering warning:

> The greatest impact of a housing downturn may be felt in consumer spending, which represents two-thirds of the US economy. Consumer spending has propped up the US economy and stock market for the past two years as capital spending languished. A primary driver of this has been the so-called 'housing ATM' phenomenon, whereby Americans tap their home equity for cash to fund their spending.... 'Our financial sectors are linked in ways they never have been before. If housing prices fall and a guy defaults on his mortgage, the pension funds that own mortgages are going to get hit, bond markets are going to get hit, everybody is going to feel it,' said hedge fund manager Jim Melcher. 'Nobody is prepared for it.'[35]

By late 2005, those unprepared were potentially in deep trouble, as 2006 would be the first year in US memory in which housing served 'as a drag on the economy', *The New York Times* reported.[36] For the third quarter of 2005, the US personal savings rate fell to −1.5 per cent, the worst-ever recorded quarterly rate (since 1947 when data begin).

Finally, another market that has taken off in a spectacularly unsustainable manner, and which may form the basis for more speculative investment in future, is energy derivatives. The number of options and futures traded has risen steadily, but does not seem to have created a 'mature' market in fields like electricity, gas and oil, as reflected in huge ongoing price fluctuations. A market in carbon emissions is also nascent but potentially enormous, given the ratification of the Kyoto Protocol by Russia, which is aiming to convert its 'hot air' allowance of emissions into trades with the world's major polluters.

DRAINING THE SOUTH

For the Third World, these multiple sources of economic volatility have important feedback effects. It is here that we might revive Trotsky's sense of capitalism's uneven and combined development, and Luxemburg's concern that capitalism needs to superexploit its non-capitalist periphery.

First, if not from foreign direct investment, where would the US get its needed capital fixes, especially financial inflows to permit the payment of more than $2 billion each workday required for imports and debt repayments? The foreign inflows were quite volatile in 2002–4, but of greatest importance, perhaps, was the rapid rise in foreign – especially East Asian – ownership of aggregate US Treasury bills, rising from 20 per cent in 1995 to 40 per cent in 2005. The contribution of emerging markets and developing countries in relation to the US rose from a net inflow of $120 billion in capital inflows in 1998 to a $120 billion net outflow by 2003. From the Euro area, Japan and other advanced economies, the flows also shifted, from a $50 billion inflow in 1991 to a $310 billion outflow by 2003.[37]

This vacuuming of available finance into the US during the early 2000s – slightly offset by capital reversals in 2005 – is important not because the supply side of capital market funding is in any way constrained. By 2004 there was, after all, roughly $124 trillion (theoretically) to draw upon within global capital markets, and an additional $36 trillion in GDP each year contributing ongoing surpluses to the markets. The distribution of these funds is notable, reflected by four major blocs of funds: the EU ($43 trillion), US ($41 trillion), Japan ($19 trillion) and Asian emerging markets ($9 trillion). The stock of capital is invested in stock markets ($31 trillion), public bonds ($20 trillion), corporate securities ($31 trillion), and banks ($41 trillion), as well as foreign exchange reserves ($3 trillion).[38] There is no shortage of liquid capital in the global markets, only a question of what rate of return will be required to maintain foreign interest in the US position. This is particularly important as one of the crucial 'pull' factors, drawing resources away from Africa and other developing countries.

The new US Federal Reserve chairperson, Ben Bernanke, offered a dangerously benign view of overaccumulated global finance, suggesting that the US can continue to suck in the world's capital:

> Over the past decade, a combination of diverse forces has created a significant increase in the global supply of saving – a global saving glut – which helps to explain both the increase in the US current account deficit and the relatively low level of long-term real interest rates in the world today. The prospect of dramatic increases in the ratio of retirees to workers in a number of major industrial economies is one important reason for the high level of global saving.[39]

As no major change in US policy is anticipated, the drain of capital to Washington continues. One result for the South, including African countries, is the need to maintain much higher interest rates than under normal conditions. To take 30 July 2004 as a snapshot point, emerging market bonds funded internationally required the highest premium in Nigeria (6.1 per cent, about twice that of South Africa, the only other major sub-Saharan Africa issuer). As for local bonds, the interest rate spreads have been stratospheric in high-risk sites like Argentina (49.1 per cent) followed in Africa by Côte d'Ivoire (33.3 per cent), Nigeria (5.3 per cent) and South Africa (1.4 per cent). But these are highly fluid financial markets and the same statistics in 2000, for example, provide interest spreads as follows: Argentina 7.7 per cent, Côte d'Ivoire 24.4 per cent, Nigeria 14.8 per cent, and South Africa 4.2 per cent.[40]

Amplified uneven development is reflected in highly divergent patterns of financial stability and volatility in these emerging markets. One set of statistics that signals perhaps the greatest danger for the Third World is that for capital outflow via unofficial routes. Capital flight has been an especially severe problem since the mid-1990s in Asia (peaking at US$100 billion in 1998) and the Middle East (US$50 billion in 1999). But, as noted in more detail below, Africa has seen an even greater share of its resources – more than US$20 billion in 1997 alone – drained out by its own citizens.[41]

Another factor reflecting potentially high risks is rising foreign indebtedness. In absolute terms, Third World debt rose from US$580 billion in 1980 to US$2.4 trillion in 2002, and much of it is now simply unrepayable, a factor recognized by the G8 finance ministers in June 2005 when they agreed to a partial write-off of $40 billion of debt owed by the 18 poorest countries.[42] In 2002, there was a net outflow of $340 billion in servicing this debt, compared to overseas development aid of $37 billion. As Brussels-based debt campaigner Eric Toussaint remarks, 'since 1980, over 50 Marshall Plans (over $4.6 trillion) have been sent by the peoples of the Periphery to their creditors in the Centre'.[43] As argued below, the Highly Indebted Poor Countries initiative demonstrably failed to change the debt servicing ratios noticeably, and the small debt relief concessions – including the June 2005 finance ministers' offer – came at the expense of deepened neoliberal conditionality.

In sum, we are left with a sense that the world economy retains features of volatility and unevenness that are untenable. These features are not accidental but are structured into economic interrelationships within the advanced capitalist world, and between the North and South. How does that structuring of underdevelopment work? At least five components of capital accumulation and class formation – trade, finance, direct investment, uneven migration and comprador relations – remain central to Africa's ongoing under-development. Most importantly, we will conclude, the home-grown nature of neoliberalism, corresponding to the formation of a trans-national neoliberal managerial elite and compliant African politicians (see Chapter 5), requires a rethink about the very nature of both liberatory and solidarity politics. The key categories for consideration are financial accounts (including aid, debt, portfolio finance and capital flight) in Chapter 3, and trade, investment and labour flows in Chapter 4.

NOTES

1 Bond, P. and A. Desai (2006), 'Explaining Uneven and Combined Development in South Africa', in B. Dunn (ed.), *The Permanent Revolution Revisited*, London, Pluto; Desai, A. and P. Bond (2006), *Crony Neoliberalism and Paranoid Nationalism: Debating South Africa's 'Developmental State'*, Pietermaritzburg, University of KwaZulu-Natal Press; and Bond, P. (1999), 'Uneven Development', in P. O'Hara (ed.), *Encyclopaedia of Political Economy*, London, Routledge. We take very seriously the mandate by Paul Zeleza for any theorist of African political economy, namely that 'Greater care needs to be taken to wed theories to facts, link structures and processes, production and exchange, integrate the relations and forces of production, society and nature, decipher the dialectic between internal and external forces, short-term and long-term trends, and capture the similarities and differences in the patterns of economic change between and within regions in Africa.' Zeleza, P. (1993), *A Modern Economic History of Africa, Volume 1: the Nineteenth Century*, Dakar, CODESRIA, p. 5.

2 The seminal work is Rostow, W. (1960), *Stages of Economic Growth*, Cambridge, Cambridge University Press.

3 See, Amin, S. (1974), *Accumulation on a World Scale*, New York, Monthly Review Press; Amin, S. (1976), *Unequal Development*, Sussex, Harvester Press; Cardoso, F. H. and E. Faletto (1979) [1970], *Dependency and Development in Latin America*, Berkeley, University of California Press; Frank, A. G. (1967), *Capitalism and Underdevelopment in Latin America*, New York, Monthly Review Press; Frank, A. G. (1969), *Latin America: Underdevelopment or Revolution*, New York, Monthly Review Press; and Frank, A. G. (1991), 'Latin American Development Theories Revisited, a Participant Review Essay', *Scandinavian Journal of Development Studies*, 10, 3; and Furtado, C. (1963), *The Economic Growth of Brazil*, Berkeley, University of California Press.

4 Marx, K. (1867) [2005], *Das Kapital*, available at <http://www.marxists.org/archive/marx/works/1867-c1/ch31.htm>.

5 See Luxemburg, R. (1968) [1923], *The Accumulation of Capital*, New York, Monthly Review Press and <www.marxists.org/archive/luxemburg/1913/accumulation-capital>; for recent interpretations see also Hart, G. (2005), 'Denaturalising Dispossession: Critical Ethnography in the Age of Resurgent Imperialism', University of KwaZulu-Natal Centre for Civil Society Research, Report 27, <http://www.ukzn.ac.za/ccs>; Harvey, D. (2003), *The New Imperialism*, Oxford and New York, Oxford University Press; and Harvey, D. (2005), *Spaces of Neoliberalization: Towards a Theory of Uneven Geographical Development*, Stuttgart, Franz Steiner Verlag.

6 See Harvey, D. (1982), *The Limits to Capital*, Chicago, University of Chicago Press; Harvey, D. (1985), *The Urbanization of Capital*, Baltimore, Johns Hopkins University Press; Harvey, D. (1996), *Justice, Nature and the Geography of Difference*, Oxford, Basil Blackwell; and Mandel, E. (1962)

[1968], *Marxist Economic Theory*, London, Merlin Press.

7 In addition to Harvey's writings, see Mandel, E. (1976), *Late Capitalism*, London, New Left Books; Smith, N. (1989), 'Uneven Development and Location Theory: Toward a Synthesis', in R. Peet and N. Thrift (eds), *New Models in Geography*, Volume 1, London, Unwin Hyman; Smith, N. (1990), *Uneven Development*, Oxford, Basil Blackwell; and Webber, M. J. and Rigby, D. L. (1996) *The Golden Age Illusion: Rethinking Postwar Capitalism*, New York, Guilford Press. See also radical geographical journals such as *Antipode*, *Economic Geography*, *Society and Space*, *Capitalism, Nature, Socialism*, and *The International Journal of Urban and Regional Research*.

8 G8 Finance Ministers (2005), 'Statement on Development and Debt: G8 Finance Ministers' Conclusions on Development', London, 10–11 June.

9 Williamson, J. (1990), 'The Progress of Policy Reform in Latin America,' Policy Analyses in International Economics, Washington, Institute for International Economics. *Business Day*, 17 December 1993.

10 Felix, D. (2003), 'The Past as Future? The Contribution of Financial Globalization to the Current Crisis of NeoLiberalism as a Development Strategy', paper presented to the conference New Pathways for Mexico's Sustainable Development, El Colegio de Mexico, Mexico City, 21 October, p. 2.

11 Harvey, D. (2005), *A Brief History of Neoliberalism*, Oxford, Oxford University Press.

12 Freeman, A. (2004), 'The Inequality of Nations', in B. Kagarlitsky and A. Freeman (eds), *The Politics of Empire: Globalization in Crisis*, London, Pluto Press.

13. World Bank, World Development Report 2006, p. 63. See Freeman, 'The Inequality of Nations', for more inequality measurement, as well as the debate over income surveys versus payroll statistics in Galbraith, J. and H. Kum (2002), 'Inequality and Globalization: Judging the Data', presentation to the World Bank, 18 June, <http://www.utip.gov.utexas.edu>.

14 See, for example, Brenner, R. (2003), *The Boom and the Bubble*, London, Verso; Foster, J. (2002), *Ecology against Capitalism*, New York, Monthly Review Press; Pollin, R. (2003), *Contours of Descent: US Economic Fractures and the Landscape of Global Austerity*, London, Verso; Wood, E. (2003), *Empire of Capital*, London, Verso.

15 Tett, G. (2004), 'The Gospel According to Paul', *Financial Times*, 23 October.

16 Harvey, D. (2003), 'The "New" Imperialism: on Spatio-temporal Fixes and Accumulation by Dispossession', in L. Panitch and C. Leys (eds), *The New Imperial Challenge: Socialist Register 2004*, London, Merlin Press and New York, Monthly Review Press.

17 Personal communication, 9 November 2004. See also Brenner, R. (1998), 'The Economics of Global Turbulence', *New Left Review*, May–June, pp. 102–11, Figure 8, Table 9; and Brenner, R. (2004), 'New Boom or New Bubble', *New Left Review*, January–February, pp. 65–9.

18 Whether Brenner offers a sufficient basis of proof has been disputed, for example by Giovanni Arrighi, who observes 'a comparatively low, and declining,

level of over-capacity.... Over-capacity in US manufacturing decreased sharply during the closing years of the long boom and increased even more sharply during the crisis of profitability that marked the transition from the boom to the long downturn. After 1973, in contrast, both indicators continue to show considerable fluctuations but provide no evidence to support Brenner's contention that the long downturn was characterized by above-normal over-capacity. The Federal Reserve Board's figures show capacity utilization settling back to where it was in the 1950s with no trend either way, while Shaikh's show capacity utilization in the 1970s at higher levels than in the 1950s and rising further in the 1980s and 1990s....' (Arrighi, G. (2003), 'The Social and Political Economy of Global Turbulence', *New Left Review*, March–April.)

Such data are not terribly useful for measuring overaccumulation, however, because year-on-year capacity measurement does not take into account either the manner in which firms add or subtract capacity (e.g., temporarily mothballing factories and equipment) or the ways that overaccumulation problems are shifted into other sectors of the economy. Brenner insists that such statistics cover merely short-term fluctuations, and more rigorous indicators of overaccumulation are not yet available in any data series. During doctoral research in Zimbabwe, I constructed a proxy based on inventory stocks drawn from the manufacturing sector in the annual, quite reliable Census of Industrial Production series for the key period when overaccumulation emerged during the 1970s–80s. See Bond, P. (1998), *Uneven Zimbabwe: A Study of Finance, Development and Underdevelopment*, Trenton, Africa World Press, Chapters 5–6.

19   Clarke, S. (1988), *Keynesianism, Monetarism and the Crisis of the State*, Aldershot, Edward Elgar, pp. 279–360; Harvey, D. (1989), *The Condition of Postmodernity*, Oxford, Basil Blackwell, pp. 180–97; Mandel, E. (1989), 'Theories of Crisis: an Explanation of the 1974–82 Cycle', in M. Gottdiener and N. Komninos (eds), *Capitalist Development and Crisis Theory: Accumulation, Regulation and Spatial Restructuring*, London, Macmillan, pp. 30–58; Shutt, H. (1999), *The Trouble with Capitalism*, London, Zed Books, pp. 34–45; and Biel, R. (2000), *The New Imperialism*, London, Zed Books, pp. 131–89.

20   According to Duménil and Lévy, 'In the first series, profits are equal to the net product minus the cost of labour, and business and profit taxes. They are divided by the net worth (total assets minus debt). For the second series, real interest is subtracted from profits, i.e. interest minus a correction for the depreciation of debt resulting from inflation.'

21   Duménil, G. and D. Lévy (2003), 'Costs and Benefits of Neoliberalism: a Class Analysis', unpublished paper, Cepremap, Paris.

22   Harvey, *The New Imperialism*; and Harvey, D. (2005), *Spaces of Neoliberalization: Towards a Theory of Uneven Geographical Development*, Stuttgart, Franz Steiner Verlag.

23   Panitch, L. and S. Gindin (2004), 'Global Capitalism and American Empire', in L. Panitch and C. Leys (eds), *The New Imperial Challenge: Socialist Register 2004*, London, Merlin Press and New York, Monthly Review Press.

24 International Monetary Fund, *Global Financial Stability Report*, Appendix, Table 10.

25 Blustein, P. (2005), 'Funds Blowing Foreign Bubbles?', *Washington Post*, 8 December.

26 One reason is that the statistics above are mainly measured in local currencies and sometimes converted to Purchasing Power Parity, so they do not fully capture the extent of global-scale volatility.

27 Simon, E. (2004), 'Weak Dollar Boosts Some Corporate Growth', *AP Business News*, 11 November.

28 Köhler, G. (1998), 'Unequal Exchange 1965–1995: World Trends and World Tables', World-Systems Archive, Working Papers, <http://csf.colorado.edu/wsystems/archive/papers/kohlertoc.htm>.

29 Ghosh, J. (2002), 'Why More Exports Have Not Made Developing Countries Richer', <http://www.networkideas.org/themes/trade/may2002/print/prnt 110502_Exports_Developing_Countries.htm>, 11 May.

30 International Monetary Fund (2004), *Global Financial Stability Report*, Washington, Appendix, Table 1.

31 International Monetary Fund (2005), 'South Africa: Selected Issues', Washington, September 2005.

32 Roach, S. (2005), 'Original Sin', Morgan Stanley, <http://www.morgan stanley.com/GEFdata/digests/20050425-mon. html#anchor0>, 25 April.

33 *The Economist* (2005), 'The Global Housing Boom: In Come the Waves', 16 June.

34 Leonhardt, D. (2005), 'Be Warned: Mr Bubble's Worried', *New York Times*, 21 August.

35 Schurr, S. (2005), 'Soft Foundations', *Financial Times*, 30 April.

36 Bajaj, V. (2005), 'Home Sales Fall 2.7 per cent, Suggesting a Drag on '06 Economy', *New York Times*, 29 November.

37 International Monetary Fund, *Global Financial Stability Report*, pp. 36, 148.

38 *Ibid.*, Appendix, Table 3.

39 Bernanke, B. (2005), 'The Global Saving Glut and the US Current Account Deficit', paper presented to the Sandridge Lecture Series, Virginia Association of Economics, Richmond, 10 March, <http://www.federalreserve.gov/board docs/speeches/2005/200503102/default.htm>.

40 International Monetary Fund, *Global Financial Stability Report*, Appendix, Table 13.

41 *Ibid.*, p. 126

42 As discussed in more detail in the next chapter, the debt relief was conditioned by standard neoliberal policy requirements, and represented an outlay of merely US$1.5 billion each year for the wealthy countries, in comparison to those states' military spending in excess of US$700 billion a year.

43 Toussaint, E. (2004), 'Transfers from the Periphery to the Centre, from Labour to Capital', unpublished paper, Committee for the Abolition of the Third World Debt, Brussels, p. 3.

3

Financial Inflows and Outflows

Phantom aid, debt peonage, capital flight

How do aid, debt, foreign financial investments and capital flight affect the way capital accumulates in Africa? The general perception of international elites is that Africa is the (often unworthy) beneficiary of 'official financial flows'. In a graph prepared for the Commission for Africa, the impression left is that there is a vast inflow of aid (because 'phantom aid' is not mentioned); that foreign direct investment in the continent has been rising steadily (without considering the special circumstances in just three recipient countries since 1997, a topic

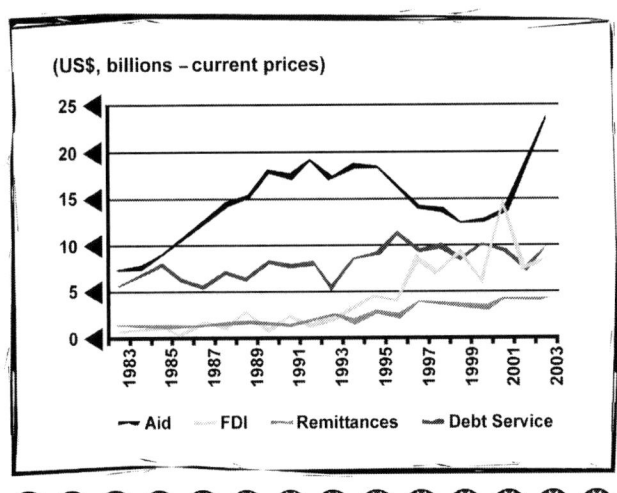

Figure 3.1 Africa Commission estimates of financial/investment flows to sub-Saharan Africa

Source: Commission for Africa (2005), *Our Common Future*, London, p. 106.

31

considered in Chapter 4); that debt service payments have been steady (although the net payment went negative during the 1990s); and that remittances are now an important factor (without factoring in capital flight by residents). It is to a reality check in each of these categories that we now turn.

AID EBBS, FLOWS AND PHANTOMS

Donor aid to Africa actually dropped 40 per cent during the 1990s, especially in the wake of the West's Cold War victory, but the general decline had begun during the late 1960s. The Commission for Africa has claimed – without providing details – that aid to Africa picked up again after 2000, doubling from US$12 billion to US$24 billion in the subsequent four years. Although during 2000–3, *per capita* aid to sub-Saharan Africa did rise by US$10 per person, the International Monetary Fund concedes that today 'it is still lower than *per capita* aid in the 1980s, when aid to the region was about US$34 *per capita* in constant 2003 prices' and, moreover, 'excluding South Africa and

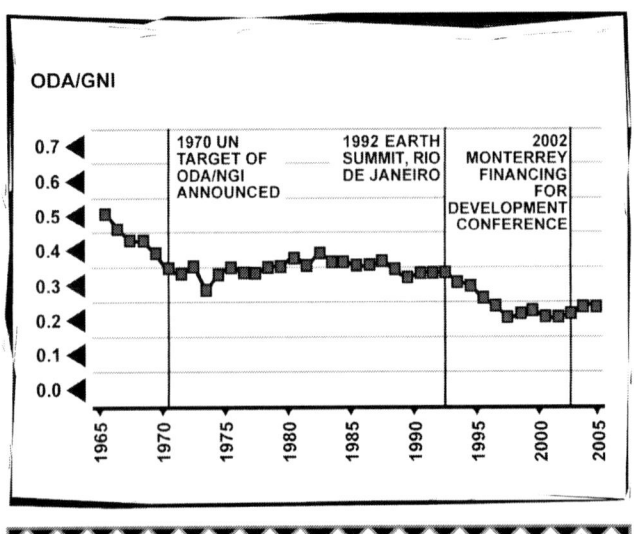

Figure 3.2 Third World aid trends, 1965–2004 (Wealthy countries' overseas development aid as percentage of gross national income, ODI/GNI)

Source: Action Aid (2005), *Real Aid: an Agenda for Making Aid Work*, Johannesburg, p. 36.

Nigeria, official grants [to sub-Saharan Africa] as a share of GDP are projected to increase to 3.2 per cent of GDP in 2005, from 3.1 per cent in 2004' – hardly evidence of a major Northern commitment to fighting poverty.[1] In any case, the use of debt relief funds to boost aid figures (such as those above) is highly dubious, since at the Monterrey Financing for Development summit in 2002, governments agreed that debt relief should be 'additional' to existing and rising aid.

Even with this and other 'phantom aid' distortions, most donor states (except the Scandinavian countries and Holland) are well below the 0.7 per cent target set thirty-five years ago in the United Nations. The US and Japanese figures of 0.12 per cent and 0.23 per cent are most egregious, if national generosity is adequately captured in this variable. Compared to military spending of $642 billion by rich countries in 2003, aid of $69 billion is a pittance. The most striking arms spender compared to aid stinginess is the US (1 per cent of government spending on aid compared to 25 per cent on the military), along with Greece (1.4 per cent compared to 26.5 per cent), the UK (1.6 per cent compared to 13.3 per cent), France (1.7 per cent compared to 10.7 per cent) and Portugal (1 per cent compared to 10 per cent).[2]

Indeed, aid and arms spending are integrally linked, given that untied money is 'fungible': that is, what comes in for one purpose (such as housing or food) permits African states to increase spending for military or repressive purposes. Donor funding received ostensibly for development activities – for example by Israel and Egypt, which for geopolitical reasons get vast amounts of US aid – can be rechannelled into military spending. Overall, according to an Action Aid correlation of *per capita* aid and UNDP Human Development Index (HDI) ratings, logically countries at the low end of the HDI scale should be receiving higher *per capita* amounts, but this is not the case. The vast majority of countries rated below number 130 on the HDI ranking get aid of US$50 per person or below, in contrast to the much higher share of countries ranked between 80 and 130, which receive upwards of at least US$90 per person.[3]

Moreover, once one factors in the vast wastage associated with the aid bureaucracy, tied aid, as well as other 'phantom' aspects such as debt relief, a further correction to the statistics can be made. Globally, according to Action Aid, total official aid of US$69 billion in 2003 was reduced to 'real' aid to poor people of just US$27 billion. About one seventh (14 per cent) of the purported aid – better considered 'phantom aid' – includes 'debt relief', which rose from around US$1.5 billion in 2000 to more than US$6 billion in 2003. As noted later, the debt relief was provided in such a way as to deepen not lessen dependence and Northern control of Africa. Other phantom aid components include the transaction and administrative costs of paying out aid funds (14 per cent). Technical assistance by Northern experts accounted for a fifth of aid; as noted below, water privatization advice by Britain's Adam Smith Institute is an example of how such donor assistance does yet more damage to the African state and society. Action Aid estimates that another 7 per cent of donor aid is spent on activities which lack any poverty focus, while 2 per cent is spent on refugees (not longer-term development). Another 4 per cent is technically 'tied' to purchase of inputs from the donor country.[4]

Even the Commission for Africa admits that only a small proportion of aid is technically 'untied', and while that amount rose from US$2.3 billion in 1999 to US$4.3 billion in 2003, it declined as a proportion of total 'aid'.[5] The worst offenders in terms of tied aid are Italy and the United States, while France and the US are the major 'phantom' donors. Even the IMF – itself regularly guilty of preventing aid from reaching its targets, on grounds that fiscal expansion threatens monetary discipline – came to admit, in 2005, that tied aid is a major problem:

> Although aid flows to Africa have been increasing since the Monterrey conference of 2002, only a small share of the incremental aid has been provided in the form of programme and project assistance.... During 2000–3, debt forgiveness accounted for 19 per cent of the total aid disbursed to this region, on average.... About 20 per cent of aid to SSA is still tied. Furthermore, the volatility of aid disbursements and the consequent unpredictability of flows make it difficult for recipient govern-ments to formulate medium-term plans.[6]

As witnessed by the IMF's repeated refusal to countenance budgetary increases to hire more African health workers, on grounds that such spending might lead to higher inflation, Northern 'condition-ality' is still pervasive, especially on the 20 per cent of aid that takes the form of technical assistance. This funding has been important to donors and allied corporations for many years, especially in areas like water and health, where relationships with water and pharmaceutical corporations appear to be continually strengthening.

According to a study by British researcher Mark Curtis,

A close look at the EU 'aid for trade' programme shows that much of this 'aid' is really about further pushing developing countries to promote trade liberalization. EU aid in this area includes, for example, 'support for the implementation of existing and future WTO agreements' and 'support for policy reforms and investments necessary to enhance economic efficiency and to ensure greater participation in the world economy'.... The Commission also states that its aid in this area helps the 'promotion of sound macroeconomic, sectoral and tax policies that improve the investment climate, as well as support for private sector development'.... The Commission states that around 70 per cent of its aid for trade is 'support for the private sector'.[7]

In East Africa, according to Curtis, EU aid has paid for a PROINVEST report that promotes privatization, including

major 'investment opportunities' for European companies, identifying one of these as public utilities: 'government authorities are increasingly open to forms of Public Private Partnerships (PPPs) (concessions, management contracts etc.) and EU operators could play a significant role'. This includes 'management and rehabilitation of water and sewage systems in major urban centres' – i.e., the privatization of water supply. The report also states that 'PROINVEST could promote and/or support initiatives aimed at analysing the complex policy and operational issues related to PPP in public utilities, bringing a more balanced "European" view to the table'. A report on West and Central Africa notes investment opportunities in health and education, concluding that 'this sector could offer interesting niche opportunities for European investors'.[8]

As another example, the British Department for International Development regularly contracted the Adam Smith Institute to design private water management programmes for African cities. In Dar es Salaam, the US$164 million water contract, funded by the World Bank, African Development Bank and European Investment Bank, was won by the British firm Biwater. British taxpayers spent £273,000 'to produce public relations materials including a pro-privatization pop song to persuade a sceptical public of the benefits of privatization', according to the World Development Movement (WDM), a progressive London-based campaigning group.

But in May 2005, the Tanzanian government deported three Biwater executives for mismanagement and cancelled the deal on the grounds that Biwater had invested only half of what it had promised

(US$8.5 million) while raising water bills precipitously. Water Minister Edward Lowassa was blunt: 'The water supply services in Dar es Salaam and in the neighbouring places have deteriorated rather than improving since this firm took over some two years ago. The revocation was made following persistent complaints by city residents over incompetence of the firm.' As interpreted by the *Financial Times,*

> Experts from multilateral agencies are understood to have taken the view that the UK–German–Tanzanian joint venture performed poorly and that the Tanzanian government had abided by its agreement.... [The Biwater deal] resulted in what many complained was worse rather than better water supply.[9]

Biwater then went to the World Bank's International Centre for Settlement of Investment Disputes to ask for compensation. According to the WDM,

> Tanzania is one of the most heavily indebted countries in the world, its external debt stands at $7.5 billion. From 1996 to 1999 privatization of Dar es Salaam's water was a condition of the IMF's Enhanced Structural Adjustment Facility and from 2000 to 2003 it was a condition of an IMF Poverty Reduction and Growth Facility. Continued restructuring and privatization of public utilities was part of Tanzania's conditions for getting debt relief under the Heavily Indebted Poor Countries initiative.... Tanzania is the 164th poorest country in the world (out of 177).

As Andrew Mushi, director of the Tanzania Association of Non-Governmental Organizations, explained, 'We are in full support of our government in cancelling the Biwater contract and we think it is very unfair of Biwater to sue our government because the burden of paying for this legal case will fall on the people of Tanzania.'[10]

The highest-profile aid interventions in recent years were probably in the field of HIV/AIDS treatment. These included a 'full-court press' – including threats of further aid cuts – against governments that made provision for generic medicines production, which Bill Clinton only backed away from in late 1999 after sustained popular protest.[11] In early 2003, George W. Bush promised a $15 billion AIDS programme, then whittled the funding down to a fraction of that, then refused to provide resources for the UN Global Fund to Fight AIDS, TB and Malaria, and then prohibited US government financing of generic medicines. Pandering to his Christian fundamentalist base, Bush's support for Third World family planning was even more conditionality-ridden.

At the same time, Bush introduced an innovative vehicle to fuse neoliberal market conditionality with, allegedly, greater social investment: the Millennium Challenge Account (MCA). With United States Agency for International Development (USAID) budgets still declining in real terms, the delinked MCA funding was meant to rise from $1 billion in 2004 to $5 billion in 2006, a 100 per cent increase on 2004 spending for all US overseas development assistance. But of 74 'low-income' countries supposedly eligible (of which 39 are from Africa), only 16 passed the first test of governance and economic freedom in May 2004. Half of these were African: Benin, Cape Verde, Ghana, Lesotho, Madagascar, Mali, Mozambique and Senegal. The criteria for funding these countries' aid programmes fall into three categories:

- *Ruling justly* – based on Freedom House rankings of civil liberties and political rights as well as World Bank Institute indices on accountability, governance and control of corruption.

- *Economic freedom* – determined by credit ratings, inflation rates, business start-up times, trade policies and regulatory regimes as measured by such institutions as the World Bank, the International Monetary Fund and the Heritage Foundation Index of Economic Freedom.

- *Investment in people* – gauged according to public expenditure on health and primary education, immunization rates and primary school completion rates as recorded by the national governments, the World Health Organization and the UN.[12]

How to interpret such a manoeuvre? The role of the US state in Africa – prior, during and after the Cold War – is invariably tied to corporate extraction of resources and backed by military might. Washington's attempt to disguise and legitimize this through aid that carries 'good governance' and 'social investment' conditionalities dates to the Clinton era,[13] but under Bush's MCA involves more sophisticated disciplinary neoliberal surveillance, especially in combination with the World Bank.[14]

The World Bank Country Policy and Institutional Assessment gave the following African countries A ratings in their 2004 quintile measures of relative performance: Cape Verde, Mauritania, Senegal, Tanzania and Uganda (South Africa is not part of the rating system, but would probably be an A performer). The number of failing (F) ratings in Africa is twice as high, and contains the most populous country: Angola, Burundi, Central African Republic, Comoros, Guinea-Bissau, Nigeria, São Tomé and Principe, Sudan, Togo and Zimbabwe. Only Nigeria and Zimbabwe score the worst across the board, in ratings that incorporate governance, economic management, structural policies, social inclusion, public sector performance and World Bank Group portfolio performance.

As Issa Bakker and Stephen Gill argue,

> A key issue for contemporary public policy is the need to minimize uncertainty (and maximize the sense of security of property) in the minds of investors/corporate decision-makers. The World Bank stresses the need to strengthen and sustain law and order, to maximize protection of private property, and to apply macroeconomic policies predictably – otherwise, investors do not consider such states credible. As such, policy rules and mechanisms to guarantee the rights and security of capital are seen as political counterparts to the discipline of market forces (for example, international capital mobility).[15]

But as I argue later, with so few African states receiving MCA funding and with so much more at stake than can be handled by the US's military expansion, it is vital for Washington to identify reliable allies in Africa – both local compradors (Chapter 5) and countries such as South Africa (Chapter 6) – to legitimize and foster both imperialist geopolitics and neoliberal economics.

DEBT REPAYMENT SQUEEZE[16]

Walter Rodney offers a strong historical critique of financiers in Africa:

> In the epoch of imperialism, the bankers became the aristocrats of the capitalist world, so in another sense, they were very much in the foreground. The amount of surplus produced by African workers and peasants and passing into the hands of metropolitan bankers is quite phenomenal. They registered a return on capital higher even than the mining companies, and each new direct investment that they made spelt further alienation of the fruits of African labour.... Furthermore, European banks transferred the reserves of their African branches to the London head office to be invested in the London money market. This was the way which most rapidly expatriated African surplus to the metropoles.[17]

These processes were crucial to colonial-era accumulation, and they continue today in an amplified way, as 'direct investment' has become

Table 3.1 Sub-Saharan African debt repayments, 2003 (US$ billion)

Country type	Bilateral lenders	Multilaterals	Private lenders	Total
HIPCs	1.1	1.1	0.1	2.3
Other low-income	1.1	0.7	1.8	3.6
Middle-income	0.3	0.2	2.3	2.7
TOTAL	2.4	2.0	4.2	8.6

Source: Commission for Africa (2005), *Our Common Future*, London, p. 349.

national sovereign debt in the post-colonial era and as African elites have transferred their society's liquid reserves to overseas accounts on an even greater scale, as we see below. Indeed, in part due to the fall-off in aid flows, Africa's debt crisis worsened during the era of globalization. Between 1980 and 2002, sub-Saharan Africa's total foreign debt rose at a faster rate than that of Latin America, the Caribbean and the Middle East – from US$61 billion to US$206 billion – and the ratio of debt to GDP soared from 23 to 66 per cent. As the poorest continent and as a recipient of much concessional finance, sub-Saharan Africa did not repay the debt at the same rate as other regions, but nevertheless retired US$255 billion of foreign credit during the 1980s–90s, a factor of 4.2 times the original 1980 debt.[18]

Indeed, Africa now repays more than it receives. In 1980, loan inflows of $9.6 billion were comfortably higher than the debt repayment outflow of $3.2 billion, so the Ponzi scheme continued: by 2000, only $3.2 billion flowed in, and $9.8 billion was repaid, leaving a net financial flows deficit of $6.2 billion.[19] If we break down the $8.6 billion considered by the Commission for Africa as gross African debt payments in 2003, bilateral ('donor') deals drain $2.4 billion, multilateral institutions (the World Bank Group, IMF and African Development Bank) receive $2 billion, and private creditors receive $4.2 billion. Arrangements in mid-2005 associated with the G8 finance ministers' debt relief announcement were notable in some respects, but ultimately did not disturb either the process of draining Africa's financial accounts, or the maintenance of debt-associated control functions.

By the early 2000s, the debt remained unbearable for at least 21 African countries, at more than 300 per cent of export earnings. For countries like Sudan, Burundi, Sierra Leone and Guinea-Bissau, it was 15 times greater than annual export earnings. For some countries (including Cameroon, the Gambia, Mauritania, Senegal and Zambia), servicing the debt far exceeded government health spending. In at least 16 countries, a very strong case could be made that the inherited debt from dictators is legally 'odious', since the citizenry were victimized both in the debt's original accumulation (and use against them), and in demands that it be repaid: Nigeria under the Buhari and Abacha regimes (1984–98: $30 billion), South Africa under apartheid (1948–93: $22 billion), the Democratic Republic of Congo under Mobutu (1965–97: $13 billion), Sudan under Numeiri (1969–85: $9 billion), Ethiopia under Mengistu (1974–91: $8 billion), Kenya under Moi (1978–2002: $5.8 billion), Congo under Sassou (1979–2005: $4.5 billion), Mali under Traore (1968–91: $2.5 billion), Somalia under Siad Barre (1969–91: $2.3 billion), Malawi under Banda (1966–94: $2.2 billion), Togo under Eyadema (1967–2005: $1.4 billion), Liberia under Doe (1980–90: $1.2 billion), Rwanda under Habyarimana (1973–94: $1 billion), Uganda under Idi Amin Dada (1971–9: $0.6 billion) and the Central African Republic under Bokassa (1966–70: $0.2 billion).[20] Other undemocratic countries – including Zimbabwe under Mugabe in recent years ($4.5 billion) – could also be added to this list, which easily exceeds 50 per cent of Africa's outstanding debt.

DEBT RELIEF SMOKE AND MIRRORS

What debt relief has been provided to these and other impoverished countries? Belatedly recognizing the unsustainability of debt financing, the World Bank and IMF introduced the Highly Indebted Poor Countries (HIPC) initiative in 1996. Nine years later, the plan was augmented by the June 2005 finance ministers' debt relief concessions for 18 countries that were near or at the HIPC 'completion point'. Of these, 14 are African: Benin, Burkina Faso, Ethiopia, Ghana, Madagascar, Mali, Mauritania, Mozambique, Niger, Rwanda, Senegal, Tanzania, Uganda and Zambia (the four others are Bolivia, Guyana, Honduras and Nicaragua). Ten others due for relief once they pass the HIPC initiative hurdles are Burundi, Cameroon, Chad, the Democratic Republic of Congo, The Gambia, Guinea, Guinea-Bissau, Malawi, Sierra Leone and São Tomé and Principe. There are at least another eight African countries waiting to enter HIPC: Central African Republic, Comoros, the Republic of the Congo, Côte d'Ivoire, Liberia, Somalia, Sudan and Togo.

Table 3.2 Sub-Saharan African debt to official creditors, 2005
(% of GDP)

Oil-producing			
Angola	25.0	Equatorial Guinea	4.0
Cameroon	34.0	Gabon	40.9
Chad	33.9	Nigeria	32.4
Congo, Rep.	71.4	São Tomé & Principe	425.6
Côte d'Ivoire	48.4		
Non-oil-producing			
Benin	35.9	Mali	60.5
Botswana	3.1	Mauritius	8.1
Burkina Faso	33.6	Mozambique	66.4
Burundi	191.5	Namibia	5.6
Cape Verde	46.6	Niger	50.6
Central African Rep.	88.1	Rwanda	73.7
Comoros	75.9	Senegal	41.8
Congo, DRC	157.0	Seychelles	39.9
Ethiopia	69.6	Sierra Leone	103.5
Gambia, The	122.1	South Africa	2.2
Ghana	73.2	Swaziland	14.0
Guinea	87.7	Tanzania	47.1
Guinea-Bissau	282.3	Togo	93.2
Kenya	27.0	Uganda	49.6
Lesotho	51.6	Zambia	60.8
Madagascar	100.3	Zimbabwe	32.2
Malawi	144.1		
Total for sub-Saharan Africa			26.4

Source: International Monetary Fund (2005), *Regional Economic Outlook: Sub-Saharan Africa*, Washington, September, p. 27. Note that the figures do not include commercial debt.

The first point to make in relation to this strategy is that HIPC debt relief largely applied to loans that *weren't being paid in any case*. Most of the countries listed in Table 3.2 have vast debts – measured as a proportion of GDP – that can never be repaid; the countries are, in accounting terms, bankrupt. The notional reduction of these debts is effectively meaningless. The 1997–2001 average official multilateral debt of HIPC completion-point countries was 80.3 per cent of GDP, a figure reduced to 57.3 per cent by late 2005. For all of sub-Saharan Africa, the equivalent figures fell from 44 per cent to 26.4 per cent.[21] Yet only very small increases in available fiscal resources resulted, with even smaller social spending increments. Moreover, for six of Africa's 14 HIPC completion-point countries – Ethiopia, Ghana, Madagascar, Niger, Rwanda and Uganda – there was insubstantial debt relief, leaving the debt/GDP burden in 2005 at roughly the same level as when the programme started nine years earlier. In another five HIPC cases – Burundi, The Gambia, Guinea, Malawi and Sierra Leone – there has been no progress in paying the debt.

The second point is that HIPC retains a deeply neoliberal set of conditionalities. HIPC country programmes and associated Poverty Reduction Strategy Papers (PRSPs) still require macroeconomic austerity and services privatization. This became evident by the time of the 2001 Pan-African meeting of Jubilee South in Kampala, which roundly rejected HIPC and PRSPs on these grounds:

- PRSPs are located within the IMF and World Bank macroeconomic framework and this is not open for debate. The poverty programmes are expected to be consistent with the neoliberal paradigm including privatization, deregulation, budgetary constraints and trade and financial liberalization. Yet these have exacerbated economic and social crises in our countries.

- They focus only on internal factors and ignore the role of international/global factors and forces in creating economic crises and poverty in our countries.

- The only aspects of our realities that are open to consultation are those 'outside' the macroeconomic realm, and even the realization of these is actively contradicted by the requirements and constraints of the macroeconomic prescriptions.

- The neoliberal paradigm is also not acceptable because it fails to locate specific programmes to tackle poverty and subordination within effective gender equity perspectives and gender frameworks. Mere gender 'mainstreaming' is totally insufficient as a remedy.

- The World Bank and IMF are manoeuvring to regain their legitimacy by offering poverty 'reduction' and debt 'relief', whereas we demand full release from all debt bondage and the total eradication of poverty.

• These so-called poverty programmes have been imposed on countries in a manner which ignores and replaces existing anti-poverty and national development programmes. As such, they are an external intervention with little or no regard for national dynamics, and are an unacceptable intrusion. But they cannot easily be ignored, given that countries have to implement these programmes as an additional conditionality even for the much-criticized HIPC debt 'relief'.[22]

Furthermore, in late November 2005, the IMF announced that there would be an additional condition for the 18 countries allegedly granted deeper debt cancellation. Its Multilateral Debt Relief Initiative

will only become effective if the 43 members who contributed to the PRGF Trust Subsidy Account consent, because debt relief under the MDRI will be financed in part with resources transferred from that account. Obtaining these consents might take some time. Fund staff will shortly prepare an assessment of whether eligible countries who are now in a position to qualify (the 18 post-completion-point HIPCs, as well as two non-HIPCs) effectively qualify for MDRI relief. As requested by the Executive Board, the assessment will be based on the countries' current performance in the areas of macroeconomic policies, poverty reduction, and public expenditure management.[23]

The third point is that ostensible 'participation' by civil society did not reform the HIPC and PRSP process. By 2001, studies sponsored by the Harare-based NGO network African Forum and Network on Debt and Development (AFRODAD) documented HIPC and PRSPs in the first five African countries to develop PRSPs: Burkina Faso, Mauritania, Mozambique, Tanzania and Uganda: 'The relationship is still one of "if you want what we have to offer, you must do things our way". At the global level, this reflects well entrenched power relations rather than anything that could be called "participatory".'[24] In the same vein, a 2002 report by a Sussex University academic found a 'broad consensus among our civil society sources in Ghana, Malawi, Mozambique, Tanzania and Zambia that their coalitions have been unable to influence macroeconomic policy or even engage governments in dialogue about it'.[25]

Hence by 2003, even the World Bank conceded some of HIPC's mistakes: its staff 'had been too optimistic' about the ability of countries to repay under HIPC, and projections of export earnings were extremely inaccurate, leading to failure by half the HIPC countries to reach their completion points.[26] As Jubilee Plus reported at the time, 'According to the original HIPC schedule, 21 countries should have fully passed through the HIPC initiative and received total debt cancellation of approximately $34.7 billion in net present value terms. In fact, only eight countries have passed Completion Point, between them receiving debt cancellation of $11.8 billion.'[27] An 'enhanced HIPC' was introduced at the Evian G8 meeting in June 2003, but was unremarkable.

By then, more than $2.2 trillion of Third World debt was outstanding. In a just world it would have been cancelled, including not just HIPC countries but also the foreign debts of Nigeria, Argentina, Brazil, South Africa and other major debtors not considered highly indebted or poor in the mainstream discourse. The Jubilee South network, with strong leadership from affiliates in Argentina, Nicaragua, the Philippines and South Africa, continued to insist upon full cancellation, Third World repudiation and G8-country reparations.

It was thus clear in the run-up to Gleneagles that the debt payments African and other Third World countries continued to make were unjustifiable. Large mobilizations of British citizens – and Blair's unpopularity because of the Iraq War, during an election year – compelled the British government to offer Africa some financial concessions so as to appear humanitarian in character. Alex Wilks of the European Network on Debt and Development explained:

> British finance minister Gordon Brown said in February 2005 that the G8 meeting in Scotland on 6–8 July would be known as the '100 per cent debt relief summit'. Both Tony Blair and George W. Bush used similar language at their White House press conference on 7 June.... In actual fact, the official plan may only write off 10 per cent of low-income country debt. Not a penny more.... The 18–38 beneficiary countries will eventually have their debts cancelled, but will also have a corresponding amount cut from the aid flows they were likely to receive.... Zambia will stop paying its debts to three creditors, but will not receive the equivalent amount in aid to spend, likely less than 20 per cent of the amount of debt cancelled. In order to get what little extra money they are eligible for, the governments of developing nations will have to accept harsh World Bank and IMF conditions. This typically means privatization and trade liberalization, misconceived policy measures which often harm poorer people and benefit international traders.[28]

What difference, then, would the finance ministers' announcement make? According to *GreenLeft Weekly*:

> The huge figures most often quoted by the press, $50–55 billion, include IMF, World Bank and African Development Bank debts owed by around 20 of the other poorest Third World countries, which may become eligible for debt cancellation in the future; possibly nine more in 12–18 months, and another 10 or so at some undetermined date. While the $1.5 billion a year made available will certainly be of use for the 18 poverty-stricken countries, it will only boost their collective budget by about 6.5 per cent per annum. The modest sum illustrates that the Western media's backslapping over their governments' 'generosity' is more than a little exaggerated and some-what premature. Those 18 countries account for only 5 per cent of the population of the Third World, and if all 38 countries become eligible in the future, it will still only affect around 11 per cent.[29]

African and global justice advocates offered harsh condemnations:

- Jubilee South in Manila: 'The multilateral debt cancellation being proposed is still clearly tied to compliance with conditionalities which exacerbate poverty, open our countries further for exploit-ation and plunder, and perpetuate the domination of the South.... Even if the debt cancellation were without conditionalities, the proposal falls far too short in terms of coverage and amounts to demonstrate a bold step towards justice by any standard.'
- Demba Moussa Dembele, director of the Forum for African Alterna-tives in Dakar: 'At the moment this is nothing but a promise.... Therefore we will wait to see how this decision is put into action and with what conditions. Caution is necessary also because the "creditor" countries are long-time masters of the arts of duplicity, manipulation and concealment.'
- Jayati Ghosh, economics professor at Nehru University, India: '[E]ven otherwise well-informed and progressive people in the developing world were fooled into thinking that, for a change, the leaders of the core capitalist countries were actually thinking about doing some good for people desperately in need of it.... The G8 debt relief deal is actually a paltry and niggardly reduction.... And this pathetic amount is being traded for yet more major concessions made by the debtor countries, in terms of sweeping and extensive privatization of public services and utilities, which is about all that is left for governments to sell in these countries, as well as large

increases in indirect taxes which fall disproportionately on the poor.'
- AFRODAD in Harare: 'Nothing short of the continuation of the chains of slavery and bondage for the citizens in those countries... The agreement does not address the real global power imbalances but rather reinforces global apartheid.'[30]

A few weeks after the finance ministers' announcement, at the African heads of state meeting during the African Union session in Sirte, Libya issued an unprecedented call for comprehensive debt cancellation for all of Africa. Although some African elites more forcefully objected to their debt burdens, most continued to do the bidding of the IMF and World Bank. In one crucial case, however, parliament and civil society advocated repudiation.

NIGERIA SCAMMED

The particular case of Nigeria is worth contemplating in the wake of its October 2005 agreement with the following Paris Club countries, which were owed US$30 billion: Austria, Belgium, Brazil, Denmark, Finland, France, Germany, Italy, Japan, the Netherlands, the Russian Federation, Spain, Switzerland, the UK and the US. As the IMF explained,

> The agreement envisages a phased approach, in which Nigeria would clear its arrears in full, receive a debt write-off up to Naples terms, and buy back the remainder of its debt. The agreement is conditional on a favorable review of its macroeconomic and structural policies supported by the Fund under a nonfinancial arrangement.[31]

The underlying agenda came to fruition on 20 October. Nigeria, $6.3 billion in arrears, would first pay $12.4 billion in up-front payments. As Rob Weissman of *Multinational Monitor* reported,

> You can celebrate this deal, as the Paris Club does, if you ignore the fact that creditors generally write down bad debts as a matter of course (not charity), the billions over principal that Nigeria has already sent out of the country, the fact that the deal imposes IMF conditionality on Nigeria (even though the IMF isn't providing credit to the country), and the reality of the severe poverty in Nigeria.[32]

According to the leader of Nigeria's Jubilee network, Rev. David Ugolor,

> The Paris Club cannot expect Nigeria, freed from over 30 years of military rule, to muster $12.4 billion to pay off interest and penalties incurred by the military. Since the debt, by President Obasanjo's own admission, is of dubious origin, the issues of the responsibilities of the creditors must be put on the table at the Paris Club. As desirable as an exit from debt peonage is, it is scandalous for a poor debt-distressed country, which cannot afford to pay $2 billion in annual debt service payments, to part with $6 billion up front or $12 billion in three months or even one year.[33]

Similarly, remarked the Global AIDS Alliance,

> The creditors should be ashamed of themselves if they simply take this money [$12.4 billion]. These creditors often knew that the money would be siphoned off by dictators and deposited in Western banks, and the resulting debt is morally illegitimate. They bear a moral obligation to think more creatively about how to use this money. Nigeria has already paid these creditors $11.6 billion in debt service since 1985.[34]

The next step in the scam was for President Obasanjo to agree to a reimposition of neoliberal policies by the IMF, under the rubric of the new Policy Support Instrument (PSI). That instrument also deserves further consideration. According to Jubilee Africa's Soren Ambrose,

> The Paris Club requires that countries applying for relief be under an IMF program, but the prospect of agreeing to one is political dynamite in Nigeria. The Paris Club was however under great pressure to complete a landmark deal with Nigeria, where the legislature had threatened to simply repudiate the debts, so the PSI was deemed an acceptable alternative. Nigerian Finance Minister Ngozi Okonjo-Iweala told Reuters on May 18 that 'the IMF makes sure it is as stringent as an upper credit tranche programme and then monitors it like a regular program, but the difference is that you develop it and you own it'.[35]

Indeed, the core message of the PSI document released by the IMF is its desire to retain effective control of African countries' macro-economic policies, *on behalf of 'donor' countries* (its shareholders):

> Around 40 per cent of donors expressed a need for on/off signals, and a majority for multidimensional assessments. According to the survey, the Fund is expected to assess, first and foremost, macroeconomic performance and policies. Like low-income members, donors consider a quantified medium-term macroeconomic framework – with quarterly or semi-annual targets – to be essential for the assessment of policies and progress made.

Most also expect the Fund to assess structural reforms that are either macro-economically critical, or within the Fund's core areas (e.g., tax system, exchange system, financial sector).[36]

This represents, simply, the expansion of the existing system of control of debtor countries to those countries which won't be so indebted in a formal sense, and hence which need more IMF 'signaling' to donors than is feasible with the standard annual Article IV surveillance reports. What the Nigerian case illustrates is that the IMF is pulling strings on behalf of the G8 'donor' countries, and that the G8 will continue to support the IMF if such functions benefit Northern countries.

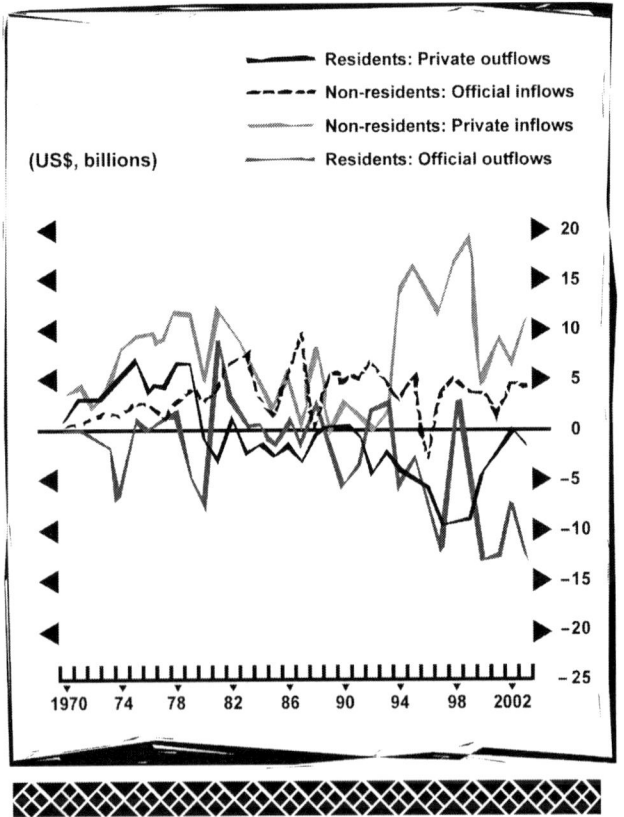

Figure 3.3 Net capital flight from Africa, 1970-2004

Source: International Monetary Fund, *Global Financial Stability Report 2004*, p. 126.

FINANCIAL PORTFOLIO (DIS)INVESTMENT AND CAPITAL FLIGHT

A related financial issue – partly captured in the 'payments to private creditors' account – is African access to 'portfolio capital', which are private credits and investments used for Africa's corporate securities, stock market investments, currency purchases and the like. This has mainly taken the form of 'hot money': speculative positions by private-sector investors. The main site of investment action has been South Africa's stock exchange, and to a much smaller extent nascent share markets in Nigeria, Kenya, Zambia, Mauritius, Botswana, Ghana and Zimbabwe (all of whose stock exchanges have at least $1 billion capitalization).

In 1995, for example, foreign purchases and sales were responsible for half the share trading in Johannesburg. But these flows have had devastating effects on South Africa's currency, with 30+ per cent crashes over a period of weeks during runs in early 1996, mid-1998 and late 2001.[37] In Zimbabwe, the November 1997 outflow of hot money crashed the currency by 74 per cent in just four hours of trading.[38]

As a result, the performance of the eight major African stock markets has been extremely erratic, sometimes returning impressive speculative-style profits to foreign investors and sometimes generating large losses. With a market capitalization of $409 billion in mid-2005, the Johannesburg Stock Exchange dwarfs the other seven (which share roughly $30 billion in capitalization). In 2000–1 and 2003, the JSE was negative, but returned 12 per cent in dollar-denominated profits in 2002, 40 per cent in 2004 and 29 per cent in the first half of 2005. (There are no exchange controls preventing foreign repatriation of recently invested dividends and profits from South Africa, and great controversy has erupted over the excessive outflows to the several huge London-registered corporations which were once South African.)

The other source of financial account outflows from Africa that must be reversed is capital flight. There are various estimates of the current (2003) accounts of African citizens in Northern banks and overseas tax havens: using Bank for International Settlements data, Eric Toussaint and Damien Millet estimate the total at $80 billion (at the same time, African countries owe $30 billion to those very banks).[39] While this is a lower figure than for other regions, it is a higher proportion of a continent's GDP than anywhere else.

The two leading scholars of the phenomenon, James Boyce and Léonce Ndikumana, argue that a core group of sub-Saharan African countries whose foreign debt was $178 billion suffered a quarter century of capital flight by elites – 1970–96 – that totalled more than $285 billion (including imputed interest earnings): 'Taking capital flight as a measure of private external assets, and calculating net external assets as private external assets minus public external debts, sub-Saharan Africa thus appears to be a net creditor *vis-à-vis* the rest of the world.'[40] In relation to foreign debt owed, the sub-Sarahan countries with the worst capital flight problems are Nigeria ($98 billion more than its foreign debt when interest on capital flight is also added), the Ivory Coast ($15 billion), the Democratic Republic of Congo ($10.1 billion), Angola ($9.2 billion) and Zambia ($5.5 billion). Overall, the main sub-Saharan African countries financed more than $100 billion more in external capital flight during that quarter century than they owed in outstanding debt. This is not surprising in some countries, like Angola, where the United Nations reports that for every billion dollars invested in the offshore oil industry, only $100,000 is spent onshore.[41]

In his book *Capitalism's Achilles Heel*, Brookings Institution scholar Raymond Baker documents 'falsified pricing, haven and secrecy structures and the illicit movement of trillions of dollars out of developing and transitional economies…. Laundered proceeds of drug trafficking, racketeering, corruption and terrorism tag along with other forms of dirty money to which the US and Europe extend a welcoming hand.' Nearly one-third of the value of annual production in sub-Saharan Africa, adds John Christensen of the Tax Justice Network, was taken offshore during the late 1990s. Across the world, eight million 'high net-worth individuals' have insulated $11.5 trillion in assets in offshore financial centres.[42]

The IMF also measures official and 'private' flows; in 2004 it found that resident African official outflows from Africa exceeded $10 billion a year, on average, from 1998. While a large portion of this would relate to changes in South African capital controls, which permitted residents to offload shares of the largest Johannesburg firms to London purchasers, very high outflows continued even after those share deals had had their impact. As for Africans' 'private outflows', they also moved from a net inflow during the 1970s to gradual outflows during the 1980s and substantial outflows during the 1990s.

Where does the money go? Caribbean and European offshore tax havens are important vehicles, leading to calls for the regulation and even prohibition of such unregulated hot money centres. But Johannesburg is also becoming a preferred hot money transit centre.

FINANCIAL LIBERALIZATION'S FALSE PROMISES

Many of these financial accounts – especially relating to capital flight – highlight the extent to which exchange control liberalization has occurred in Africa. Ironically, IMF researchers – including the then chief economist, Kenneth Rogoff – finally admitted in 2003 that severe damage had been inflicted by two decades of financial liberalization. Rogoff and his colleagues (Eswar Prasad, Shang-Jin Wei and Ayhan Kose) admitted 'sobering' findings, namely 'evidence that some countries may have experienced greater consumption volatility as a result.... Recent crises in some more financially integrated countries suggest that financial integration may in fact have increased volatility.'[43] These conclusions are also conceded by the World Bank, which promoted financial liberalization with a vengeance during the 1980s–90s. By 2005, even Bank staff had to concede that central objectives were not met:

> To be sure, most African countries have introduced market-based reforms in their financial sectors. But post-liberalization problems still need to be addressed. Financial reform programmes anticipated an initial increase in the spread between lending and deposit rates, but the spread continues to widen in many countries. Moreover, since liberalization, many financial systems have seen high real interest rates. There has also been little financial deepening. While normally liberalization was expected to encourage financial deepening, with a positive effect on savings mobilization and credit allocation, for most of Africa, ratios of money and credit to GDP have not increased.[44]

Within Africa, the main driving force behind the liberalized, integrated financial system is the South African government.[45] Pretoria removed its main exchange control – the Financial Rand – in 1995 and permitted the offshore listing of the largest firms in 1998–2000. Results, during a period of alleged post-apartheid macroeconomic 'stability', included severe currency crashes in 1996, 1998 and 2000–1, followed by very high interest rate increases. The high rates exacerbated the already serious problem of stagnant investment, which was also affected by the late 1990s liberalization of restrictions on movement of corporate financial headquarters. But because of prevailing power relations in Pretoria and Johannesburg, South Africa's official agenda is to amplify liberalization, a point taken up again in Chapter 6. Meanwhile, now that we have considered various aspects of Africa's financial portfolio, looting via trade and investment routes can now be addressed.

NOTES

1 International Monetary Fund (2005), *Regional Economic Outlook: Sub-Saharan Africa*, Washington, September, p. 7.
2 United Nations Development Programme (2005), *Human Development Report 2005: International Cooperation at a Crossroads*, New York, UNDP, p. 94.
3 Action Aid (2005), *Real Aid: an Agenda for Making Aid Work*, Johannesburg, Action Aid, p. 22.
4 *Ibid.*, p. 18.
5 Commission for Africa (CfA) (2005), *Our Common Future*, London, p. 349.
6 IMF (2005), *Regional Economic Outlook: Sub-Saharan Africa*, September, pp. 7–8.
7 Curtis, M. (2005), '17 Ways the European Commission is Pushing Trade Liberalization on Poor Countries', London, Christian Aid.
8 *Ibid.*
9 White, D. (2005), 'Tanzanian Spat Puts Focus on Aid Dilemma', *Financial Times*, 29 June.
10 World Development Movement (2005), 'UK Water Company to Sue One of World's Poorest Countries', WDM press release, London, 1 December.
11 Bond, P. (1999), 'Globalization, Pharmaceutical Pricing and South African Health Policy: Managing Confrontation with US Firms and Politicians', *International Journal of Health Services*, 29, 4.
12 Cited in SA Institute for International Affairs, *e-Africa*, May 2004.
13 Bond, P. (2003), *Against Global Apartheid: South Africa Meets the World Bank, IMF and International Finance*, London, Zed Books and Cape Town, University of Cape Town Press, Chapter 4.
14 Alexander, N. (2004), 'Triage of Low-Income Countries? The Implications of the IFI's Debt Sustainability (DS) Proposal', Washington, <http://www.services forall.org/ html/otherpubs/ judge_jury_ scorecard.pdf>.
15 Bakker, I. and S. Gill (2003), 'Ontology, Method and Hypotheses', in I. Bakker and S. Gill (eds), *Power, Production and Social Reproduction*, Basingstoke, Palgrave Macmillan, p. 31.
16 One of the strongest recent overviews of African debt is Capps, G. (2005), 'Redesigning the Debt Trap', *International Socialism*, 107.
17 Rodney, W. (1972), *How Europe Underdeveloped Africa*, Dar es Salaam,

Tanzania Publishing House and London, Bogle L'Ouverture Publications; all citations are from this edition, available at <http://www.marxists.org/subject/africa/rodney-walter/how-europe/>.

18 Toussaint, E. (2004), *Your Money or Your Life*, Chicago, Haymarket Books, p. 150.

19 World Bank (2002), *Global Finance Tables*, Washington, World Bank.

20 Toussaint, *Your Money or Your Life*, p. 384. See also <http://www.jubilee plus.org/analysis/reports/dictatorsreport.htm>.

21 IMF (2005), *Regional Economic Outlook: Sub-Saharan Africa*, May, p. 45.

22 Jubilee South (2001), 'Pan-African Declaration on PRSPs', Kampala, 12 May.

23 IMF (2005), 'Multilateral Debt Relief: Questions and Answers', Washington, <http://www.imf.org/external/np/exr/mdri/eng/mdrians.htm>, 8 December.

24 AFRODAD (2001), 'Civil Society Participation in the Poverty Reduction Strategy Paper Process: a Synthesis of Five Studies Conducted in Burkina Faso, Mauritania, Mozambique, Tanzania and Uganda', Harare, April.

25 McGee, R. (2002), 'Assessing Participation in Poverty Reduction Strategy Papers: a Desk-Based Synthesis of Experience in Sub-Saharan Africa', University of Sussex Institute of Development Studies.

26 *Financial Times*, 27 February 2003.

27 Jubilee Plus (2003), 'Real Progress Report on HIPC', London, September.

28 Wilks, A. (2005), 'Selling Africa Short', European Network on Debt and Development, Brussels, 21 June.

29 *GreenLeft Weekly* (2005), 'Africa Needs Justice not Charity', 29 June.

30 Ambrose, S. (2005), 'Assessing the G8 Debt Proposal and Its Implications', *Focus on Trade*, 25 September 2005.

31 IMF (2005), *Regional Economic Outlook: Sub-Saharan Africa*, September, p. 10.

32 Weissman, R. (2005), 'Nigeria Debt Disgrace', *Multinational Monitor*, Washington, 20 October.

33 Cited by Jubilee USA (2005), 'Nigerian Threat to Repudiate Helps Force Paris Club to Deliver Debt Cancellation', press release, Washington, 20 October.

34 Global AIDS Alliance (2005), 'Nigeria's Creditors Should Be Ashamed', press release, Washington, 20 October.

35 Ambrose, S. (2005), 'IMF Adds a New Tool to its Bag of Tricks', *Economic Justice News (50 Years Is Enough)*, 8, 3, http://www.50years.org/cms/ejn/v8n3, September.

36 IMF (2005), 'Policy Support and Signaling in Low-Income Countries', Policy Development and Review Department, Washington, Annex 1, p. 25.

37 Bond, *Against Global Apartheid*, Afterword.

38 Bond, P. and M. Manyanya (2003), *Zimbabwe's Plunge: Exhausted National-ism, Neoliberalism and the Search for Social Justice*, London, Merlin Press, Pietermaritzburg, University of KwaZulu-Natal Press and Harare, Weaver Press.

39 Toussaint, *Your Money or Your Life*, p. 171.

40 Boyce, J. and Léonce Ndikumana (2000), 'Is Africa a Net Creditor? New Estimates of Capital Flight from Severely Indebted Sub-Saharan African

Countries, 1970–1996', Occasional Paper, University of Massachusetts/Amherst Political Economy Research Institute.

41 United Nations Integrated Regional Information Network (2006), 'Angola: Resource Curse?', 10 January.

42 Baker, R. (2005), *Capitalism's Achilles Heel*, London, Wiley; and Christensen cited in Campbell, D. (2005), 'Where They Hide the Cash', *Guardian*, 5 December.

43 Prasad, E., K. Rogoff, S. J. Wei and M. Ayhan Kose (2003), 'Effects of Financial Globalization on Developing Countries: Some Empirical Evidence,' Washington, IMF, 17 March, pp. 6–7, 37.

44 World Bank (2005), 'Meeting the Challenge of Africa's Development: a World Bank Group Action Plan', Africa Region, Washington, 7 September, pp. 32–3.

45 Bond, P. (2004), 'Bankrupt Africa: Imperialism, Subimperialism and Financial Politics', *Historical Materialism*, 12, 4.

4

Unequal Exchange Revisited
Trade, investment, wealth depletion

Unfair trade and investment relationships are nothing new for Africa. When *Time* magazine entitled an article 'Looting Africa', its authors acknowledged a long tradition for a continent: 'Africa, its people already plundered by slavers, its animals by poachers and its mineral wealth by miners, is now yielding up its cultural heritage. Across the continent, artifacts are looted from museums, from universities and straight from the ground.' The latest form of value export, rare antiquities (sometimes nominally protected in legislation as critical to national heritage), are often sold by impoverished Africans dirt-cheap for resale in trendy New York, London and Johannesburg markets:

> It is the West's growing enthusiasm for African objects that has placed many of them in jeopardy. Most of Mali's archaeological sites, including graves built into the cliffs along the World Heritage-listed Bandiagara escarpment, have been looted. Ethiopia is struggling to protect its oldest silver Coptic Christian crosses and medieval manuscripts. Since 1970, illegal traders in Kenya and Tanzania have carted off hundreds of *vigango*, or Swahili wooden grave markers. When fighting erupted in the Somali capital of Mogadishu in 1991, one of the first casualties was the National Museum. Within weeks many of its prized exhibits, including ancient Egyptian pottery, were on sale to tourists in neighboring Kenya.[1]

This form of plunder alone, *Time* and experts estimate, robs Africa of US$450 million a year. A single notorious 1994 robbery from the (uninsured) Ile-Ife National Museum cost Nigeria US$200 million worth of terracotta and brass heads dating from the twelfth and thirteenth centuries.

More broadly, according to John Saul and Colin Leys, many of the multifaceted problems the continent faces follow from long-standing trends that reflect capital's inability to accumulate in a balanced way:

> Some forms of capital see plenty of profitable opportunities in sub-Saharan Africa, but the likelihood that the region is going to be developed by capitalism seems smaller than ever. On a continent of household-based agrarian economies with very limited long-distance trade, colonialism imposed cash-crop production for export, and mineral extraction, with manufacturing supposed to come later.... Takeoff into manufacturing for internal consumption is blocked by an inability to compete with imports and by tiny domestic markets; meanwhile collapsing infrastructures, political risk, and poorly trained workforces tend to make manufacturing for export uncompetitive, even at very low wages.[2]

Hence, having considered Africa's deteriorating financial accounts in the last chapter, it is crucial to look more closely at the underlying economic basis for the continent's unprofitable insertion into the world economy, via trade, investment and labour flows.

TRADE TRAPS

A slight upturn in the terms of trade for African countries in recent years should not disguise the profoundly unequal and unfair system of export-led growth, which has impoverished Africans in many ways. Given that many of the continent's elites and allied aid agencies such as Oxfam believe that it is possible to achieve growth through exports, a draft mid-2005 report by the World Bank is important to cite at the outset. By considering natural resources depletion – petroleum, other subsoil mineral assets, timber resources, non-timber forest resources, protected areas, cropland and pastureland – associated with trade, the Bank calculates that much of Africa is poorer, not wealthier than it would have been without this emphasis on the export of primary products.

The Bank report, *Where Is the Wealth of Nations,* makes several crucial adjustments to gross national income and savings accounts, and by subtracting fixed capital depreciation, adding education spending, subtracting resource depletion and subtracting pollution damage, the Bank finds that some countries are vast losers via export processing. For example, according to this methodology, Gabon's citizens lost US$2,241 each in 2000, followed by citizens of the Republic of the

Congo (–$727), Nigeria (–$210), Cameroon (–$152), Mauritania (–$147) and Côte d'Ivoire (–$100). Even the continent's strongest economy, South Africa, has lost net wealth in large part via trade. In addition to mineral depletion worth 1 per cent of national income each year, the Bank acknowledges that South Africans lose forests worth 0.3 per cent; suffer pollution ('particulate matter') damage of 0.2 per cent; and emit CO_2 that causes another 1.6 per cent of damage. In total, adding a few other factors, the actual 'genuine savings' of South Africa is reduced from the official 15.7 per cent to just 6.9 per cent of national income.[3]

However, trade liberalization's damage is not limited to the primary product export drive with all its adverse implications. In addition, African elites have lifted protective tariffs excessively rapidly, leading to the premature deaths of infant industries and manufacturing jobs, as well as a decline in state customs revenue. As a result, according to Christian Aid, 'Trade liberalization has cost sub-Saharan Africa $272 billion over the past 20 years.... Overall, local producers are selling less than they were before trade was liberalized.'[4] Deconstructing African

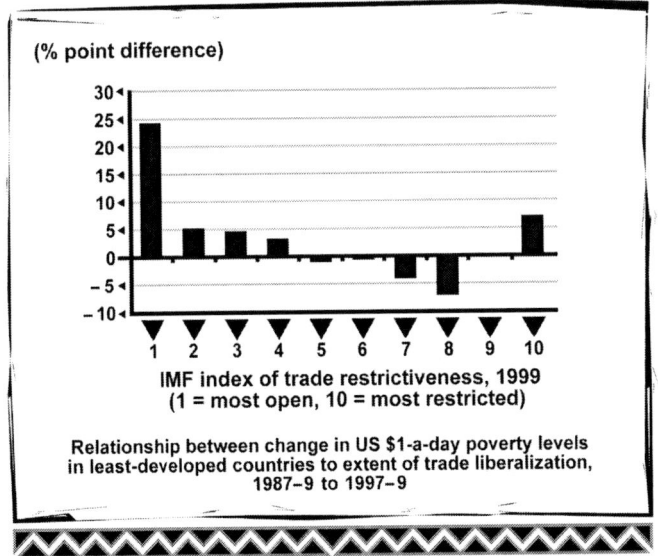

Figure 4.1: Poverty and free trade

Source: Christian Aid, 'The Economics of Failure', London, p. 6.

countries according to whether there was rapid or slow trade liberalization during 1987–99, Christian Aid found a close correlation between trade openness and worsening poverty.

COMMODITY EXPORT DEPENDENCY AND FALLING TERMS OF TRADE

The most important myth of neoliberal economics is that production for export inexorably creates prosperity. That myth was contested by Frantz Fanon just as African countries came to independence:

> The national economy of the period of independence is not set on a new footing. It is still concerned with the ground-nut harvest, with the cocoa crop and the olive yield. In the same way there is no change in the marketing of basic products, and not a single industry is set up in the country. We go on sending out raw materials; we go on being Europe's small farmers who specialize in unfinished products.[5]

Like financial imbalances, 'unequal exchange' in trade – including the rising African trade deficit with South Africa – is another route for the extraction of superprofits from Africa. The continent's share of world trade declined over the past quarter century, but the volume of exports increased. 'Marginalization' of Africa occurred, hence, not because of insufficient integration, but because other areas of the world – especially East Asia – moved to the export of manufactured goods, while Africa's industrial potential declined thanks to excessive deregulation associated with structural adjustment.

Overall, primary exports of natural resources accounted for nearly 80 per cent of African exports in 2000, compared to 31 per cent for all developing countries and 16 per cent for the advanced capitalist economies. According to the UN Conference on Trade in Development, in 2003 a dozen African countries were dependent upon a single commodity for exports, including crude petroleum (Angola 92 per cent, Congo 57 per cent, Gabon 70 per cent, Nigeria 96 per cent and Equatorial Guinea 91 per cent); copper (Zambia 52 per cent); diamonds (Botswana 91 per cent); coffee (Burundi 76 per cent, Ethiopia 62 per cent, Uganda 83 per cent), tobacco (Malawi 59 per cent) and uranium (Niger 59 per cent).[6] Excluding South Africa, the vast bulk (63 per cent) of sub-Saharan exports in recent years has been petroleum-related, largely from Nigeria, Angola and other countries in the Gulf of Guinea. The next largest category of exports from the subcontinent (not including South Africa) is food and live animals (17 per cent).[7] The problems associated with primary product export dependence are not only high levels of price volatility and downward price trends for many natural resources. In addition, especially for minerals, production is highly capital-intensive, offers low incentives for educational investments, and provides a greater danger of intervention by parasitical rentiers.[8]

Although more than two-thirds of Africa's trade is with developed countries, from the early 2000s China has become a bigger factor, in the process attracting growing geopolitical controversy (because, from Sudan to Zimbabwe to Angola, Chinese loans and investments have propped up corrupt regimes) and having a marked deindustrialization effect. Well-grounded concerns over employment practices and product quality turned into xenophobia against Chinese merchants

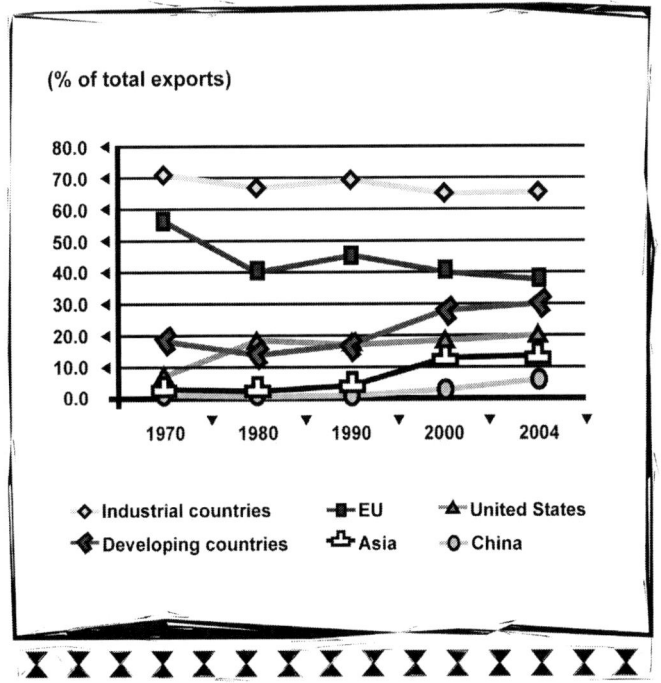

Figure 4.2 Sub-Saharan Africa's trading partners, 1970–2004

Source: International Monetary Fund (2005), *Regional Economic Outlook: Sub-Saharan Africa*, Washington, September, p. 15.

Table 4.1 Commodity price decline, 1980–2001

Product, Unit	1980	1990	2001
Coffee (Robusta) cents/kg	411.70	118.20	63.30
Cocoa cents/kg	330.50	126.70	111.40
Groundnut oil dollars/ton	1090.10	963.70	709.20
Palm oil dollars/ton	740.90	289.90	297.80
Soya dollars/ton	376.00	246.80	204.20
Sugar cents/kg	80.17	27.67	19.90
Cotton cents/kg	261.70	181.90	110.30
Copper dollars/ton	2770.00	2661.00	1645.00
Lead cents/kg	115.00	81.10	49.60

Source: Touissant, E. (2005), *Your Money or Your Life*, Chicago, Haymarket Books, p. 157.

(leading to 'yellow peril' sloganeering from otherwise internationalist activists within the Southern African Social Forum in late 2005). The Chinese threat to African industry is profound, with Nigeria losing 350,000 jobs directly (and 1.5 million indirectly) owing to Chinese competition in 2000–5. Lesotho's garment industry collapsed when the Africa Growth and Opportunity Act benefits evaporated in 2005 once China joined the WTO.[9]

But the main damage continues to be inflicted by the long-term decline in primary product price trends. As Michael Barrett Brown explains: 'The value added in making up manufactured goods has been greatly increased compared with the raw material required; synthetics continue to replace natural products in textiles, shoes and rubber goods; and the elasticity of demand for agricultural products (the proportion of extra incomes spent on food and beverages) has been steadily falling.' Notwithstanding the 2002–5 price increases – especially for oil, rubber and copper thanks to Chinese import demand – the value of the coffee, tea and cotton exports that many African countries rely upon continues to stagnate or fall. Falling prices for most cash crops pushed Africa's agricultural export value down from US$15 billion in 1987 to US$13 billion in 2000.[10] Far greater declines were witnessed for most agricultural commodities if the period 1980–2001 is considered.

In historical terms, the prices of primary commodities (other than fuels) have risen and fallen according to a deeper rhythm. Exporters of primary commodities, for example, fared particularly badly when financiers were most powerful. The cycle for an exporting country typically begins with falling commodity prices, then leads to rising foreign debt, dramatic increases in interest rates, a desperate intensification of exports which lowers prices yet further, and bankruptcy. Using 1970 as a base index year of 100, from 1900 to 1915, the prices of commodities rose from 130 to 190, and then fell dramatically to 90 in 1919. From a low point of 85 in 1930, as the Great Depression began, the commodity price index rose, mainly during the Second World War, to 135, as demand for raw materials proved strong and shipping problems created supply-side problems. Prices fell during the subsequent globalization process until 1968 (to 95 on the index), but soared to 142 at the peak of a commodity boom in 1973. The subsequent crash of commodity prices took the index down steadily to well below 40 by the late 1990s.[11] In Ethiopia, to illustrate, coffee exports rose from 1992, with the volume of output doubling by 2003. But the export value fell from $450 million to less than $100 million during the same period, according to the United Nations Development Programme.[12]

Falling prices were sometimes arrested, and such respites might even last a few years. The 2002–5 minor boom in some commodity prices reflected strong Chinese import demand and the East Asian recovery from the 1997–8 crash. From a very low base in early 2002, the prices of agricultural products rose 80 per cent and metals/minerals doubled. Most spectacularly, the rise of the oil price from $11/barrel to $70/barrel in 1998–2005 meant that price volatility did indeed assist a few countries. But the soaring price of energy came at the expense of most African countries, which import oil.

Supporters of the *status quo* argue that there are mitigating factors in the world trading system designed to offer Africa a safety net. But 'preferential access' that permits somewhat greater Northern imports from Africa represents only 1 per cent of world trade volume. And the Special and Differential Treatment (SDT) concessions grudgingly provided to some Third World exports are typically hard-fought and minimal; as Tetteh Hormeku of the Africa Trade Network explains:

> Countries at different stages of growth and development should not assume the same level of responsibilities in international agreements as these are unequal partners. But by the end of the Uruguay Round the spirit of SDT was reduced to a narrower concept: developing countries had to essentially

accept the same obligations as developed countries, and may be exempted from implementing some measures, as well as allowed different time scales. But almost all obligations would be adopted by them.... [At Doha,] over 200 proposals were made relating first to strengthening SDT and second to resolving implementation issues. Since the Round has been launched, all discussions on SDT and implementation issues have made no progress, except on 22 issues which are widely described as of having little or no commercial value.[13]

Notwithstanding overwhelming evidence of the dangers of export dependency under these circumstances, the policy debate continues. As Nancy Alexander of the Services for All campaign in Washington has shown, a 2002 World Bank paper promoting export-led growth revealed how two dogmatic economists – David Dollar and Aart Kraay – tortured trade data until, as the saying goes, the numbers confessed.[14] Dollar and Kraay termed certain countries 'globalizers' – including China and India – and others 'non-globalizers': mainly commodity producers whose prices fell dramatically during the 1980s–90s, even if during that period they were *more* not less dependent upon the whims of globalized markets. By adding a commodity dependence dummy variable to the Dollar-Kraay growth equation, Alexander notes, the importance of openness to growth falls by at least half:

> These findings are significant because, whereas some development experts assert that low-income countries are caught in a 'poverty trap', they are actually caught in a 'commodity trap' – signified by a long-term decline of commodity prices, especially relative to the cost of manufactures.... In their calculation of the impact of openness on growth, Dollar and Kraay use changes in the volume of trade as a proxy for changes in trade policy. However, volumes of trade vary due to many influences other than policy changes.... Openness is generally the outcome of growth rather than its cause; its 'fruit, not its root'. The most successful globalizers in the World Bank study, such as China and India, follow heterodox policies, rather than those advocated by donors and creditors.[15]

China and India have substantial tariffs to protect their own agricultural industries, as well as rigorous exchange controls which shielded them from the turmoil that rocked their Asian neighbours in 1997–8, for example.

At least other Bank economists, Ataman Aksoy and John Beghin, were honest enough to admit that their employer 'oversold' the benefits of exporting commodities in a context of diminishing world prices: 'A development strategy based on agricultural commodity exports is likely to be impoverishing in the current agricultural policy environment.' They also conceded that during 1970–97 the cumulative loss resulting from declining terms of trade for sub-Saharan African non-oil exporting countries amounted to 119 per cent of their total GDP.[16]

Finally, in another embarrassing reversal just before the Hong Kong WTO summit, two other Bank economists – Kym Anderson and Will Martin – released a report on 'Agricultural Trade Reform and the Doha Development Agenda' which claimed a $287 billion world GDP gain from a successful WTO.[17] But as the Center for Economic and Policy Research pointed out, Anderson and Martin conceded several crucial countervailing facts:

- Removal of all rich country agricultural export subsidies and domestic support programmes would actually cause a net loss for developing countries. This is mainly because the removal of these subsidies would raise the world price of food and agricultural products.
- The developing countries as a group would gain $86 billion, or 0.8 per cent of GDP, from complete trade liberalization. However, about half of these gains would come from liberalization of developing countries' own trade barriers. This means that even if the Doha round were to collapse, much of the gains from liberalization would still be available to these countries, since any country can liberalize its own imports at any time, without any rule requiring them to do so.
- The $287 billion gains are for complete liberalization, which is not expected from the Doha round; the Bank's estimates of gains from various more realistic scenarios are much smaller gains for the world: between $17.9 billion and $119.3 billion, or just 0.04 to 0.28 per cent of world GDP. Again, much of this very small gain would still be available to developing countries even if the Doha round collapsed.
- Even a very successful Doha round would barely make a dent in poverty rates: according to the study, the number of people living in poverty in 2016 would be reduced by somewhere between 0.4 and 1 per cent (2.5 to 6.3 million people).[18]

RURAL INEQUALITY AND PERVERSE SUBSIDIES

Under colonialism, Walter Rodney showed,

> The unequal nature of the trade between the metropole and the colonies
> was emphasized by the concept of the 'protected market', which meant even
> an inefficient metropolitan producer could find a guaranteed market in the
> colony where his class had political control. Furthermore, as in the
> preceding era of pre-colonial trade, European manufacturers built up useful
> sidelines of goods which would have been sub-standard in their own
> markets, especially in textiles.[19]

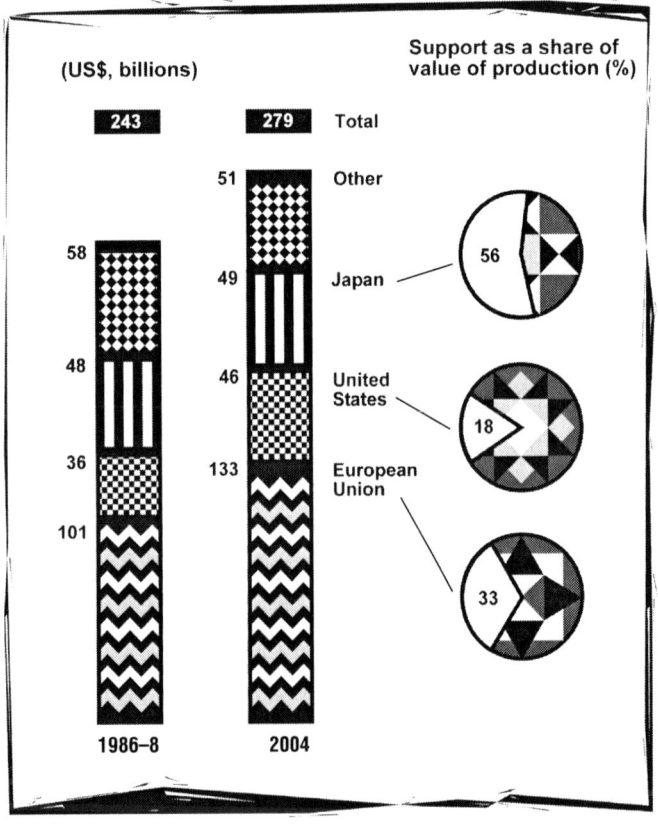

Figure 4.3 Agricultural subsidies in Japan, the EU and the US

Source: United Nations Development Programme, *Human Development Report 2005*, p. 129.

In contemporary times, Northern agricultural subsidies worth nearly several hundred billion dollars a year, whether for domestic market stabilization (in an earlier era) or export promotion, have been an enormous bone of contention. Inefficient European, US and Japanese agro-industrial producers find African markets in the form of dumped grains and foodstuffs. Rarely examined, however, are the differential impacts of subsidies, especially when associated with glutted global agricultural markets. This is a general problem associated with export-led growth, but is particularly acute in the farming sector because of uneven access to state subsidies, especially affecting export crops.

It is not only a matter of much lower national-scale productive potential in the Third World than would have been the case had liberalization not decimated many local industries, including domestic farming. In the process, rapid trade-related integration caused growing social inequality, as Branco Milanovic of the World Bank has reported.[20] Those who benefited most include the import/export firms, transport/shipping companies, plantations and large-scale commercial farmers, the mining sector, financiers (who gain greater security than in the case of produce designed for the domestic market), consumers of imported goods, and politicians and bureaucrats who are tapped into the commercial/financial circuits.

Agricultural subsidies are merely one aspect of growing rural inequality. Farm subsidies today mainly reflect agro-corporate campaign contributions and the importance of rural voting blocs in advanced capitalist countries. (In the 1930s, the first generation of US farm subsidies instead reflected the dangers of agricultural over-production to society and ecology, for the 'dust bowl' phenomenon in the Midwest emerged when many family farmers simply left their failing lands fallow after markets were glutted.)

The power of the agro-corporate lobby is substantial and getting stronger. The UN Development Programme found that agricultural subsidies had risen 15 per cent between the late 1980s and 2004, from $243 billion to $279 billion (a figure Vandana Shiva considers a vast underestimate), with Japan's subsidies the highest in relation to the total value of agricultural production.

Unlike earlier periods when farming was smaller-scale and atomized, advanced capitalist countries' agricultural subsidies today overwhelmingly benefit large agro-corporate producers. Subsidies in the EU's fifteen major countries are even more unequally distributed than in the US, with beneficiaries in Britain including Queen Elizabeth II ($1.31 million), Prince Charles ($480,000) and Britain's richest man, the Duke of Westminster ($1.13 million).[21] Studies of the Gini coefficients of Northern agriculture subsidy recipients, as reported by the UNDP, confirm that large farming corporations benefit far more than do small farmers. In 2001, the EU 15's Gini coefficient was .78 and the US coefficient was .67, both far higher than income distribution in the world's most unequal countries.[22] Were political power relations to change, a massive redirection of subsidies to small, lower-income, family farmers in the North would be more equitable and could have the effect of moving agricultural production towards more organic (and less petroleum-intensive) farming.

A detailed debate regularly occurs over whether subsidies are 'trade-distorting'. If they represent export subsidies or price supports, these subsidies belong in what the WTO terms an 'Amber Box', targeted for elimination. Export subsidies of $7.5 billion in 1995 were reduced, as a result, to $3 billion by 2001. Formerly trade-distorting subsidies were reformed by the EU, with the new aim of limiting production of crops (farmers are paid to simply leave land fallow), and are hence 'Green Box': not subject to cuts. In a transition from Amber to Green Box subsidies, another category – Blue Box – subsidies are allegedly less damaging. But the US government proposed that the large counter-cyclical payments it makes to US cotton producers when the price declines be considered Blue Box, even though the WTO itself agreed with Brazilian complaints that the subsidies still distort trade by increasing US output and lowering world prices. Generally, the complexity associated with the subsidy regimes reflects Northern capacity to maintain their subsidies but continually dress them up in new language.

According to Delhi-based agriculture trade researcher Devinder Sharma, Europe especially has taken advantage of Third World powerlessness in the WTO:

> Between 1995 and 2004, Europe alone has been able to increase its agricultural exports by 26 per cent, much of it because of the massive domestic subsidies it provides. Each percentage increase in exports brings in a financial gain of $3 billion. On the other hand, a vast majority of the developing countries, whether in Latin America, Africa or Asia, in the first 10 years of WTO have turned into food importers. Millions of farmers have

lost their livelihoods as a result of cheaper imports. If the WTO has its way, and the developing countries fail to understand the prevailing politics that drives the agriculture trade agenda, the world will soon have two kinds of agriculture systems – the rich countries will produce staple foods for the world's 6 billion plus people, and developing countries will grow cash crops like tomato, cut flowers, peas, sunflower, strawberries and vegetables.[23]

What impact would the removal of Northern agricultural subsidies have in Africa? The explicit export subsidies that are most damaging – less than 1 per cent of the total and mainly provided by the EU – will finally cease in 2013, thanks to concessions at the Hong Kong WTO summit. (Implicit EU export subsidies worth US$65 billion will continue, however.) This trivial reform aside, the most important debate is over whether substantive reductions from at least $360 billion in current annual subsidies would genuinely benefit African peasants.

One problem is that power relations prevailing in the world agricultural markets allow huge cartels to handle shipping and distribution, and they usually gain the first round of benefits when prices change. A second problem is that local land ownership patterns typically emphasize plantation-based export agriculture, with the danger that further cash crop incentives will crowd out land used for food cropping by peasants. No reliable studies exist to make definitive statements. There are, indeed, African heads of state in food-importing countries who advocate continuing EU agricultural subsidies for a third reason: because lower crop prices reduce the cost of feeding their own citizenry.

In sum, two crucial questions associated with subsidies and agricultural exports are typically elided by neoliberal economists and other pro-trade campaigners: which forces in Northern societies benefit from subsidies that promote export orientation, in both the short and long terms; and which forces in Southern societies would win, and which would lose, if subsidies were lifted. Furthermore, the crucial strategic question is whether self-reliant development strategies – which were the necessary (if insufficient) condition for most industrialization in the past – can be applied if low-income exporting countries remain mired in the commodity trap.

The same points must be raised again below with respect to Africa's mineral exports, where depletion of non-renewable resources drains the wealth of future generations. However, before doing so, let us consider problems associated with trade negotiations as the action moved to Hong Kong in December 2005.

FROM DOHA TO HONG KONG

The Doha Development Agenda – the name of the post-Uruguay round of WTO liberalization negotiations which began in November 2001 – did not address most of the distortions in international markets that keep Third World exporters down and limit national sovereignty, especially with respect to food security.

Interimperial rivalry between the major exporting blocs is an issue, to be sure. Competition was, for example, a factor limiting US arrogance in the largely unsuccessful attempt by Monsanto to introduce genetically modified (GM) agriculture in Africa, mainly via South Africa and Kenya. In opposition, Zambia, Zimbabwe and Angola rejected World Food Programme and US food relief during the early 2000s because of fears of future GM threats both to their citizens and, not coincidentally, to immediate European market access, given the banning of GM crops in the European Union (a ban that the US successfully contested as this book was going to press).

Linking its relatively centralized aid regime to trade through bilateral regionalism, the EU regularly tries to win major Africa-Caribbean-Pacific (ACP) country concessions on investment, competition, trade facilitation, government procurement, data protection and services. Along with grievances over agriculture, industry and intellectual property, the ACP's rejection of EU pressure was the basis for withdrawal of consent from the Cancún WTO summit in 2003.

Subsequently, the EU's Economic Partnership Agreements (EPAs) under the Cotonou Agreement (which replaced the much more generous Lomé Convention) signified a new, even harsher regime of 'reciprocal liberalization' to replace the preferential agreements that tied so many African countries to their former colonial masters via cash-crop exports. If the EPAs are agreed upon, what meagre organic African industry and services that remain after two decades of structural adjustment will probably be lost to European-scale economies and technological sophistication. An April 2004 meeting of parliamentarians from East Africa expressed concern 'that the pace of the negotiations has caught our countries without adequate consideration of the options open to us, or understanding of their implications, and that we are becoming hostage to the target dates that have been hastily set without the participation of our respective parliaments'. As even Botswana's neoliberal president Festus Mogae admitted in 2004,

'We are somewhat apprehensive towards EPAs despite the EU assurances. We fear that our economies will not be able to withstand the pressures associated with liberalization.'[24]

As for the WTO, a July 2004 deal in Geneva permitted the elites a chance to regroup. Notwithstanding continued recalcitrance by the EU and US on agricultural subsidies, the selection of Pascal Lamy – the EU's former trade commissioner – as WTO head confirmed the unbalanced power relationships, and Blair's appointment of Peter Mandelson to replace Lamy at the EU was a final signal that hardline neoliberalism would continue. Mandelson let slip his trading bloc's agenda in late 2005: 'Through regional market building and the Doha Development Round of trade negotiations, we need to chip away at the tariff walls that still surround many individual developing countries in Africa.'[25] Of particular importance were the residual industries of Africa and services such as national and municipal utilities, ranging from telecommunications and energy (often highly profitable) to water. According to Mark Curtis, the EU's liberalization agenda spanned the following areas:

> agricultural produce, industrial goods, services, investment policy, public utilities, the role of companies, intellectual property, competition policy, and government procurement. Many of these areas in reality go well beyond countries' trade policy as such; the EU's push for liberalization is in reality a push to promote neoliberal domestic economic policies in all countries. It is to deepen the process of corporate globalization primarily to benefit businesses in the rich world.[26]

As Walden Bello correctly predicted a month before the December 2005 WTO summit, 'The only possible deal that could emerge out of Hong Kong is a deal that would have the developing countries make damaging concessions in agriculture, non-agricultural market access (NAMA), and services, while the EU and US make cosmetic concessions in agriculture and pursue offensive interests in the other areas.'[27]

In Hong Kong, a series of vibrant street protests – especially by militant South Korean farmers (arrested in their hundreds by Chinese police) – were not enough to prevent most of the Third World delegates from caving in to EU/US pressure. With mandatory openings replacing the previous, more flexible, request-offer system in the General Agreement on Trade in Services, Third World privatizations will intensify. Moreover, there will be severe deindustrialization in many more Third World locations (Mexico, for example, has seen its *maquiladora* sector devastated), especially as the Chinese expand their exports. And any hopes that trade ministers from the South might stand up to Lamy, Mandelson and other Northern negotiators were also dashed. As Vandana Shiva summed up,

> Total failure of the WTO Doha round was averted by the fig leaf of withdrawal of export subsidies in agriculture by 2013 (while most of the $400 billion subsidies for rich-country industrialized corporate agriculture will remain) and the fig leaf of 'aid-for-trade'. The agreements on liberalization of services and industrial goods which had been totally rejected by the developing countries were sneaked in through a divide and rule policy of US and EU which have started to treat Brazil and India as 'developed', thus splitting the unity of the G20 forged in Cancún, and turning into an empty shell the new forged alliance of the G20 and G90. If the G110 had negotiated as G110, instead of merely announcing the grand alliance, services and NAMA would not have gone through.[28]

Sharma likewise concluded:

> Despite making loud noises, threatening and fuming over the injustice done to the poor and developing countries, the trade ministers of the G110 countries, comprising the entire developing world, finally bowed before the rich and mighty.... Developing countries have agreed to a 'high level of ambition for market access in agriculture and non-agriculture goods'. The text links the market access in both areas, stating that the 'ambition is to be achieved in a balanced and proportionate manner'. This is exactly what the developed countries had been keenly looking forward to, and this is where the developing countries gave in.[29]

For Bello, the most disturbing political development was that India and Brazil structurally shifted their location from an alliance with 110 Third World countries to the core of the 'Five Interested Parties' (joining the US, the EU and Australia) that cut the final deal:

> In the end, the developing country governments caved in, many of them motivated solely by the fear of getting saddled with the blame for the collapse of the organization. Even Cuba and Venezuela confined themselves to registering only 'reservations' with the services text during the closing session of the ministerial.... The main gain for Brazil and India lay not in the impact of the agreement on their economies but in the affirmation of their new role as power brokers within the WTO.[30]

According to Bello, South Africa was a problem in so far as it sold out on services privatization at the last moment (alongside Indonesia and the Philippines). Pretoria's stance compared favourably with earlier negotiations, when Alec Erwin was Trade Minister and a 'Friend of the Chair'. But the demise of the G20 as an allegedly counterhegemonic force – so highly touted by Erwin in Cancún – reveals the larger problem of subimperial interests, a topic revisited in Chapter 6.

INVESTMENT, PRODUCTION AND EXPLOITATION

From trade to direct investment, the patterns of exploitation are similar. Walter Rodney described foreign direct investment in stark terms:

> Under colonialism the ownership was complete and backed by military domination. Today, in many African countries the foreign ownership is still present, although the armies and flags of foreign powers have been removed. So long as foreigners own land, mines, factories, banks, insurance companies, means of transportation, newspapers, power stations, etc. then for so long will the wealth of Africa flow outwards into the hands of those elements. In other words, in the absence of direct political control, *foreign investment ensures that the natural resources and the labour of Africa produce economic value which is lost to the continent* [original emphasis].[31]

In recent years, Africa has not been overwhelmed by interest from foreign corporate suitors. During the early 1970s, roughly a third of all FDI to the Third World went to sub-Saharan African countries, especially apartheid South Africa. By the 1990s, that statistic had dropped to 5 per cent. Aside from oil field exploitation, the only other substantive foreign investments over the past decade were in South Africa, for the partial privatization of the state telecommunications agency and for the expansion of automotive-sector branch plant activity within global assembly lines. These inflows were offset by far by South Africa's own outflows of foreign direct investment, in the form of relocation of the largest corporations' financial headquarters to London, which in turn distorted the Africa FDI data – not to mention the repatriation of dividends/profits and payments of patent/royalty fees to transnational corporations.

To consider investment/production with the rigour required compels us also to dwell upon a wide range of historical processes and production issues which cannot be reduced to foreign firms' holdings in Africa. Such firms have many different and sometimes contradictory agendas, and the economic and eco-social impacts of their investments are diverse and often incalculable. Moreover, investment and production systems of the North have an indirect – and sometimes a direct – adverse effect in Africa because the *global* commons, including the world's carbon sink capacity, is subject to looting. Hence it is appropriate to consider, amongst the investment/production-related exploitation issues, the ecological debt that the North owes the South, especially Africa. Another feature of foreign investment activity is distortion of local African politics, a feature taken up in the next chapter.

Many authors can be cited to document the economic logic behind foreign corporate domination of African economies. One of the most careful, UN Research Institute for Social Development director Thandika Mkandawire, recently studied African economies' 'maladjustment' and concluded, 'Little FDI has gone into the manufacturing industry. As for investment in mining, it is not drawn to African countries by macroeconomic policy changes, as is often suggested, but by the prospects of better world prices, changes in attitudes towards national ownership and sector specific incentives.' Moreover, 14 per cent of FDI was 'driven by acquisitions facilitated by the increased pace of privatization to buy up existing plants that are being sold, usually under "fire sale" conditions'. What little new manufacturing investment occurred was typically 'for expansion of existing capacities, especially in industries enjoying natural monopolies (e.g. beverages, cement, furniture). Such expansion may have been stimulated by the spurt of growth that caused much euphoria and that is now fading away.'[32]

African elites' futile search for FDI seems to have grown increasingly frantic, especially with the 2001 New Partnership for Africa's Development. According to Mkandawire, leaders have not applied their minds fully to the evidence:

> It is widely recognized that direct investment is preferable to portfolio investment, and foreign investment in 'green field' investments is preferable to acquisitions. The predominance of these [portfolio and acquisition] types of capital inflows should be cause for concern. However, in their desperate efforts to attract foreign investment, African governments have simply ceased dealing with these risks or suggesting that they may have a preference for one type of foreign investment over all others. Finally, such investment is likely to taper off within a short span of time, as already seems to be the case in a number of African countries.

Thus, for Ghana, hailed as a 'success story' by the Bretton Woods Institutions, FDI, which peaked in the mid-1980s at over $200 million annually – mainly due to privatization – was rapidly reversed to produce a negative outflow. It should be noted, in passing, that rates of return of direct investments have generally been much higher in Africa than in other developing regions. This, however, has not made Africa a favourite among investors, largely because of considerations of the intangible 'risk factor', nurtured by the tendency to treat the continent as homogeneous and a large dose of ignorance about individual African countries. There is considerable evidence that shows that Africa is systematically rated as more risky than is warranted by the underlying economic characteristics.[33]

The critique of foreign investors in Africa must now extend beyond the EU, US and Japan, to China. For example, the Chinese National Petroleum Corporation (CNPC) and two other large Chinese oil firms are active in 17 African countries. In Sudan, despite the Darfur genocide, US$2 billion in investment is under way, responsible already for 5 per cent of China's import requirements, along with Chinese-financed development of a home-grown Sudanese military capacity. (Arms sales to Robert Mugabe are also dubious.) As Ben Schiller reports,

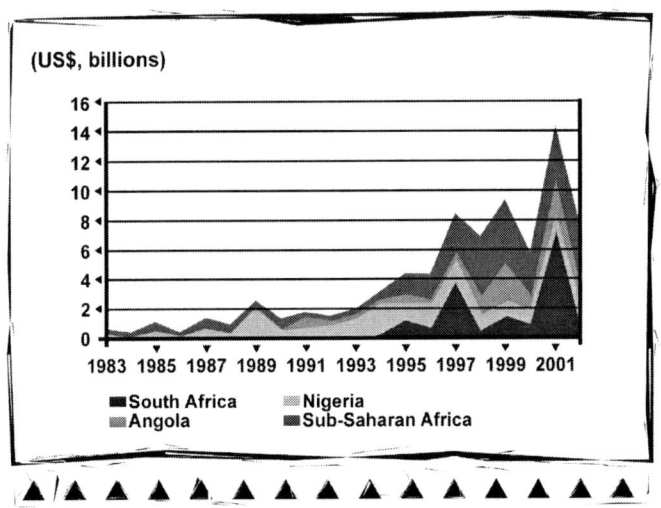

Figure 4.4 African recipients of FDI

Source: Commission for Africa (2005), *Our Common Future*, London, p. 295.

Concerns have been raised over the environmental impact of various Chinese-run mining operations in Africa, including copper mines in Zambia and Congo, and titanium sands projects in ecologically sensitive parts of Mozambique, Kenya, Tanzania, and Madagascar.

Moreover, China is a major importer of illegal timber from forests in Indonesia, Cameroon, Congo, and Equatorial Guinea. Though accurate figures are hard to access, www.globaltimber.org.uk says that up to 50 per cent of all timber imported to China in 2004 was illegal. Chinese businesses have also been implicated in ivory smuggling, notably in Sudan and Zimbabwe. According to Care for the Wild International, Chinese companies buy up to 75 per cent of Sudan's ivory.

In its rush to expand, development experts say China is reinvigorating an older, crude style of development, re-establishing an era of 'white elephants' and 'prestige projects' with little benefit to local people. In Ethiopia, the Chinese state-owned Jiangxi International built $4 million worth of new housing, after a flood left hundreds destitute. But instead of accommodating the homeless, the blocks ended up being used by military officials. A Jiangxi manager later told the *Wall Street Journal*: 'It was a political task for us and so long as Ethiopia officials are happy, our goal is fulfilled.'

Another feature of Chinese investment overseas is the use of Chinese rather than local workers. Thousands of Chinese labourers and engineers have been imported to build Ethiopia's $300 million Takazee Dam. In Sudan, Chinese workers have constructed an oil pipeline; 74,000 Chinese remain in the country, 10,000 employed by CNPC. Chinese workers are also being used in Namibia, Zimbabwe, and a host of other African states.[34]

Given that mining houses have been central to looting Africa for at least a century and a half, it is fitting next to consider the damage done by depletion of minerals and other non-renewable natural resources.

FDI AND NATURAL RESOURCE DEPLETION

Notwithstanding the recent drought, in absolute terms the volume of FDI to sub-Saharan Africa began rising again, overtaking financing by private lenders in 1988 and from 1991 staying level with financial flows. The story of FDI becomes more complex at that stage, during the late 1990s, particularly when one factors in the major two forces on the continent: South African capital and resurgent oil investments. The former is taken up below, in Chapter 6, while the latter requires consideration of new data from, surprisingly, the World Bank.

A delicately nuanced approach is required to deconstruct the brief rise of investment in sub-Saharan Africa, especially from 1997, for it appears that the peaks are associated with special circumstances. The Angolan 1999 oil investment peak was limited to the offshore Cabinda fields, while, on the Angolan mainland, a repressive, corrupt state regime waged war against a right-wing guerrilla army. The 1990s investments in Nigerian oil occurred largely under Sani Abacha's dictatorial rule, and were negated by his looting of state resources to private Swiss and London accounts. The other peak of foreign investment, into South Africa, reflects statistical accounting changes associated with the relisting of the country's largest firms to London.

The oil sector is a clear case in which profit and dividend outflows, often lubricated by corruption, have had extremely negative consequences. As demonstrated by the Open Society-backed campaign 'Publish What You Pay', elites in Africa's oil-producing countries – Angola, Chad, Congo, Equatorial Guinea, Gabon, Nigeria and Sudan – are amongst the world's least transparent.[35] In Nigeria, demands by the Ogoni people relate not only to the massive destruction of their Delta habitat, but also to the looting of their natural wealth by Big Oil. According to Sam Olukoya,

> Reparations is a crucial issue in the struggle for environmental justice in Nigeria. Many of the ethnic groups in the Niger Delta have drawn up various demands. A key document is the Ogoni Bill of Rights which seeks reparations from Shell for environmental pollution, devastation and ecological degradation of the Ogoni area. Shell's abuses in Ogoniland were made infamous by the late playwright and activist Ken Saro-Wiwa, who was executed by the Nigerian government.[36]

In all these respects, diverse forces in society have moved away from considering oil merely a matter of private property, to be negotiated between corporations and governments, as was the case during much of the twentieth century. Instead, these forces now treat oil as part of a general 'commons' of a national society's natural resources. George Caffentzis explains:

> There are three levels of claims to petroleum as common property, correlating with three kinds of allied communities that are now taking shape, for there is no common property without a community that regulates its use:

- first, some local communities most directly affected by the extraction of petroleum claim to own and regulate the petroleum under their territory as a commons;
- second, Islamic economists claim for the Islamic community of believers, from Morocco to Indonesia, and its representative, the twenty-first-century Caliphate in formation, ownership of and the right to regulate the huge petroleum fields beneath their vast territory;
- third, UN officials claim for the 'coming global community' the right to regulate the so-called global commons: air, water, land, minerals (including petroleum) and 'nous' (knowledge and information). This imagined global community is to be represented by a dizzying array of 'angels' that make up the UN system, from NGO activists to UN environmentalist bureaucrats to World Bank 'green' advisers.[37]

From a September 2005 conference in Johannesburg organized by the South African NGO groundWork, delegates petitioned the World Petroleum Congress:

> At every point in the fossil fuel production chain where your members 'add value' and make profit, ordinary people, workers and their environments are assaulted and impoverished. Where oil is drilled, pumped, processed and used, in Africa as elsewhere, ecological systems have been trashed, peoples' livelihoods have been destroyed and their democratic aspirations and their rights and cultures trampled....
>
> Your energy future is modelled on the interests of over-consuming, energy-intensive, fossil-fuel-burning wealthy classes whose reckless and selfish lifestyles not only impoverish others but threaten the global environment, imposing on all of us the chaos and uncertainty of climate change and the violence and destruction of war. Another energy future is necessary: yours has failed![38]

We turn to the political implications of these different claims to the commons at the end of the book. But it would be a mistake to neglect another political feature created in the process. In a remarkable essay, 'Seeing Like an Oil Company', anthropologist James Ferguson argues that 'capital "hops" over "unusable Africa"', alighting only in mineral-rich enclaves that are starkly disconnected from their national societies. The result is not the formation of standardized national grids, but the emergence of huge areas of the continent that are effectively "off the grid".' In the process, there emerges 'a frightening sort of political-economic model for regions that combine mineral wealth with political intractability', ranging from African oil zones to occupied Iraq. The model includes protection of capital by 'private military companies' (in Baghdad, Blackwater, Erinys and Global Risk Strategies), and protection of the 'Big Man' leader (Paul Bremer, John Negroponte) 'not by his own national army but, instead, by hired guns'.[39] The bottom line is enhanced profit for international capital and despotism for the citizenry.

Of interest, though, is that because of the environmental movement, some of the costs of this model are now being measured, even at the World Bank. If we take as given that there is some merit in considering 'natural resource' as a global commons, its depletion plus associated negative externalities – such as the social devastation caused by mining operations – must, by all accounts now, be taken seriously. That entails at least a rough accounting of the costs associated with tearing resources from the ground, forests and fisheries, no matter that many aspects of valuation – human life, indigenous people's traditions and culture, aesthetics of the natural environment – are impossible to quantify.

ACCOUNTING FOR NATURE

Because of the legacy of environmental economists like Herman Daly, even the World Bank has addressed the question of natural resource depletion, in *Where is the Wealth of Nations?*[40] The Bank methodology for correcting bias in GDP wealth accounting is nowhere near as expansive as that, for instance, of the San Francisco group Redefining Progress, which, as shown in Chapter 2, estimates that global GDP began declining in absolute terms during the mid-1970s, once we account for natural resource depletion, pollution and a variety of other factors. Nevertheless, the Bank's tentative approach is at least a step forward in recognizing that extractive investments may not contribute to net GDP, and indeed may cause net national savings and wealth to actually shrink.

The Bank's first-cut method subtracts from the existing rate of savings factors such as fixed capital depreciation, depletion of natural resources and pollution, but then adds investments in education (defined as annual expenditure). The result, in most African countries dependent upon primary products, is a net negative rate of national savings to gross national income (GNI). Notwithstanding some problems, the Bank's methodology at least indicates some of the trends associated with raw materials extraction.[41] In particular, the attempt to

Table 4.2 Adjustment to Ghana's 2000 savings rate,
based upon tangible wealth and resource depletion (US$ *per capita*)

Tangible wealth		Adjusted net saving	
Subsoil assets	$65	Gross national saving	$40
Timber resources	$290	Education expenditure	$7
Non-timber forest resources	$76	Consumption fixed capital	$-19
Protected areas	$7	Energy depletion	$0
Cropland	$855	Mineral depletion	$-4
Pastureland	$43	Net forest depletion	$-8
Produced capital	$686		
Total tangible wealth	$2022	Adjusted net saving	$16
Population growth	1.7%	Change in wealth *per capita*	$-18

Source: World Bank (2005), *Where Is the Wealth of Nations?*, Washington, pp. 64-5.

generate a 'genuine savings' calculation requires adjusting net national savings to account for resource depletion. The Bank suggests the following steps:

> From gross national saving the consumption of fixed capital is subtracted to give the traditional indicator of saving; net national savings. The value of damages from pollutants is subtracted. The pollutants carbon dioxide and particulate matter are included. The value of natural resource depletion is subtracted. Energy, metals and mineral and net forest depletion are included. Current operating expenditures on education are added to net national saving to adjust for investments in human capital.[42]

Naturally, given oil extraction, the Middle East region (including North Africa) has the world's most serious problem of net negative gross national income and savings under this methodology. But sub-Saharan Africa is second worst, and several years during the early 1990s witnessed net *negative* GNI for the continent once extraction of natural resources was factored in. Indeed, for every percentage point increase in a country's extractive-resource dependency, that country's potential GDP declines by 9 per cent (as against the real GDP recorded), according to the Bank.[43] African countries with the combined highest resource dependence and lowest capital accumulation included Nigeria, Zambia, Mauritania, Gabon, Congo, Algeria and South Africa. In comparing the *potential* for capital accumulation – if, that is, resource

Table 4.3 African countries' adjusted national wealth and
'savings gaps', 2000

	Income per capita ($)	Population growth rate (%)	Adjusted net saving per capita ($)	Change in wealth per capita ($)	Saving gap % GNI
Benin	360	2.6	14	-42	11.5
Botswana	2925	1.7	1021	814	n.a.
Burkina Faso	230	2.5	15	-36	15.8
Burundi	97	1.9	-10	-37	37.7
Cameroon	548	2.2	-8	-152	27.7
Cape Verde	1195	2.7	43	-81	6.8
Chad	174	3.1	-8	-74	42.6
Comoros	367	2.5	-17	-73	19.9
Congo, Rep.	660	3.2	-227	-727	110.2
Côte d'Ivoire	625	2.3	-5	-100	16.0
Ethiopia	101	2.4	-4	-27	27.1
Gabon	3370	2.3	-1183	-2241	66.5
The Gambia	305	3.4	-5	-45	14.6
Ghana	255	1.7	16	-18	7.2
Kenya	343	2.3	40	-11	3.2
Madagascar	245	3.1	9	-56	22.7
Malawi	162	2.1	-2	-29	18.2
Mali	221	2.4	20	-47	21.2
Mauritania	382	2.9	-30	-147	38.4
Mauritius	3697	1.1	645	514	n.a.
Mozambique	195	2.2	15	-20	10.0
Namibia	1820	3.2	392	140	n.a.
Niger	166	3.3	-10	-83	50.3
Nigeria	297	2.4	-97	-210	70.6
Rwanda	233	2.9	14	-60	26.0
Senegal	449	2.6	31	-27	6.1
Seychelles	7089	0.9	1162	904	n.a.
South Africa	2837	2.5	246	-2	0.1
Swaziland	1375	2.5	129	8	n.a.
Togo	285	4.0	-20	-88	30.8
Zambia	312	2.0	-13	-63	20.4
Zimbabwe	550	2.0	53	-4	0.7

Source: World Bank, *Where Is the Wealth of Nations?*, p. 66.

rents were not simply extracted (and exported) and resources depleted
– on the one hand and, on the other, the *actual* measure of capital
accumulation, Bank researchers discovered that,

> In many cases the differences are huge. Nigeria, a major oil exporter, could
> have had a year 2000 stock of produced capital five times higher than the
> actual stock. Moreover, if these investments had taken place, oil would play
> a much smaller role in the Nigerian economy today, with likely beneficial
> impacts on policies affecting other sectors of the economy.[44]

A more nuanced breakdown of a country's estimated 'tangible wealth'
is required to capture not just obvious oil-related depletion and rent
outflows, but also other subsoil assets, timber resources, non-timber
forest resources, protected areas, cropland and pastureland. The 'produced capital' normally captured in GDP accounting is added to tangible
wealth. In the case of Ghana, that amounted to $2,022 per person in
2000. The same year, the gross national saving of Ghana was $40 and
education spending was $7. These figures require downward adjust-
ment to account for the consumption of fixed capital ($19), as well as
the depletion of wealth in the form of stored energy ($0), minerals
($4) and net forest assets ($8). In Ghana, the adjusted net saving was
$16 per person in 2000. But given population growth of 1.7 per cent,
the country's wealth actually shrank by $18 per person in 2000.[45]

How much of this exploitation is based on transnational capital's
extractive power? In the case of Ghana, $12 of the $18 decline in 2000
could be attributed to minerals and forest-related depletions, a large
proportion of which now leave Ghana.[46] The largest indigenous (and
black-owned) mining firm in Africa, Ashanti, was recently bought by
AngloGold, so it is safe to assume that an increasing amount of
Ghana's wealth flows out of the country, leaving net negative *per
capita* tangible wealth. Other mining houses active in Africa which
once had their roots here – Lonrho, Anglo American, DeBeers, Gencor/
Billiton – are also now based offshore.

It is thus logical to assume that an increased drive by London, New
York and Sydney shareholders for profits results in accumulation of
capital within Africa being systematically stymied. The central question
is whether any of the financial capital that returns to Africa – by way
of royalties on minerals or profits to local shareholders (still significant
in the case of South Africa) – is reinvested, or merely becomes the
source of further capital flight.

Ghana was an interesting example, given that it has often played the role of the World Bank's poster child. Other African countries whose economies are primary-product-dependent fare much worse, according to the Bank methodology. Gabon's citizens lost $2,241 each in 2000, as oil companies rapidly depleted the country's tangible wealth. The Republic of the Congo (–$727), Nigeria (–$210), Cameroon (–$152), Mauritania (–$147) and Côte d'Ivoire (–$100) are other African countries whose people lost more than $100 each in tangible national wealth in 2000 alone. (Angola would rank high amongst these, were data available for the Bank's analysis.) A few countries did benefit, according to the tangible wealth measure, including the Seychelles (+$904), Botswana (+$814) and Namibia (+$140), but the majority of African countries saw their wealth depleted.[47]

Even Africa's largest economy, South Africa, which from the early 1980s has been far less reliant upon minerals extraction, recorded a $2 drop in *per capita* wealth in 2000 using this methodology. According to the World Bank, the natural wealth of $3,400/person in South Africa included subsoil assets (worth $1,118 per person);[48] timber ($310); non-timber forest resources ($46); protected areas ($51); cropland ($1,238); and pastureland ($637). This sum can be compared to the value of produced capital (plant and equipment) and urban land (together worth $7,270 per person in 2000). Hence, even in Africa's most industrialized economy, the estimated value of natural resources is nearly half of the measurable value of plant, equipment and urban land.[49]

Given the constant depletion of these natural resources, South Africa's official gross national savings rate of 15.7 per cent of GDI should be adjusted downwards. By substracting consumption of fixed capital at 13.3 per cent, the net national savings is actually 2.4 per cent, to which should be added education expenditure (amongst the world's highest) at 7.5 per cent. Then subtract mineral depletion of 1 per cent; forest depletion of 0.3 per cent; 0.2 per cent pollution damage (limited to 'particulate matter', a small part of South Africa's waste problem); and CO_2 emissions worth 1.6 per cent of GDI (a serious undervaluation). In total, the actual 'genuine savings' of South Africa is reduced to just 6.9 per cent of national income.[50] How much of this deficit from the 15.7 per cent savings rate can be attributed to foreign investors? Not only is mineral depletion biased to benefit overseas mining houses, but CO_2 emissions and many other pollution flows (especially SO_2) are largely the result of energy consumption by metal smelters owned by large multinational corporations (Mittal Steel, BHP Billiton and the Anglo American group).

In sum, the role of extractive FDI in oil- and resource-rich countries must take into account the net negative impact on national wealth, including natural resources. Ironically, given the source of leadership at the World Bank (Paul Wolfowitz of the US petro-military complex), the Bank's new accounting of genuine savings is a helpful innovation. Taking the methodology forward to correct biases, and rigorously estimating an Africa-wide extraction measure in order to better account for the way extractive FDI generates net negative welfare/savings are important tasks.

FOREIGN INVESTMENT IN PRIVATIZATION

The other concern noted above is the manner in which foreign acquisitions of existing domestically owned plant and equipment also have unintended negative consequences. Perhaps the worst case was on the Zambian copperfields, when Anglo American invested during the late 1990s but then simply closed down one of the most important mining sites, leaving thousands of victims in its wake.

But even South Africa has been victimized by privatization-related FDI. Indeed, the large foreign investments in South Africa that appear as a blip on the FDI graph are mainly accounted for by the 1997 privatization of the telecommunications sector and the 2001 rejigging of statistics to claim large formerly domestic corporations as foreign, once they had changed their primary share listing to London. The implications of the telecommunications investments are now well-known, in the wake of the 30 per cent share purchase in the state-owned Telkom by a Houston/Kuala Lumpur alliance. Critics such as the Freedom of Expression Institute[51] point to subsequent problems as being inexorably related to FDI and privatization, including the sky-rocketing cost of local calls as cross-subsidization from long-distance (especially international) calls was phased out; the disconnection of 2.1 million lines (out of 2.6 million new lines installed) due to unafford-ability; the firing of 20,000 Telkom workers, leading to ongoing labour strife; and an Initial Public Offering on the New York Stock Exchange in 2003 which raised only $500 million, with an estimated $5 billion of Pretoria's own funding of Telkom's late 1990s capital expansion lost in the process. Ironically, the South African state repurchased the shares of Telkom held by the foreign investment consortium in 2004 (although Pretoria did not materially change policies and practices subsequently). There are several similar experiences with failed foreign investment in South Africa's other privatized state assets, including transport (where renationalization occurred in the cases of Sun Air and South African Airways), water (where remunicipalization occurred in the case of Suez in Nkonkobe and is likely to occur in Johannesburg) and electricity.

Meanwhile, South Africa witnessed very few foreign investments in 'greenfield' projects (as opposed to existing acquisitions). Behind the overall slowdown in South African fixed investment lies not only global overcapacity combined with national industrial uncompetitiveness, but also South Africa's own overcapacity constraints on new investment. In manufacturing especially, there has been a long-term decline in capacity utilization, due to overproduction and excessive concentration in the major industrial sectors. South Africa is, thus, a more complicated and perhaps extreme example of so many other African countries where the private sector was stagnant and in need of privatization opportunities, yet, in spite of the fire-sale character of privatization, did not subsequently succeed in turning its acquisition investments into sustained productive investments.

Another query is also worth raising: to what extent do the foreign investors cover their own initial equity stake? The case of the partially privatized Airports Company of South Africa is instructive, for Aeroporti Di Roma earned a vast profit – R785 million – on its initial 1998 investment of R890 million for 20 per cent of the company. In September 2005, the South African state's investment arm bought back the stake for R1.67 billion. Adding R180 million in dividends paid since 1998, the Italian firm took home more than a 108 per cent rate of return over seven years, exceptionally high by any measure.[52] At the same time, the repurchase of the company by a state agency demonstrated that there was no particular reason to have a foreign investor in the first place. Although 'technical expertise' is sometimes considered a valid reason for inviting foreign investment, the South African air transport industry's operations management and logistics operations were always sufficiently sophisticated to handle the expansion of airports.

These experiences are not uncommon, according to Transparency International's Lawrence Cockcroft:

The most common and important form of corruption has been one in which, in spite of a conventional bidding process, an award has been made to a company which has committed itself to specific additional investment, often amounting to large sums. The real, but very untransparent arrangement, has been that a key figure in the privatization panel has taken a bribe for the award of the contract and will ensure that no further investment need be made, and even that the initial downpayment should be very modest. This is certain to have disastrous consequences for the long-term viability of the operation in question.[53]

FOREIGN INVESTMENT, TAX FRAUD AND TRANSFER PRICING

Many other modes of surplus and resource extraction through FDI involve swindling. For example, corporate failure to pay taxes and state failure to collect them is a point stressed by Cockcroft:

Most African countries operate some form of tax break for new investors, with varying degrees of generosity. In fact such incentive schemes are frequently deceptive in that the real deal is being done in spite of them and alongside them, with a key cabinet minister or official coming to an alternative arrangement which may well guarantee an offshore payment for the individual in question as well as a 'tax holiday' for the company concerned....

One of the most common instruments of state-sponsored corruption is the award of import permits to well-placed individuals which undermines this legitimate protection. The Kenyan sugar industry and the Nigerian feedmilling and poultry industry have been ruined for several years at a stretch through this process.

As access to prime land becomes more and more competitive in African countries where there is a formal market in land the corruption surrounding the award of title has become more and more severe. A recurrent problem is one in which a title, once awarded, is re-awarded to a competitor by the Registrar of Lands or the senior politician who controls the Registrar.

Facilitation payments, also known as grease payments, may be usefully defined as payments designed to ensure that a standard service is performed more quickly than would be the case without the payment. The clearance of customs and the installation of a telephone are illustrations of such cases. Obviously payments of this kind are regarded as standard practice in many countries of the world, and Africa is no exception to this. They have been permitted under the US Foreign Corrupt Practices Act since its revision in 1988, and in a guarded form are permitted under the 1997 OECD AntiBribery Convention.

Official statistics have never properly picked up the durable problem of transfer pricing, whereby foreign investors misinvoice inputs drawn from abroad. Companies cheat Third World countries on tax revenues by artificially inflating their imported input prices so as to claim lower net income. It is only possible to guess the vast scale of the problem on the basis of case studies.

The Oxford Institute of Energy Studies estimated that, in 1994, 14 per cent of the total value of exported oil 'was not accounted for in national trade figures as a result of various forms of transfer pricing and smuggling'.[54] According to a 1999 United Nations Conference on Trade and Development survey on income shifting as part of transfer pricing,

> Of the developing countries with sufficient evidence to make an assessment, 61 per cent estimated that their own national transnational corporations (TNCs) were engaging in income shifting, and 70 per cent deemed it a significant problem. The income-shifting behaviour of foreign-based TNCs was also appraised. 84 per cent of the developing countries felt that the affiliates they hosted shifted income to their parent companies to avoid tax liabilities, and 87 per cent viewed the problem as significant.[55]

Similarly, another kind of corporate financial transfer aimed at exploiting weak African countries is the fee that headquarters charge for patent and copyright fees on technology agreements. Such payments, according to Yash Tandon, are augmented by management and consultancy fees, as well as other Northern corporate support mechanisms that drain the Third World. For the year 2000, Tandon listed export revenue for non-agricultural products of more than $30 billion denied to the South by Northern protectionism.[56]

PRODUCTION, TRANSPORT AND THE ECOLOGICAL DEBT

Most of the systems of unequal exchange have been identified (aside from labour, which is considered below), but not the ecological implications. In an indirect manner, such that victims are not aware of the process, another crucial outlet for Northern investors seeking to exploit Africa is in their consumption of the global commons, particularly the earth's clean air. During the early 1990s, the idea of the North's ecological debt to the South began gaining currency in Latin America thanks to NGOs, environmentalists and politicians (including Fidel Castro of Cuba and Virgilio Barco of Colombia). According to Joan Martinez-Alier,

> The notion of an ecological debt is not particularly radical. Think of the environmental liabilities incurred by firms (under the United States Super-fund legislation), or of the engineering field called 'restoration ecology', or the proposals by the Swedish government in the early 1990s to calculate the country's environmental debt. Ecologically unequal exchange is one of the reasons for the claim of the Ecological Debt. The second reason for this claim is the disproportionate use of Environmental Space by the rich countries.[57]

In the first category, ecologically unequal exchange, Martinez-Alier lists:

- unpaid costs of reproduction or maintenance or sustainable management of the renewable resources that have been exported;
- actualized costs of the future lack of availability of destroyed natural resources;
- compensation for, or the costs of reparation (unpaid) of the local damages produced by exports (for example, the sulphur dioxide of copper smelters, the mine tailings, the harms to health from flower exports, the pollution of water by mining), or the actualized value of irreversible damage;
- (unpaid) amounts corresponding to the commercial use of inform-ation and knowledge on genetic resources, when they have been appropriated gratis ('biopiracy'). For agricultural genetic resources, the basis for such a claim already exists under the Food and Agri-culture Organization's Farmers' Rights.

In the second, he cites 'lack of payment for environmental services or for the disproportionate use of Environmental Space':

- (unpaid) reparation costs or compensation for the impacts caused by imports of solid or liquid toxic waste;
- (unpaid) costs of free disposal of gas residues (carbon dioxide, CFCs, etc.), assuming equal rights to sinks and reservoirs.

These aspects of ecological debt defy easy measurement. Each part of the ecological balance sheet is contested, and information is imperfect. As Martinez-Alier shows in other work, tropical rainforests used for wood exports have an extraordinary past we will never know and on-going biodiversity whose destruction we cannot begin to value. However, he acknowledges, 'although it is not possible to make an exact account-ing, it is necessary to establish the principal categories [of ecological debt] and certain orders of magnitude in order to stimulate discussion'.[58]

The sums involved are potentially vast. Vandana Shiva and Tandon estimate that acts of biopiracy including 'wild seed varieties have contributed some $66 billion annually to the US economy'.[59] As Shiva observes, oligopolistic concentration in the firms that transform ecology into profit is now an 'epidemic':

- the world's top ten seed companies have increased their control from one-third to one-half of the global seed trade;
- the top ten biotech enterprises have raised their share from just over half to nearly three-quarters of world biotech sales; and
- the top ten pharmaceutical companies control almost 59 per cent in market share of the world's leading 98 drug firms (previously the top ten accounted for 53 per cent in market share of 118 companies).[60]

A 2005 study commissioned by the Edmonds Institute and African Centre for Biosafety identified nearly three dozen cases of African resources captured by firms for resale without adequate 'access and benefit sharing' agreements between producers and the people who first used the natural products. The values expropriated are impossible to calculate but easily run into billions of dollars. They include a diabetes drug produced by a Kenyan microbe; a Libyan/Ethiopian treatment for diabetes; antibiotics from a Gambian termite hill; an antifungal from a Namibian giraffe; an infection-fighting amoeba from Mauritius; a Congo (Brazzaville) treatment for impotence; vaccines from Egyptian microbes; multipurpose medicinal plants from the Horn of Africa; the South African and Namibian indigenous appetite suppressant Hoodia; antibiotics from giant West African land snails; drug addiction treatments and multipurpose kombo butter from Central and West Africa; skin whitener from South African and Lesotho aloe; beauty and healing from Okoumé resin in Central Africa; skin and hair care from the argan tree in Morocco; skin care plus from Egyptian 'Pharaoh's Wheat'; skin care from the *bambara* groundnut and 'resurrection plant; endophytes and improved fescues from Algeria and Morocco; nematocidal fungi from Burkina Faso; groundnuts from Malawi, Senegal, Mozambique, Sudan and Nigeria; Tanzanian *impatiens*;

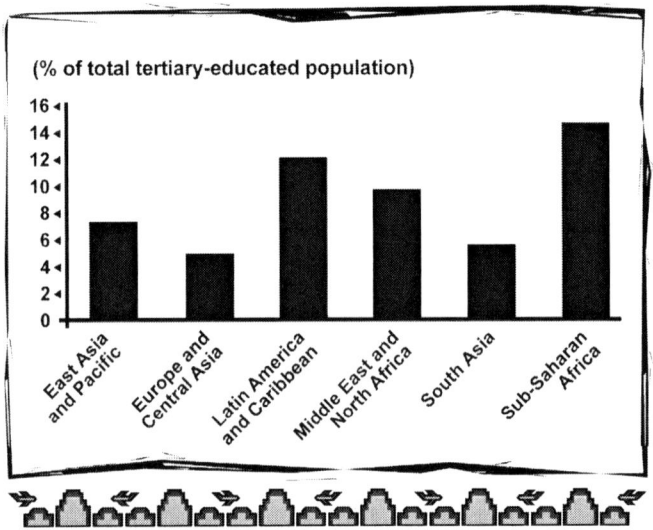

Figure 4.5 Emigration of skilled workers with tertiary education, 2000

Source: World Bank (2005), *Global Economic Prospects, 2006*, Washington, World Bank, p. 72.

and molluscicides from the Horn of Africa. As author Jay McGown concluded,

> It's a free-for-all out there, and until the parties to the Convention on Biological Diversity solve the problems of access and benefit sharing, the robbery will continue. They've got to declare a moratorium on access until a just protocol on access and benefit sharing is finished and implemented. Until they slog through that terrible work – and that includes all the hard questions indigenous peoples and local communities are asking and all the hard questions about the sources of biodiversity mentioned in patent applications – until that work is done, the biopirates will keep on shouting in the ears of their victims, 'There's no such thing as biopiracy!'[61]

Moreover, in the case of CO_2 emissions, according to Martinez-Alier,

> Jyoti Parikh (a member of the UN International Panel on Climate Change) [argues that] if we take the present human-made emissions of carbon, the average is about one tonne per person per year. Industrialized countries produce three-fourths of these emissions, instead of the one-fourth that would correspond to them on the basis of population. The difference is 50 per cent of total emissions, some 3,000 million tons. Here the increasing marginal cost of reduction is contemplated: the first 1,000 million tons

could be reduced at a cost of, say, $15 per ton, but then the cost increases very much. Let us take an average of $25: then a total annual subsidy of $75 billion is forthcoming from South to North.[62]

Depletion of minerals and other non-renewable resources, dumping of toxics, biopiracy and excess use of the planet's CO_2 absorption capacity are some of the many ways in which the South is being exploited by the North on the ecological front. Africans are most exploited in this regard because non-industrialized economies have not begun to utilize more than a small fraction of what should be due under any fair framework of global resource allocation. The amounts involved would easily cover debt repayments.

LABOUR MIGRATION AS RESOURCE DEPLETION

A final way in which Africa's wealth is depleted is via skilled labour migration. This problem has become important, even if it is slightly mitigated by the inflow of migrant remittance payments to families at home. Approximately 20,000 skilled workers leave Africa each year. The World Bank's estimate of the share of Africa's skilled workers with a tertiary education who emigrate is more than 15 per cent, higher than any other region.

It is true that remittances from both skilled and unskilled labour flow back to Africa as a result, and in some cases represent an important contribution to GDP: Lesotho, 26 per cent (measured in 2004); The Gambia, 7 per cent (1998); Mali, 6 per cent (1994); Uganda, 4 per cent (1999); Burkina Faso, 3 per cent (1998); Kenya, 3 per cent (1997); and Senegal, 3 per cent (1995). But as the World Bank concedes, there are extremely high transaction costs imposed upon the small sums that are transferred by migrants (Western Union branches in Brussels and Paris charge 21 per cent of the principal amount in a wire transfer below 40 euros; 13 per cent for 41–75 euros; 10 per cent for 76–150 euros; and decreasing subsequent amounts).[63] For this reason, a great deal of migration-related inflows to Africa have become informal in nature, via black market systems, according to Sarah Bracking. In turn, once the flows reach their home destination, further problems often emerge:

> While money sent from the 'other side' has a beneficial effect on close kin, remittances can also undermine the purchasing power of those households

without migrating members. This is in part a result of asset price inflation, and in part due to the inflationary effects of parallel currency markets. The situation for those excluded from benefiting from foreign currency inputs is aggravated by chronic scarcity in the availability of consumables.[64]

The progressive position on migration has always been to maintain support for the 'globalization of people' (while opposing the 'globalization of capital') and in the process to oppose border controls and arduous immigration restrictions, as well as all forms of xeno-phobia. In contrast, the Blair Commission for Africa has already given up the battle, arguing that even for temporary migration, full liberalization of borders 'is unlikely to happen, and may be politically unfeasible – even though there are substantial gains to "temporary movement". Most OECD governments, their public and media, are extremely sensitive to immigration issues, and more recently to security concerns.'[65]

That 'sensitivity' was on display in October 2005 when North Africans were expelled from the Moroccan-Spanish border at Granada by lethal force, and the supposedly progressive Zapatero regime announced it would build the equivalent of Israel's notorious apartheid wall at the border. It was, according to Slavoj Žižek, just another symptom of Fortress Europe:

A couple of years ago, an ominous decision of the EU passed almost unnoticed: a plan to establish an all-European border police force to secure the isolation of the Union territory, so as to prevent the influx of the immigrants. *This* is the truth of globalization: the construction of *new* walls safeguarding the prosperous Europe from a flood of immigrants....

The segregation of the people is the reality of economic globalization. This new racism of the developed world is in a way much more brutal than the previous one. Its implicit legitimization is neither naturalist (the 'natural' superiority of the developed West) nor culturalist (we in the West also want to preserve our cultural identity). Rather, it's an unabashed economic egotism – the fundamental divide is the one between those included into the sphere of (relative) economic prosperity and those excluded from it.[66]

According to Tandon and the UN Development Programme, there is a substantial 'loss of revenue on account of blockage on the free movement of people', which they estimated to amount to at least $25 billion annually during the 1980s. But setting such numbers aside, in migration and many other forms of North–South power, it is also important to recognize an important basis for superexploitation within patriarchal power relations. In many (though not all) cases, women face such disempowering conditions across Africa that political-economic and human-environmental systems permit the processes discussed above – debt/finance, trade, investment and labour migration – to maintain inordinately high rates of exploitation. This is just one of the ways that a group of elites plays an accommodating role in the looting of Africa, as we see next in Chapter 5. Another, termed 'subimperialism', is considered in Chapter 6.

NOTES

1 Labi, A. and S. Robinson (2001), 'Looting Africa', *Time International*, 6 August.

2 Saul, J. and C. Leys (1999), 'Sub-Saharan Africa in Global Capitalism', *Monthly Review*, July, p. 6.

3 World Bank (2005), *Where Is the Wealth of Nations? Measuring Capital for the Twenty-first Century*, Washington, World Bank, Table 5.2, p. 66.

4 Christian Aid (2005), 'The Economics of Failure: the Real Cost of "Free" Trade for Poor Countries', London, p. 3. See also Kraev, E. (2005), 'Estimating Demand Side Effects of Trade Liberalization on GDP of Developing Countries', London, Christian Aid, May.

5 Fanon, F. (1963), *The Wretched of the Earth*, Chapter 3, New York, Grove Press.

6 Cited in Oxfam (2005), 'Africa and the Doha Round: Fighting to Keep Development Alive', Oxfam Briefing Paper 80, Oxford, November, p. 21.

7 Commission for Africa, *Our Common Future*, London, p. 250.

8 Cornia, G. (1999), 'Liberalization, Globalization and Income Distribution', United Nations World Institute for Development Economic Research Working Papers No. 157, Helsinki, March.

9 Chiahemen, J. (2005), 'Africa Fears "Tsunami" of Cheap Chinese Imports', Reuters, 18 December.

10 Barratt-Brown, M. (2004), 'Africa's Trade Today', paper for the *Review of African Political Economy* and CODESRIA 30th Anniversary Conference, Wortley Hall, Sheffield, 27 May. See also Barratt-Brown, M. and P. Tiffen (1992), *Short Changed: Africa and World Trade*, London, Pluto Press.

11 Leon, J. and R. Soto (1997), 'Structural Breaks and Long-term Trends in Commodity Prices', *Journal of International Development*, 9, p. 350.

12 United Nations Development Programme (2005), *Human Development Report 2005: International Cooperation at a Crossroads*, New York, p. 141.

13 Hormeku, T. (2005), 'The "Development Package" That Isn't', Third World Network Info Service on WTO and Trade Issues, Accra, <http://www.twnside.org.sg>, 16 December.

14 Dollar, D. and A. Kraay (2002), 'Trade, Growth and Poverty', Washington,

World Bank.

15 Alexander, N. (2005), 'The Ideological Economics of Commodity Production', Services for All listserve, 9 December. As other critics – including Dani Rodrik of Harvard and Mark Weisbrot of the Center for Economic Policy and Research (<www.cepr.net>) – argue, Dollar and Kraay made an elementary statistical mistake by confusing the source of causality.

16 Aksoy, A. and J. Beghin (2005), *Global Agricultural Trade and Developing Countries*, Washington, World Bank.

17 <http://web.worldbank.org/WBSITE/EXTERNAL/TOPICS/TRADE/0,,content MDK:20716308~pagePK:64020865~piPK:149114~theSitePK:239071,00.html >; see the Anderson/Martin article at <http://www.worldbank.org/trade/wto>.

18 Center for Economic and Policy Research (2005), 'World Bank's Claims on WTO Doha Round Clarified: Banks Research Shows Little at Stake in Hong Kong Ministerial', press release, Washington, 22 November.

19 Rodney, W. (1972), *How Europe Underdeveloped Africa*, Dar es Salaam, Tanzania Publishing House and London, Bogle L'Ouverture Publications; all citations are from this edition, available at <http://www.marxists.org/subject/africa/rodney-walter/how-europe/>.

20 Milanovic, B. (2002), 'Can We Discern the Effect of Globalization on Income Distribution?, Evidence from Household Budget Surveys', World Bank Policy Research Working Paper 2876, Washington, April.

21 Sharma, D. (2005), 'Farm Subsidies: The Report Card', ZNet commentary, 27 November. Sharma argues that in response, 'Developing countries should ask for: agricultural subsidies to be classified under two categories: one which benefits small farmers and the remaining which goes to agri-business companies and the big farmers/landowners; and since less than 20 per cent of the $1 billion farm subsidies being doled out every day genuinely benefit small farmers, the remaining 80 per cent subsidies need to be outright scrapped before proceeding any further on agriculture negotiations.'

22 United Nations Development Programme, *Human Development Report 2005*, p. 130.

23 Sharma, D. (2005), 'Much Ado about Nothing', *ZNet Commentary*, 24 December.

24 <http://www.epawatch.net/general/text.php?itemID=161&menuID=28>, <http://www.twnafrica.org/atn.asp>.

25 Cited in Curtis, '17 Ways the European Commission is Pushing Trade Liberalization on Poor Countries'. The 17 strategies were as follows: (1) through unfair deals; (2) through Economic Partnership Agreements; (3) through bilateral trade agreements; (4) by pushing for market access for agricultural exports; (5) by pushing for market access for industrial goods; (6) by trying to open up markets for services; (7) by using aid to promote trade liberalization; (8) through its 'Trade barriers regulation'; (9) through the WTO's 'Dispute settlement' mechanism; (10) through pushing new issues onto the agenda; (11) by seeking to liberalize government spending contracts; (12) by seeking new

rules on international investment; (13) by seeking new rules on competition policy; (14) by seeking to strengthen intellectual property rights; (15) by promoting business interests; (16) by decreasing regulation of corporations; (17) by offering not very special treatment.

26 *Ibid.*

27 Bello, W. (2005), email communication, 10 November.

28 Shiva, V. (2005), 'Beyond the WTO Ministerial in Hong Kong', *ZNet Commentary*, 26 December.

29 Sharma, 'Much Ado about Nothing'.

30 Bello, W. (2005), 'The Meaning of Hong Kong: Brazil and India Join the Big Boys' Club', unpublished paper, Bangkok, Focus on the Global South. Bello particularly blames Brazilian foreign minister Celso Amorim and Indian commerce minister Kamal Nath.

31 Rodney, *How Europe Underdeveloped Africa*.

32 Mkandawire, T. (2005), 'Maladjusted African Economies and Globalization', *Africa Development*, 30, 1–2, p. 6.

33 *Ibid.*, p.7.

34 Schiller, B. (2005), 'The China Model of Development', <http://www.open democracy.net/democracy-china/china_development_3136.jsp>, 20 December.

35 <www.opensociety.org>.

36 Olukoya, S. (2001), 'Environmental Justice from the Niger Delta to the World Conference Against Racism', special report in *CorpWatch*, 30 August, <http://www.corpwatch.org/article.php?id=18>.

37 Caffentzis, G. (2004), 'The Petroleum Commons: Local, Islamic and Global', *The Progress Report*, <http://www.progress.org/2004/water26.htm>.

38 <www.groundwork.org.za>.

39 Ferguson, J. (2005), 'Seeing Like an Oil Company: Space, Security and Global Capital in Neoliberal Africa', *American Anthropologist*, 107, 3, p. 381.

40 World Bank (2005), *Where Is the Wealth of Nations?*

41 In making estimates about the decline in a country's wealth due to energy, mineral or forest-related depletion, the World Bank has a minimalist definition based upon international pricing (not potential future values when scarcity becomes a more crucial factor, especially in the oil industry). The Bank does not fully calculate damages done to the local environment, to workers' health/ safety, and especially to women in communities around mines. Moreover, the Bank's use of average – not marginal – cost resource rents also probably leads to underestimations of the depletion costs.

42 World Bank, *Where is the Wealth of Nations?*, p. 39.

43 *Ibid.*, p. 55.

44 *Ibid.*

45 *Ibid.*, pp. 64–5.

46 *Ibid.*

47 *Ibid.*, p. 66.

48 According to a different study by the United Nations Development Programme,

the value of natural minerals capital in the soil fell from $112 billion in 1960 to $55 billion in 2000. See United Nations Development Programme (2004), *South Africa Human Development Report 2003*, Pretoria, Appendix 12.

49 World Bank, *Where is the Wealth of Nations?*, p. 179.

50 *Ibid.*

51 <http://www.fxi.org.za>; see also <http://www.helkom.co.za>.

52 Faniso, M. (2005), 'PIC Purchases One-Fifth of ACSA for R1.67 billion', *Business Report*, 22 September 2005.

53 Cockcroft, L. (2001), 'Corruption as a Threat to Corporate Behaviour and the Rule of Law', London, Transparency International UK, p. 2.

54 *Ibid.*

55 UN Conference on Trade and Development (1999), 'Transfer Pricing', Geneva, UNCTAD, p. 167.

56 <http://www.globalpolicy.org/socecon/develop/devthry/well-being/2000/tandon.htm>.

57 Martinez-Alier, J. (2003), 'Marxism, Social Metabolism and Ecologically Unequal Exchange', paper presented at Lund University Conference on World Systems Theory and the Environment, 19–22 September. Martinez-Alier elaborates with examples of ecological debt that are never factored into standard trade and investment regimes: 'nutrients in exports including virtual water ... the oil and minerals no longer available, the biodiversity destroyed. This is a difficult figure to compute, for several reasons. Figures on the reserves, estimation of the technological obsolescence because of substitution, and a decision on the rate of discount are needed in the case of minerals or oil. For biodiversity, knowledge of what is being destroyed would be needed.' Some of these cases are considered in the discussion earlier concerning depletion of natural capital. See also <www.deudaecologica.org>.

58 Martinez-Alier, J. (1998) 'Ecological Debt – External Debt', unpublished paper, Quito, Acción Ecológica.

59 <http://www.globalpolicy.org/socecon/develop/devthry/well-being/2000/tandon.htm>.

60 Shiva, 'Beyond the WTO Ministerial in Hong Kong'.

61 McGown, J. (2006), 'Out of Africa: Mysteries of Access and Benefit Sharing', Edmonds Washington, the Edmonds Institute and Johannesburg, the African Centre for Biosafety.

62 Martinez-Alier cites Parikh, J. K. (1995), 'Joint Implementation and the North and South Cooperation for Climate Change', *International Environmental Affairs*, 7, 1.

63 World Bank, *Global Economic Prospects, 2006*, Washington, World Bank.

64 Bracking, S. (2003), 'Sending Money Home: Are Remittances Always Beneficial to Those who Stay Behind?', *Journal of International Development*, 15, p. 633.

65 Commission for Africa, *Our Common Future*, p. 106.

66 Žižek, S. (2005), 'The Subject Supposed to Loot and Rape: Reality and Fantasy in New Orleans', *In These Times*, 20 October.

5

Global Apartheid's African Agents

Home-grown neoliberalism, repression, failed reform

Is bad implementation of otherwise good public policy to blame for the overall state of African underdevelopment? Tony Blair's Commission for Africa would have us believe that 'internal factors have been the primary culprit for Africa's economic stagnation or decline over the past three decades'.[1] No one can deny the orientation of so many African state elites towards parasitical, consumptive, unproductive activities. It may be that the main complaint made by the Bretton Woods Institutions, of African elites who go 'off track' because they cannot stand the pressures of reform, has a grain of truth. But the full picture requires a focus that does not privilege the viewpoints of the elites alone, but also includes those of their grassroots and shopfloor opponents.

Walter Rodney was unforgiving about

> the minority in Africa which serves as the transmission line between the metropolitan capitalists and the dependencies in Africa. The importance of this group cannot be underestimated. The presence of a group of African sell-outs is part of the definition of underdevelopment. Any diagnosis of underdevelopment in Africa will reveal not just low *per capita* income and protein deficiencies, but also the gentlemen who dance in Abidjan, Accra and Kinshasa when music is played in Paris, London and New York.[2]

Initially, according to critics of African compradorism such as Rodney, Frantz Fanon or Amilcar Cabral, there emerged a post-independence cadreship of leaders amenable to Northern objectives. In the first phase of class formation, the new state-based ruling elites were compelled to issue statements about the need for national developmental projects. However, those elites failed to challenge the North–South order substantively. A second phase of elite formation during the 1980s allowed a 'home-grown' technocratic neoliberalism to prosper, typically within finance ministries and central banks in African capitals, as well as allied thinktanks. As Jimi Adesina explains, 'Ministries of Finance, central banks, bureaux with oversight mandate for privatization and commercialization often became the first-line soldiers for the emergent neoliberal orthodoxy. "Capacity building" projects by the Bretton Woods institutions and similarly oriented Western agencies focused on reinforcing this ideological commitment.'[3]

One key agent for this process was the World Bank. Geoffrey Lamb – formerly a member of the South African Communist Party, then dean at the Sussex Institute of Development Studies, and later a top Bank official – argued cleverly in 1987 that

> Building an independent technocratic policy capacity within member countries is therefore important to encourage domestic political accountability for policy decisions over the longer run and for improving the credibility of economic advice to countries' political leaderships – provided that support for technocratic 'policy elites' does not too drastically compromise the recipients' influence.[4]

Several decades earlier, Cabral had explained the pressure under which such policy elites would be placed after liberation:

> To retain the power which national liberation puts in its hands, the petty bourgeoisie has only one path: to give free rein to its natural tendencies to become more bourgeois, to permit the development of a bureaucratic and intermediary bourgeoisie in the commercial cycle, in order to transform itself into a national pseudo-bourgeoisie, that is to say in order to negate the revolution and necessarily ally [with imperialist capital]. In order not to betray these objectives the petty bourgeoisie has only one choice: to strengthen its revolutionary consciousness, to reject the temptations of becoming more bourgeois and the natural concerns of its class mentality, to identify itself with the working classes and not to oppose the normal development of the process of revolution. This means that in order to truly fulfil the role in the national liberation struggle, the revolutionary petty bourgeoisie must be capable of committing suicide as a class in order to be reborn as revolutionary workers, completely identified with the deepest aspirations of the people to which they belong. This alternative – to betray the revolution or to commit suicide as a class – constitutes the dilemma of the petty bourgeoisie in the general framework of the national liberation struggle.[5]

Fanon was also aware of these dangers, as he signalled in *The Wretched of the Earth*:[6]

> The national middle class which takes over power at the end of the colonial regime is an underdeveloped middle class. It has practically no economic power, and in any case it is in no way commensurate with the bourgeoisie of the mother country which it hopes to replace. In its wilful narcissism, the national middle class is easily convinced that it can advantageously replace the middle class of the mother country. But that same independence which literally drives it into a corner will give rise within its ranks to catastrophic reactions, and will oblige it to send out frenzied appeals for help to the former mother country.

As a result, the 'policy elites' – who, Lamb hoped, could be shielded from criticism – are often exposed as comprador allies of those exploiting Africa, according to Fanon:

> Seen through its eyes, [the new bourgeoisie's] mission has nothing to do with transforming the nation; it consists, prosaically, of being the transmission line between the nation and a capitalism, rampant though camouflaged, which today puts on the masque of neocolonialism. The national bourgeoisie will be quite content with the role of the Western bourgeoisie's business agent, and it will play its part without any complexes in a most dignified manner. But this same lucrative role, this cheap-jack's function, this meanness of outlook and this absence of all ambition symbolize the incapability of the national middle class to fulfil its historic role of bourgeoisie.

Not limited to national sites of power, Fanon warns, the implications of compradorism extend unevenly into outlying regions and locales, as well:

> We know that colonial domination has marked certain regions out for privilege. The colony's economy is not integrated into that of the nation as a whole. It is still organized in order to complete the economy of the different mother countries. Colonialism hardly ever exploits the whole of a country. It contents itself with bringing to light the natural resources, which it extracts, and exports to meet the needs of the mother country's industries, thereby allowing certain sectors of the colony to become relatively rich. But the rest of the colony follows its path of underdevelopment and poverty, or at all events sinks into it more deeply.

In attempting to disguise their role in amplifying uneven development within Africa, projects such as the New Partnership for Africa's Development (NEPAD) pose a unified African partnership

with the North. In the process, their proponents suffer from a psycho-
logical sense of grandeur and collaboration, rather than displaying the
tougher mentality of struggle and material analysis which, according
to Fanon, won liberation in the first place:

> African unity, that vague formula, yet one to which the men and women of
> Africa were passionately attached, and whose operative value served to
> bring immense pressure to bear on colonialism, African unity takes off the
> mask, and crumbles into regionalism inside the hollow shell of nationality
> itself. The national bourgeoisie, since it is strung up to defend its immediate
> interests, and sees no farther than the end of its nose, reveals itself
> incapable of simply bringing national unity into being, or of building up the
> nation on a stable and productive basis. The national front which has forced
> colonialism to withdraw cracks up, and wastes the victory it has gained.

Fanon's view corresponds to arguments made by a variety of progressive African civil society organizations in relation to NEPAD, the
WTO and trade (especially the EU's Economic Partnership Agreements),
the Bretton Woods institutions and debt, transnational corporations
and ecological imperialism. The contrast with the viewpoint from the
North's major institutions, especially the IMF and World Bank and
Tony Blair's Commission for Africa, deserves consideration.

AFRICAN NEOLIBERALISM DERAILED?

The Bretton Woods institutions describe matters in a rather different
way, of course. From the early 2000s, the IMF began publishing lists
of good African countries that stayed the structural adjustment course,
and those that were, as the Fund put it, 'off track'. A country would lose
its ordained 'track' if half or more of its programmes in a given five-
year period experienced an 'irreversible interruption' due to 'policy
slippages', leading to cancellation or a lapsing of the programme.
There were 29 African countries under IMF advice by 1990. By 1994,
however, only 20 African countries were performing on track, while 11
were off. The ratio worsened during the late 1990s, according to the
IMF, when 16 were on and 14 off track.[7]

This kind of disaggregation, however, is easy in retrospect. If we
consider perhaps the most extreme case of anti-IMF dirigisme in
Africa, Zimbabwe, the picture becomes surprisingly nuanced. After all,
Zimbabwe's 1991–5 Economic Structural Adjustment Programme
(ESAP) was not judged 'off track' by the World Bank, but, on the

contrary, received the highest possible score in the Bank's *Project Completion Report*: 'highly satisfactory'.[8] The Mugabe regime's liberalization of trade and finance caused mass deindustrialization during the early 1990s, with the share of manufacturing in GDP dropping from a peak of 32 per cent in 1992 to 17 per cent in 1998, *before relations with the IMF and World Bank broke down.*[9]

The power of the IMF over Africa was also witnessed in the shrinkage of state spending in relation to national income nearly everywhere. The main reason was the decision by elites to repay their Northern creditors, instead of increasing social support to the needy majority. On average, Africa recorded a decline of early 1990s deficit/GDP statistics from around 6 per cent to just under 4 per cent a decade later. Naturally this was led by oil-producing countries, which benefited from price windfalls. Ironically, the fastest-growing African economies actually increased their deficits by a full percentage point between the two periods, while the medium- and especially the slowest-growing economies cut their fiscal deficits furthest. John Maynard Keynes would have smiled knowingly.

Likewise, monetary policy was tightened and central banks were discouraged from printing money (which can fuel inflation), in line with the standard neoliberal menu. The major benefits of a high-interest rate policy accrue to bankers, for it is their asset – money – that is devalued during inflation. In most cases, it is a country's banking fraternity that typically drives neoliberal financial deregulation and monetary processes. Hence sub-Saharan African inflation was reduced from double-digit rates prior to 2004, to on average 9 per cent more recently.

It should thus be evident that the reason Africa is suffering is *not* because it rejected a full neoliberal makeover during the 1980s–90s. The imposition of such policies generally requires a reshaped state: with a loyal police and army standing by to quell dissent, highly centralized power must be located in a neoliberal finance ministry and an increasingly independent central bank. Invariably, these institutions enjoy a 'revolving door', permitting senior staff to flow in and out of relationships with both domestic and international financiers. Finally, the neoliberal class configuration also requires a decline in direct democratic participation in government, which translates to 'leadership' in the language of the Bretton Woods institutions.

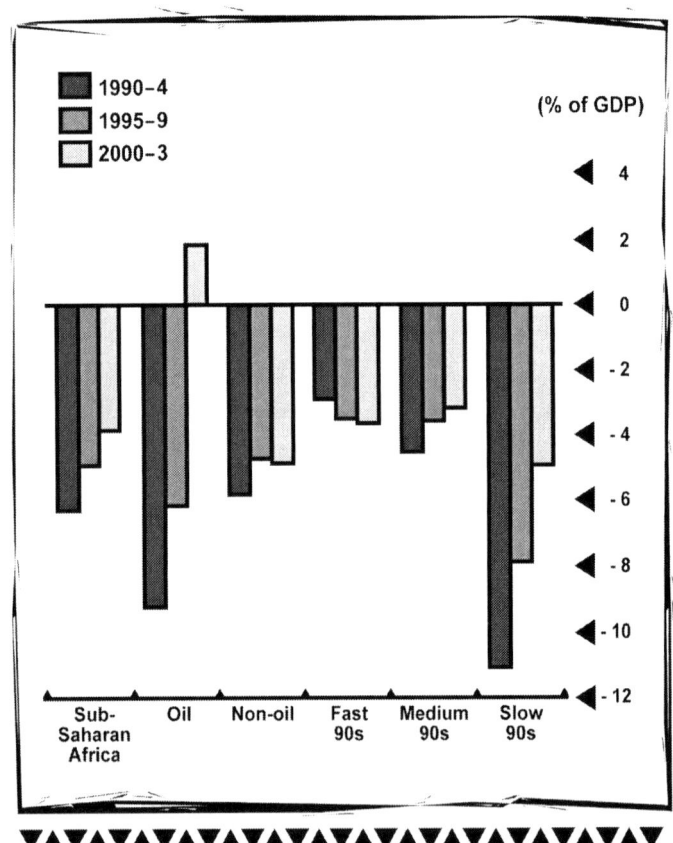

Figure 5.1 African fiscal deficits, 1990–2003

Source: International Monetary Fund (2005), *Regional Economic Outlook: Sub-Saharan Africa*, Washington, May, p. 4.

ELITE OPPORTUNITIES LOST

During 2005 the World Bank began to highlight the need for renewed neoliberal 'leadership' in Africa, with Paul Wolfowitz hosting Nelson Mandela at the Bank/IMF annual meetings in September, stressing African elite power. But serious embarrassments befell the Blair government in its attempt to find reliable African elite partners in

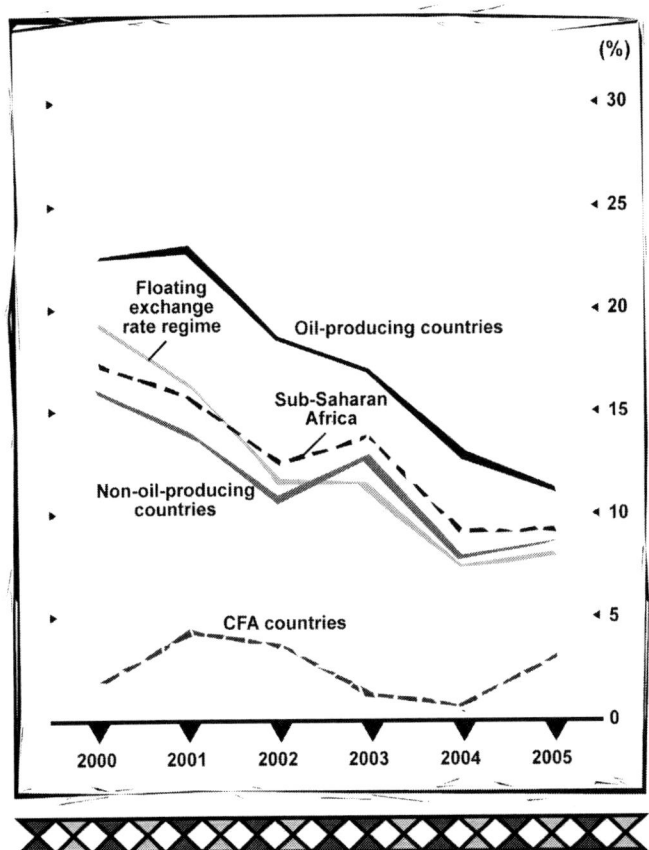

Figure 5.2 African inflation rates, 2000–5

Source: International Monetary Fund (2005), *Regional Economic Outlook:*
Sub-Saharan Africa, May, p. 25.

2005. Manchester professor of politics Paul Cammack described the nine chosen to join the Commission for Africa as

> a web of bankers, industrialists and political leaders with connections to the IMF and the World Bank, all committed to spreading the gospel of free market capitalism. Benjamin Mkapa, president of Tanzania since 1994, has steered his country directly into the arms of the IMF and World Bank over the past decade. Former Marxist guerrilla leader Meles Zenawi has done the

same as Ethiopia's prime minister. Trevor Manuel, South Africa's finance minister, is chair of the IMF/World Bank Development Committee, a vehicle for the dissemination of neoliberal reform around the developing world. He'll probably have come across Ghana's Kingsley Amoako, who went from the World Bank to head the UN Economic Commission for Africa, and Linah Mohohlo, Botswana Central Bank governor, who has represented African countries at the IMF. Tidjiane Thiam, senior executive of global insurance giant Aviva, was nominated for the 1999 Davos 'Dream Cabinet'; merchant banker Fola Adeola chairs FATE, a charitable foundation promoting entrepreneurship among the Nigerian youth; William Kalema, an industrialist and banker, is founder of the Private Sector Foundation and board chairman of the Development Finance Company of Uganda; and Anna Tibaijuka combines an active role in Tanzanian civil society forums with directorships in private companies dedicated to encouraging entrepreneurship and efficiency in the marketing of agricultural commodities.[10]

Blair did not make good choices. Within a few months, as Reuters reported, his reliance on the East African presidents had become a messy embarrassment:

The recent turbulence across east Africa – and the often heavy-handed official responses – must be particularly galling for British leader Tony Blair, who made the continent a priority of his leadership of the EU and G8 blocs this year. He appointed both Ethiopian prime minister Meles Zenawi and Tanzanian president Benjamin Mkapa to his prestigious Africa Commission as examples of good democratic governance. But the international image of former rebel leader Meles has been badly tarnished by a questionable May election win, two subsequent bouts of clashes between police and protesters killing some 70 people, and an uncompromising stance towards a border dispute with Eritrea. Tanzania's Mkapa, in turn, is under pressure for his security forces' repression of opposition protesters and fraud allegations at the recent Zanzibar elections. While reporters saw police pummelling protesters with rifle-butts, sticks and boots as they arrested them on the main Zanzibar island of Unguja, worse was alleged on the smaller island Pemba. There, at least one person was killed and residents speak of rape and looting.[11]

Widespread poverty in Uganda has coincided with 20 years of neo-liberal rule by former leftist Yoweri Museveni, who is periodically celebrated by the Bretton Woods institutions and Washington/London politicians as a star performer, an Mbeki-style new African leader who breaks the mould of authoritarian dictator. By late 2005, however, his reputation was sullied by his disregard for democratic succession (and announced intent to rule until 2013 once term limits were removed), his decision to arrest opposition leader Kizza Besigye, and his refusal to countenance a peace deal with the Lord's Resistance Army (LRA) in one of the world's longest military conflicts. In an open letter to Museveni, Mahmood Mamdani suggested six reasons for his protracted campaign against the LRA:

First, has not the ongoing war channelled a growing proportion of the official budget to military uses, and created a vigorous constituency inside the army for a continued war and against a negotiated solution to it?

Second, has this constituency not been further reinforced by those civilian leaders who realize that the security budget is relatively immune from scrutiny by outside agencies, such as the IMF?

Third, is it not significant that every major regional intervention by Uganda – whether in Rwanda, Congo or Sudan – has been launched from the north, in light of the fact that the northern war provides a theatre for constant military mobilization?

Fourth, is not the most evident consequence of the war a brutalization of the society in the north – particularly the million plus interned – and a militarized distortion of its politics?

Fifth, is there not a corresponding political advantage gained by holding up [LRA leader] 'Kony' as an alternative in the wings, a threat to the population should it demand that the government resolve Uganda's own local 'war on terror' politically?

And, finally, has not the continuation of this 'war on terror' in the north secured for your government a place as a front-line state in the global 'war on terror', thereby assuring it the uncritical protection of an American political umbrella?[12]

Along with Mamdani, other African citizens, including many in the diaspora, are not as quiescent as in earlier times. In mid-November 2005, eleven days after violence in Ethiopia in which police killed 24 protesters, more than 2,000 Ethiopians marched in Washington, from the World Bank to the White House, protesting 'that George Bush and his cronies were supporting the fixed elections'.[13]

In spite of the often deadly foibles associated with African elite gambits to remain in power, the Bank, nevertheless, is sufficiently confident in home-grown neoliberalism and compradorism to give extensive lip service to ownership of – and indeed to civil society participation in – Washington-designed structural adjustment programmes:

There is an increase in 'country ownership' of development support. Development partners are relying more on the African countries' national poverty reduction strategies – most often embodied in their Poverty Reduction Strategy Papers – as the instrument around which to align assistance. The recent Paris Declaration binds both multilateral and bilateral development partners to accelerated progress on harmonization and alignment to national outcome objectives.[14]

The Bank elides the fact that its role in donor coordination – with respect not only to financing but also to concrete conditionality – has provoked strenuous objections from progressive African civil society groups like Jubilee Africa. Jubilee's objections are also based upon the decline of national sovereignty associated with neoliberalism. The unpatriotic character of elite compliance with neoliberalism has not gone unnoticed by the majority of African citizens. Even the World Bank cannot deny the legitimacy deficit, admitting in 2005 that, according to *Afrobarometer* surveys and the *World Values Survey,*

> Africans believe democracy is good for the economy and prefer democratic political systems to authoritarian alternatives. The African public expects democracy to deliver access to the basic necessities of life, like food, water, shelter and education. The value surveys also show that Africans care about equity and public action to reduce poverty. They are less comfortable with wide wealth differentials, and have a strong commitment to political equality. About 75 per cent of the respondents agree that African governments are doing too little for people trapped in poverty.[15]

Do opportunities for a few NGOs and academics to participate in structural adjustment redesign – including the dubious NEPAD peer review process – solve the legitimacy problem? On NEPAD, South African finance minister Trevor Manuel confessed in 2004 that, 'it was shameful that a year after the African peer-review mechanism was launched, less than half of African countries had signed up to be independently reviewed' because they had 'misbehaving governments'.[16]

The most famous case of African malgovernance tabled at the Bank is systemic corruption in the Lesotho Highlands Water Project. Bank staff at first defended Masupha Sole – the main organizer and financier of the apartheid-era (sanctions-busting) dam project and the man ultimately found guilty of bribery receipts – thus keeping him in his job for four years longer than might have been expected, until 1998. The Bank then dithered for years before finally debarring a major Canadian firm (Acres International) that had been guilty of paying the official. It was only because the US Senate Foreign Relations Committee intervened and put pressure on the Bank that the debarment went forward in 2003. The project is still subject to regular protests – including a march by 500 activists from Survivors of the Lesotho Dams in Maseru in September 2005 – over lingering grievances arising from thousands of displacements, submerged farmlands, forests and sacred places, destroyed fisheries and the like.[17]

Even the Bank's high-profile intervention in the $4.2 billion, 1,070-kilometre Chad–Cameroon pipeline, allegedly aimed at halting oil-related malgovernance, apparently failed in 2005. According to Amnesty International, the project 'risks freezing human rights protection for decades to come for the thousands of people who live in its path' in part because the Bank worked to assure profits for export credit agencies, private banks and three oil corporations – Exxon Mobil, Chevron and Petronas – instead of heeding local and international warnings about the Chadian dictatorship run by Idriss Deby.[18] The Bank had to withdraw support hastily in early 2006 when Deby blatantly broke several commitments on the use of oil revenues.

There are many similar cases, ranging from Nigeria in the west to Sudan in the east, from Libya in the north to Angola in the south, where petroprofits vastly outweigh human and environmental considerations – not only for corporations but also for the Northern governments and financial agencies that support them. As a result, it is crucial to look deeper at the revitalized pro-Africa rhetoric, and to unearth the more durable, exploitative factors associated with allegedly increased amounts of aid, credit and debt relief to dictatorial regimes. Likewise, talk of reformed 'global governance', whether coming from the Bretton Woods institutions or the United Nations, is generally hot air. To maintain the façade, Northern elites continue to need African allies, and there are always a willing few.

GLOBAL GOVERNANCE GIMMICKS AT THE BRETTON WOODS INSTITUTIONS

There are two primary sites where the global democracy deficit has been most obvious in recent years: the Bretton Woods institutions and the UN Security Council. In March 2005, President George Bush made an extremely controversial choice in appointing Iraq War architect Paul Wolfowitz as the World Bank's leader. The historic tradition that the US appoints the Bank president was simply not challenged, even by African finance ministers, in spite of the 2002 commitment by partici-pants in the UN's Financing for Development conference at Monterrey to support Bretton Woods democratization.[19]

The democracy deficit actually worsened in the wake of Monterrey, as witnessed by the controversial appointments of Spanish and US neoconservatives Rodrigo Rato and Wolfowitz in 2004–5. At the Bretton Woods institutions, nearly fifty sub-Saharan African countries are represented by just two directors, while eight rich countries enjoy a director each and the US maintains veto power by holding more than 15 per cent of the votes. (There is no transparency as to which board members take what positions on key votes.) The leaders of the Bank and the IMF are chosen from the US and EU, respectively, with the US Treasury Secretary holding the power of hiring or firing.

Can the undemocratic Bretton Woods board of executive directors be reformed? The *Financial Times* reported that a 2003 Bank/Fund strategy emanating from the Bank/IMF Development Committee – chaired by South African finance minister Trevor Manuel – offered only 'narrow technocratic changes', such as adding *one* additional representative from the South to the 24-member board.[20] In 2003, a leaked World Bank paper proposed raising developing country voting power from 39 to 44 per cent and adding one new African executive director. But IMF governance and Bank/IMF board transparency and senior management selection were all neglected in the proposals.[21]

The African comprador who sweet-talked the world into accepting this state of affairs was Manuel, who chaired the Bretton Woods institutions' Development Committee during 2001–5, after a year as chair of the two agencies' board of governors. Manuel came to accept the democracy deficit with grace. As he put it at a press conference during the September 2003 IMF/Bank annual meeting in Dubai, when asked why no progress was made on governance reform, 'I don't think that you can ripen this tomato by squeezing it.'[22]

By the time of the April 2005 meetings, after Wolfowitz's appointment, reform had obviously failed. As Manuel conceded during a Development Committee press conference, 'The difficulty about the present arrangement is that the process in fact masks the individuals, and of course, Jim [Wolfensohn] is correct – both Rodrigo here and Paul Wolfowitz are wonderful individuals, perfectly capable. But unfortunately, the process hasn't helped. It's not their fault. It is a governance issue.'[23] At the September 2005 annual meetings, Manuel remarked that the process was simply not going to change: 'Part of the difficulty in the present milieu is that it is more comfortable for too many countries to live with what we have, because there's a comfort zone around this, and that, I think, is a challenge.' Who was to blame? According to Manuel, 'we who are elected into office in the respective 184 member states have passed the buck'.[24]

UN SECURITY COUNCIL OBSTINACY

It is clear that the World Bank and IMF aren't capable of democratic self-reform, and that the G8 offers no route out. But can the UN be saved? The world body's role within the circuitry of neoliberal power attracts increasingly formidable protest, certainly in South Africa. In September 2001, at the World Conference Against Racism, the UN's failure to address reparations for slavery/colonialism and Israeli apartheid led to a hostile demonstration outside the Durban convention centre by 20,000 activists. In August 2002, the Johannesburg World Summit on Sustainable Development's drive to privatize basic services and its utter failure to address most major ecological problems (such as global warming) were grounds for 25,000 people marching 12 kilometres from an impoverished township to the luxury suburb of Sandton, demanding that the UN delegates disband before doing yet more damage. The UN's complicity in the 1994 Rwandan genocide, the mid-1990s NATO bombing of Yugoslavia, the 1991–2003 sanctions against Iraq which killed at least half a million people, and George Bush's occupation of Iraq (endorsed at the UN on 22 May 2003) were also a source of great concern to peace activists.

Subsequent attempts to democratize the UN Security Council stalled in August 2005. One reason was that at an African Union summit that month, Robert Mugabe and his allies foiled a comprador strategy by South African Foreign Minister Nkosazana Dlamini-Zuma. Officials from Pretoria, Berlin, Tokyo, New Delhi and Brasilia had agreed to lobby for permanent seats on the Security Council but without veto rights. Mugabe won an AU rejection on grounds that two African permanent members would have 'second-class status'.[25] On this, and in making other *rhetorical* critiques of global power relations, Mugabe was just as powerful an opponent of Pretoria and the aspirant world elite as he was, simultaneously in mid-2005, of his urban poor and working citizenry (as witnessed by the 'Operation Murambatsvina' – 'clear the rubbish' – mass displacements against an estimated 700,000 urban poor people).

The crucial lesson is that the South African politicians were perfectly content to play the role of Bantustan rulers, in hopes of being given a seat at the Security Council table albeit without any chance of first-class citizenship. (Ironically, in order to undercut the early 1980s anti-apartheid struggle, white South African leader P. W. Botha provided an opportunity for blacks to gain second-class political citizenship in parliament and municipal councils, but the African National Congress and its allies rejected this emphatically as a sell-out.)

On the one hand, the failure to reform the UN Security Council can be blamed mainly upon the blocking role of one malevolent man, US ambassador to the UN John Bolton. On the other hand, it is reasonable to ask whether institutions and agents supporting the Washington Consensus – including local elites and much of the UN – can play any *non-destructive* role in African economic development or political governance, given the prevailing balance of forces. Nicola Bullard of Focus on the Global South answers:

> Where is the potential for democratizing the global system when the main sources of the 'democracy deficit' – the market and militarized, globalized capitalism – are outside the UN system? Is it realistic to imagine that the UN could 'control' the market and curtail the world's superpower? And, most importantly here, what sort of reforms, if any, would address the concerns of peoples' organizations and social movements, especially those struggling for basic rights such as land, water, work, housing, health and education?...
>
> It is difficult to imagine what sort of institutional reforms would be useful in this struggle. What use would an expanded Security Council be to the coca farmers of Bolivia? Would an Economic Security Council defend the peoples' resources against the multinationals? It seems most unlikely.[26]

In Africa, the most important site of power to target when one is asking these kinds of question is Pretoria.

NOTES

1 Commission for Africa (2005), *Our Common Future*, London, p. 106.
2 Rodney, W. (1972), *How Europe Underdeveloped Africa*, Dar es Salaam, Tanzania Publishing House and London, Bogle L'Ouverture Publications;

<http://www.marxists.org/subject/africa/rodney-walter/how-europe/>.

3 Adesina, J. (2002), 'NEPAD and the Challenge of Africa's Development: Towards the Political Economy of a Discourse', unpublished paper, Department of Sociology, Rhodes University, Grahamstown.

4 Lamb, G. (1987), 'Managing Economic Policy Change: Institutional Dimensions', Washington, World Bank, p. 10.

5 Cabral, A. (1966), 'The Weapon of Theory', address delivered to the first Tricontinental Conference of the Peoples of Asia, Africa and Latin America, Havana.

6 Excerpts below are from Fanon, F. (1963), *The Wretched of the Earth*, New York, Grove Press, Chapter Three, Pitfalls of National Consciousness.

7 International Monetary Fund (2005), *Regional Economic Outlook: Sub-Saharan Africa*, Washington, May, p. 27.

8 World Bank (1995), *Project Completion Report: Zimbabwe: Structural Adjustment Program*, Country Operations Division, Washington, p. 23.

9 Bond, P. (1998), *Uneven Zimbabwe: a Study of Finance, Development and Underdevelopment*, Trenton, Africa World Press, Chapters 11–12; Bond, P. (2005), 'Zimbabwe's Hide and Seek with the IMF: Imperialism, Nationalism and the South African Proxy', *Review of African Political Economy*, 106.

10 Cammack, P. (2005), 'Blair's Commissioners', *Red Pepper*, July. As for their counterparts from the North, 'Alongside Geldof, Blair, Brown and UK development minister Hilary Benn, the "African nine" worked with former IMF managing director Michel Camdessus, Republican senator Nancy Baker and Canadian finance minister Ralph Goodale, who also represents Ireland and Caribbean countries at the IMF. The report was also heavily influenced by the Commission's secretariat. Chief writer was Paul Vallely, associate editor of the *Independent*, who co-authored Geldof's autobiography. He was assisted by the secretariat's head, Myles Wickstead of DfID, and director of research, former World Bank chief economist Sir Nick Stern, who spent the 1990s steering eastern Europe and the former Soviet Union towards free market capitalism.'

11 Cawthorne, A. (2005), 'Once Favoured E. African Leaders' Lustre Fades', Reuters, 13 November.

12 Mamdani, M. (2005), 'Reconcile with the Living, Not Just the Dead: an Open Letter to President Museveni', Kampala, 4 December.

13 Indymedia (2005), 'Ethiopians Rally Against US-Supported Torture, Terror and Zenawi', <http://dc.indymedia.org/newswire/display/131285/index.php>.

14 World Bank (2005), 'Meeting the Challenge of Africa's Development: a World Bank Group Action Plan', Africa Region, Washington, 7 September, p. 3.

15 *Ibid.*, p. 5.

16 South African Press Association (SAPA) (2004), 'Response to Peer Review Dismal', *Business Day*, 16 September.

17 See Bond, P. (2002), *Unsustainable South Africa: Environment, Development and Social Protest*, London, Merlin Press and Pietermaritzburg, University of KwaZulu-Natal Press, Chapter Three.

18 Amnesty International (2005), press release, 7 September.

19 United Nations (2002), 'Report of the International Conference on Financing for Development', Final Resolution, Monterrey, paragraphs 62–3.

20 *Financial Times*, 13 February 2003.

21 World Bank (2003), 'Issues Note: Enhancing the Voice of Developing and Transition Countries at the World Bank', Washington, 9 June, <http://www. brettonwoodsproject.org/topic/governance/WBgovissuesnote.pdf>.

22 World Bank (2003), 'Proceedings of Press Conference', Dubai, <http://www. worldbank.org>, 22 September.

23 World Bank (2005), 'Proceedings of Press Conference', Washington, <http:// www.worldbank.org>, 17 April.

24 World Bank and International Monetary Fund (2005), 'Transcript of a Joint IMF/World Bank Town Hall with Civil Society Organizations', Washington, 22 September, <http://www.imf.org/external/np/tr/2005/tr050922a.htm>.

25 Fabricius, P. (2005), 'Mugabe Helps Scupper SA's Bid for a UN Seat', *Sunday Independent*, 7 August.

26 Bullard, N. (2005), 'Why UN Reform Is not a Priority', *Focus on Trade*, Focus on the Global South, <http://www.focusweb.net>, September. For longer critiques of the 'international community's ability' to create genuinely democratic space, see Abrahamsen, R. (2000), *Disciplining Democracy: Development Discourse and Good Governance in Africa*, London, Zed Books, and Wilson, Z. (2006), *The United Nations and Democracy in Africa: Labyrinths of Legitimacy*, New York, Routledge.

6

Militarism and Looming Subimperialism in Africa

Washington, London, Pretoria

Imperialism, subimperialism and anti-imperialism are all settling into durable patterns and alignments in Africa – especially South Africa – even if the continent's notoriously confusing political discourses sometimes conceal the collisions and collusions. 'All Bush wants is Iraqi oil,' the highest-profile African, Nelson Mandela, charged in January 2003. 'Their friend Israel has weapons of mass destruction but because it's [the US's] ally, they won't ask the UN to get rid of them.... Bush, who cannot think properly, is now wanting to plunge the world into a holocaust. If there is a country which has committed unspeakable atrocities, it is the United States of America.'[1] Mandela's remarks were soon echoed at a demonstration of 4,000 people outside the US embassy in Pretoria, by African National Congress (ANC) secretary-general Kgalema Motlanthe: 'Because we are endowed with several rich minerals, if we don't stop this unilateral action against Iraq today, tomorrow they will come for us.'[2]

This was not merely conjunctural anti-war rhetoric. Mandela's successor Thabo Mbeki was just as vitriolic when addressing the broader context of imperial power in welcoming dignitaries to the August 2002 World Summit on Sustainable Development in Johannesburg: 'We have all converged at the Cradle of Humanity to confront the social behaviour that has pity neither for beautiful nature nor for living human beings. This social behaviour has produced and entrenches a global system of apartheid.'[3] Mbeki's efforts to insert the phrase 'global apartheid' in the summit's final document were thwarted by then US Secretary of State Colin Powell, who in turn was heckled by both civil society activists and Third World leaders in the final plenary session.

111

A year later, in the immediate run-up to the World Trade Organization ministerial in Cancún, Malaysia's *Straits Times* reported Mbeki's comment on the global justice movements at a Kuala Lumpur seminar: 'They may act in ways you and I may not like and break windows in the street but the message they communicate relates.'[4] Moreover, in the light of Pretoria's centrality to the India-Brazil-South Africa bloc and the G20 group often credited (incorrectly) with causing the Cancún WTO summit's collapse and threatening the Hong Kong WTO summit, the logical impression is that the anti-imperialist cause has an important state ally in Africa.

But these outbursts can best be understood as 'talking left, walking right', in so far as they veil the underlying dynamics of accumulation, class struggle and geopolitics.[5] Alongside parallel economic, ideological and military functions played by the governments of Nigeria, Ghana, Senegal, Algeria, Uganda and Kenya (amongst others), Pretoria's crucial role as Washington's main subimperial African partner requires unpacking.

For example, in early 2003, at the same time as Mandela's outburst, the ANC government permitted three Iraq-bound warships to refuel in Durban, and the state-owned weapons manufacturer Denel sold US$160 million worth of artillery propellants and 326 hand-held laser range-finders to the British army, and 125 laser-guidance sights to the US Marines.[6] South Africa's independent left immediately formed a 300-organization Anti-War Coalition which periodically led demonstrations of 5,000–20,000 protesters in Johannesburg, Pretoria and Cape Town. Despite the embarrassment, Pretoria refused the Coalition's demands to halt the sales. George W. Bush rewarded Mbeki with an official visit just as the dust from the Baghdad invasion had settled, in July 2003. As *Business Day* editorialized, the 'abiding impression' left from Bush's Pretoria stopover was 'of a growing, if not intimate trust'.[7]

Organizing large demonstrations against Bush in Pretoria and Cape Town, the Anti-War Coalition complained: 'The ANC's public relations strategy around the war directly contradicts their actions, which are pro-war and have contributed to the deaths of thousands of Iraqi civilians.'[8] But public relations finally caught up to reality, as Mandela, too, recanted his criticism of Bush in May 2004.[9]

How much of this political inconsistency linking Pretoria and the Washington–London imperialist axis was merely contingent? In contrast, how badly does the world capitalist empire need Africa for surplus and resource extraction and the deepening of global neo-liberalism, and South Africa for legitimacy and deputy-sheriff support? After all, it should be clear that the imposition of neoliberal logic, in the form of concrete policies, has amplified Africa's uneven and combined development.

Stephen Gill has shown how imperialism requires continual enforce-ment, through both a 'disciplinary neoliberalism' entailing surveillance and a 'new constitutionalism' that locks these policies in over time.[10] Leo Panitch and Sam Gindin have conducted emphatic studies of empire's management capacities via the power and centrality of Washington, linking the neoconservative military-industrial complex in the Bush White House and Pentagon to the Washington Consensus nexus of the US Treasury, Bretton Woods institutions and Wall Street.[11] Sub-Saharan Africa may be a site to demonstrate *both* the structurally rooted need to extract surpluses (based on crisis tendencies discussed in Chapter 2) and agency: the importance of Washington's combined political and economic power. In his recent survey, Robert Biel identi-fied two central contradictions in US imperialism *vis-à-vis* Africa:

> First, central accumulation always tends to siphon away the value which could form the basis of state-building, bringing with it the risk of 'state failure', leading to direct intervention. Second, the international system becomes increasingly complex, characterized by a range of new actors and processes and direct penetration of local societies in a way which bypasses the state-centric dimension.[12]

Because of the complexity associated with indirect rule, and especially the difficulty of coopting all relevant actors, Biel continues, 'A reversion to the deployment of pure power is always latent, and the post-September 11 climate has brought it directly to the fore. This is a significant weakness of international capitalism.'

If modern imperialism necessarily combines neoliberalism and 'accumulation by dispossession' in peripheral sites like Africa, along with increasing subservience to the USA's indirect, neocolonial rule, the next logical step is to locate South Africa's own position as regional subimperial hegemon within the same matrices. That requires identify-ing areas where imperialism is facilitated in Africa by the Pretoria–Johannesburg state-capitalist nexus, in part through Mbeki's New Partnership for Africa's Development and in part through the independent (though related) logic of private capital. Finally, in response to this subjugation, we can consider what kinds of analyses, strategies, tactics and alliances are being posed by serious African anti-imperialists. First, however, we must clarify imperialism's militarist and geopolitical inclinations.

WASHINGTON'S REACH

What are US planners up to in Africa? The period during the 1990s after the failed Somali intervention, when Washington's armchair warriors let Africa slide out of view, may have come to an end with September 11, 2001. One of the most acute critics of US Africa policy, Bill Martin, argues that

> Bill Clinton broke new ground by forcefully applying free market policies to Africa and, often unnoticed, by placing Africa on the US foreign policy map by casting it as a transnational security threat.... Secretary of State Madeleine Albright was blunt in 1999: 'Africa is a major battleground in the global fight against terror, crime, drugs, illicit arms-trafficking, and disease.' Bush's discourse and web of military engagements after 9/11 have turned these Democratic policy statements into concrete actions, sustaining compliant allies in the hope they can contain local unrest and resistance to corrupt local states, international capital, and imperial interventions. The discourse of internal and international terrorism is thus not simply substituting for the ideology of the Cold War, but is forging new military and ideological networks as capable of repressing internal dissent as pursuing 'foreign' terrorists.[13]

The US has developed an Africa Contingency Operations and Assistance Program to strengthen favoured militaries, but to do so under civilian control to prevent rogue forces from emerging (such as the Venezuelan precedent), according to David Wiley. The Pentagon's goal appears to be the deployment of 200 US troops at a half-dozen light bases which maintain stores of petrol, runways and 24-hour operations.[14]

Army General Charles Wald, who controls the Africa Programme of the European Command, told the BBC in early 2004 that he aims to have five brigades with 15,000 men working in cooperation with regional partners including South Africa, Kenya, Nigeria and two others still to be chosen.[15] NATO's Supreme Allied Commander for Europe, General James Jones, confirmed the US geographical strategy in May 2003: 'The carrier battle groups of the future and the expeditionary strike groups of the future may not spend six months in the Mediterranean Sea but I'll bet they'll spend half the time down the West Coast of Africa.'[16] Within weeks, that coast was graced by 3,000 US troops deployed offshore from Liberia (and briefly onshore to stabilize the country after Charles Taylor departed). Potential US bases were suggested for Ghana, Senegal and Mali, as well as the North African countries of Algeria, Morocco and Tunisia.[17] Another base was occupied by 1,500 US troops in the small Horn country of Djibouti. Botswana and Mozambique were also part of the Pentagon's strategy, and South Africa would remain a crucial partner.

Central and Eastern Africa remains a problem area, and not merely because of traditional French and Belgian neocolonial competition with British and US interests. President Clinton's refusal to cite the Rwanda massacre as definitive genocide in 1994 was an infamous failure of nerve in terms of the emerging doctrine of 'humanitarian' imperialism – in comparison to intervention in the white-populated Balkans. The lesson Wald drew was the need to engage more carefully, using proxy forces, rather than disengage. Hence in northern Uganda, the US has cooperated in state counter-insurgency efforts against the persistent guerrillas of the Lord's Resistance Army. Ian Taylor summarized the subregion's geopolitical alignment in the late 1990s: 'Pro-American leaders in Asmara, Addis Ababa, Kampala and Kigali seemed to be constructing a new bloc of regimes friendly to Washington's interests, linking up with South Africa as a group of states that America could do business with.'[18]

With an estimated three million dead in Central African wars, partly because of their proximity to zones of access to coltan and other mineral riches, conflicts worsened between and within the Uganda/Rwanda bloc, *vis-à-vis* the revised alliance of Kabila's Democratic Republic of Congo (DRC), Zimbabwe, Angola and Namibia. Only with Kabila's assassination in 2001 and Pretoria's management of elite peace deals in the DRC and Burundi are matters settling, however briefly, into a fragile peace combining neoliberalism and opportunities for mineral extraction. Another particularly difficult site is Sudan, where US Delta Force troops have been sighted in informal operations, perhaps because, after China broached oil exploration during the country's civil war chaos, US firms are now active in the country.

Bridging sub-Saharan Africa and North Africa is another subregion of crucial importance to US imperialism. Not only is Libya being brought into the fold of weapons certification and control. Already, US troops have been deployed for small-scale interventions in Mali, Chad and Mauritania. A site of future extraction lies between northern Nigeria and southern Algeria, where gas pipeline options have been contracted by the US multinationals Halliburton and Bechtel. The major petro prize remains the Gulf of Guinea. With African routes to Louisiana oil-processing plants many weeks less time-consuming for tanker transport than the Persian Gulf, the world's shortage of supertankers is eased by direct sourcing from West Africa's offshore oil-fields.

In continent-wide settings, the US military is also ambitious. For example, of $700 million destined to develop a 75,000-strong UN peacekeeping force in coming years, $480 million is dedicated to African soldiers.[19] But Africa is also a site for recruiting private mercenaries, as an estimated 1,500 South Africans – reportedly including many of Mbeki's own personal security forces – joined firms such as Executive Outcomes in Johannesburg and British-based Erinys to provide more than 10 per cent of occupied Iraq's bodyguard services.[20] Some African countries joined the Coalition of the Willing against Iraq in 2003, including Angola, Eritrea, Ethiopia and Rwanda, although temporary UN Security Council members Cameroon, Guinea and the Republic of the Congo were opponents, notwithstanding Washington's bullying. In addition, Martin warns of the

> $100 million Eastern Africa Counter-Terrorism initiative involving Kenya, Ethiopia, Uganda, Tanzania and Eritrea as well as Djibouti. Another new State Department program, the Pan-Sahel Initiative, is being implemented by Pentagon and civilian contractors in Mali, Mauritania, Chad, and Niger. These actions suggest the obvious targeting and encirclement of Islamic Africa. Yet the number of African armies involved extends well beyond Islamic or oil-rich areas.... More than 120 senior African military officers and defense officials from 44 states participated, for example, in seminars this past February [2004] at the Pentagon's Africa Center for Strategic Studies.
>
> Compliant African states and militaries offer Washington far more than checks to radical Islam; they are increasingly seen as a counterweight to rival core powers in the North and unruly states and leaders in the South. African peacekeeping forces, the thinking goes, may be especially valuable in replacing, as the occupation of Iraq has so starkly indicated, European and other allies now unwilling to occupy areas conquered by direct US

military action or deploy to areas the US is unwilling or unable to (due to overextension in Iraq and Afghanistan).

And even if South African troops are not sent to Iraq, the South African government seems more than willing to allow their mercenaries, now converted into 'private military contractors', to play major roles in the US occupation. African states are clearly judged by some US policy makers to be more politically compliant as well as more militarily dependent – and have a proven track record. This may prove especially valuable as the 'war on terrorism' transmutes into a broader discourse that supports a global, post-liberal order including repressive regimes in the South. The current top ten contributors to UN operations are Third World states, with Africa providing four of the ten (Nigeria, 2,930 troops; Ghana, 2,790 troops; Kenya, 1,826 troops; Ethiopia, 1,822 troops).[21]

Africa remains an important site in Washington's campaigns against militant Islamic networks, especially in Algeria and Nigeria in the north-west, Tanzania and Kenya in the east, and South Africa. Control of African immigration to the US and Europe is crucial, in part through the expansion of US-style incarceration via private sector firms like Wackenhut, which has invested in South African privatized prison management, along with the notorious Lindela extradition camp for 'illegal immigrants'. The development of a highly racialized global detention and identification system is proceeding apace.

Of course, the US military machine does not roll over Africa entirely unimpeded. Minor potholes have included Pretoria's rhetorical opposition to the belligerent parties in the Iraq war, conflicts within the UN Human Rights Commission (especially over Zimbabwe), and the controversy over US citizens' extradition to the International Criminal Court. Regarding the latter, on the eve of Bush's first-ever Africa trip in July 2003, the Pentagon announced it would withdraw $7.6 million worth of military support to Pretoria, because the South African government – along with 34 military allies of Washington (and 90 countries in total) – had not agreed to give US citizens immunity from prosecution at The Hague. Relations with Pretoria became somewhat more complicated, as noted below, but several other countries, including four on Bush's itinerary (Botswana, Uganda, Senegal and Nigeria) signed these blackmail-based immunity deals and retained US military spending.[22]

It is in these functions that we can observe the ongoing relevance of the national state, not only to accumulation via traditional facilitative functions (securing property rights, the integrity of money, and the monopoly on violence), but also to the 'coauthorship' of the neoliberal project, in turn reflecting a shift in the balance of forces within societies and state bureaucracies. Thanks largely to capitalist crisis tendencies and the current orientation to accumulation by dispossession, imperialism can neither deliver the goods nor successfully repress sustained dissent in Africa. It is here, therefore, that the ideological legitimation of 'free markets and free politics' requires renewal. Sub-Saharan Africa is so rife with state failure and '*un*disciplined neo-liberalism' (witnessed in repeated IMF riots) that Washington needs a subimperial partner, even (maybe especially) one whose politicians are as cheeky as those in Pretoria – and who have thus become just as vital for broader systemic legitimation as other talk-left, walk-right allies in Delhi and Brasilia.[23] After all, anti-imperial critique continues to emerge across Africa, not just rhetorically (as cited at the outset) but even in practical form – as when African ministers withdrew consensus from the WTO's Seattle and Cancun summits. Thus NEPAD becomes especially important as a surrogate for imperialism, as argued below.

In July 2004, the Center for Strategic and International Studies publicly launched a bipartisan US–Africa policy blueprint, requested by Colin Powell and the US Congress. That document, 'Rising US Stakes in Africa', recommends seven interventions: political stabilization of Sudan, whose oil is craved by Washington; support for Africa's decrepit capital markets, which could allegedly 'jump start' the Millennium Challenge Accounts; more attention to energy, especially the 'massive future earnings by Nigeria and Angola, among other key West African oil producers'; promotion of wildlife conservation; increased 'counter-terrorism' efforts, which include 'a Muslim outreach initiative'; expanded peace operations, which can be transferred to tens of thousands of African troops thanks to new G8 funding; and more attention to AIDS patients, whose treatment is feared by pharmaceutical corporations because it will require generic drugs. In all but Sudan, South African cooperation will be crucial for the new US imperial agenda.[24]

Does Pretoria qualify as subimperialist? Aside from Mandela's vacillation, there is much to consider in the hectic activities of Mbeki and his two main internationally oriented colleagues: Finance Minister Trevor Manuel (chair of the IMF/World Bank Development Committee, 2001–5) and Trade/Privatization Minister Alec Erwin. The question will be put: are these gentlemen breaking or shining the chains of global apartheid?

SOUTH AFRICA'S SUBIMPERIAL FUNCTIONS

During an August 2003 talk to business and social elites at Rhodes House in Cape Town, Mandela offered the single most chilling historical reference possible: 'I am sure that Cecil John Rhodes would have given his approval to this effort to make the South African economy of the early twenty-first century appropriate and fit for its time.'[25] (In the same spirit, Mandela took that opportunity to publicly criticize, for the first time and at a crucial moment, activists from the Jubilee South Africa anti-debt movement and apartheid-victims support groups. As discussed in the conclusion, their sin was filing lawsuits in New York demanding reparations from corporations for their pre-1994 South African profits, along the lines of the Nazi-victims' ancestors' banking and slave labour cases. Mandela backed Mbeki, who formally opposed the suits on grounds that Pretoria had its own reconciliation strategy, and that such litigation would, if successful, deter future foreign investors.)

Is the Rhodes comparison apt? We do have much to learn from revisiting late-nineteenth-century imperial rule in Africa, in part because no other buccaneer did as much damage to the possibilities for peace and equitable development in Africa as Cecil Rhodes. As diamond merchant, financier and politician (Governor of the Cape Colony during the 1880s–90s), Rhodes received permission from Queen Victoria to plunder what are now called Gauteng Province (greater Johannesburg) once gold was discovered in 1886, and then Zimbabwe, Zambia and Malawi; his ambition was to paint the map British imperial red, stretching along the route from the Cape to Cairo. Rhodes's two main vehicles were the British army, which invented the concentration camp and in the process killed 14,000 blacks and 25,000 Afrikaner women and children during the 1899–1902 Anglo-Boer War, and the British South Africa Company (BSAC), a for-profit firm which in 1890 began systematically imposing settler colonialism across the region. The BSAC's charter, following the notorious Rudd Concession which Rhodes obtained deceitfully from the Ndebele king Lobengula, represented a structural switch: from informal control of trade, to trade with rule. British imperialists assumed that competition for control of Africa would continue beyond the 1885 Berlin Conference, which partitioned Africa, and that only BSAC-style 'imperialism on the cheap', as it was termed, would ensure geographical dominance over the interior of the continent in the face of hostile German, Portuguese and Boer forces. Such a strategy was critical, they posited, to the protection of even the Nile Valley, which in turn represented the lifeline to the prize of India.[26]

But, as today, there was also a crucial economic dynamic under way in Britain (and much of Europe) beyond the never-ending search for gold which undergirded Rhodes's conquests: chronic overaccumulation of capital, especially in the London financial markets, combined with social unrest. The easy availability of foreign portfolio funding for nascent Southern African stock markets stemmed from a lengthy international economic depression, chronic excess financial liquidity (a symptom of general overaccumulation), and the global hegemony enjoyed by City of London financiers.[27] From the standpoint of British imperialism, the main benefit of Rhodes's role in the region was to ameliorate the contradictions of global capitalism by channelling financial surpluses into new investments (such as the telegraph connections, railroad building and surveying projects that tamed and commodified the land known as Rhodesia), extracting resources (especially gold, even if in tiny amounts compared to the Rand), and assuring political allegiance to South African corporate power, which was in harmonious unity with the evolving British-run states of the region.

Can Mandela claim he is faithfully following in these footsteps? Today, for Victoria, substitute the White House. Instead of the old-fashioned power plays of the Rudd Concession and similar BSAC tricks of dispossession, read NEPAD and its many corporate backers. Likewise, the SA National Defence Force stands ready to follow British army conquests, what with its invasion of Lesotho in September 1998, justified by Pretoria's desire to protect a controversial, corrupt mega-dam from an alleged sabotage threat. As Rhodes had his media cheerleaders from Cape Town to London, so too do many Western publications regularly promote Mandela and Mbeki as Africa's saviours, and so too does the South African Broadcasting Corporation beam pro-Pretoria propaganda to the continent's luxury hotels and other satellite broadcast receivers.

Mandela's less honourable foreign policy intentions were also difficult to disguise. Although South Africa can claim one intervention worthy of its human rights rhetoric – leadership of the 1997 movement to ban landmines (and hence a major mine-clearing role for South African businesses which helped lay the mines in the first place) – the first-ever democratic regime in Pretoria recognized the Myanmar military junta as a legitimate government in 1994; gave the country's highest official award to Indonesian dictator Suharto three months before his 1998 demise (in the process extracting $25 million in donations for the ANC); and sold arms to countries which practised mass violence, such as Algeria, Colombia, Peru and Turkey.

Another moment of ideological confusion was cleared up in 2004. As noted above, in mid-2003 the US House of Representatives extended a ban on military assistance to 32 countries – including South Africa – which agreed to cooperate in future with the International Criminal Court against alleged US war criminals. Nevertheless, Washington's ambassador to Pretoria, Cameron Hume, quickly announced that several bilateral military deals would go ahead in any case. According to Peter McIntosh of the journal *African Armed Forces*, the US 'had simply re-routed military funding for South Africa through its European Command in Stuttgart'. Hume reported the Pentagon's desire 'to train and equip two additional battalions to expand the number of forces the [South African armed services] have available for peacekeeping in Africa'. In the wake of two successful joint US/SA military manoeuvres in 2003–4, South African newspaper *ThisDay* pointed out that 'Operations such as Medflag and Flintlock clearly have applications other than humanitarian aid, and as the US interventions in Somalia and Liberia have shown, humanitarian aid often requires forceful protection.'[28]

The two countries' military relations were fully 'normalized' by July 2004, in the words of Deputy Foreign Minister Aziz Pahad. In partnership with General Dynamics Land Systems, state-owned Denel immediately began marketing 105 mm artillery alongside a turret and light armoured vehicle hull, in support of innovative Stryker Brigade Combat Teams ('a 3500-personnel formation that puts infantry, armour and artillery in different versions of the same 8x8 light armoured vehicle'). According to one report, 'The turret and gun is entirely proprietary to Denel, using only South African technology. At sea level, it can fire projectiles as far as 36 km.'[29] This followed a period of serious problems for the arms firm and others like it (Armscor and Fuchs), which were also allowed full access to the US market in July 2004 after paying fines for apartheid-era sanctions-busting.[30]

Given Pretoria's 1998 decision to invest $6 billion in mainly offensive weaponry such as fighter jets and submarines, there are growing fears that peacekeeping is a cover for a more expansive geopolitical agenda, and that Mbeki is tacitly permitting a far stronger US role in Africa – from the oil-rich Gulf of Guinea and Horn of Africa, to training bases in the South and North – than is necessary.[31] On the surface, Pretoria's senior roles in the mediation of conflicts in Burundi and the Democratic Republic of the Congo (DRC) during 2003 appeared positive. However, closer to the ground, the agreements more closely resemble the style of elite deals that lock in place 'low-intensity democracy' and neoliberal economic regimes. Moreover, because some of the belligerent forces were explicitly left out, the subsequent weeks and months after declarations of peace witnessed periodic massacres of civilians in both countries and a near-coup in the DRC. By mid-2004, the highly regarded intellectual and leader of the Rassemblement Congolais pour la Démocratie, Ernest Wamba dia Wamba, was publicly critical of Pretoria's interference:

> When a [transition process] takes off on a wrong footing, unless a real readjustment takes place on the way, the end cannot be good.... Some feel like South Africa has actively put us in the situation we are in. They had a lot of leverage to make sure that certain structural problems were anticipated and solutions proposed. They seem to have fallen into the Western logic of thinking that mediocrity is a lesser evil for Congolese, if it stops the war. They also have a lot of leverage to get a clear ongoing commitment to resolve the contradictory fears of both the DRC and Rwanda; they do not seem to use it. This is why some feel that South Africa is too close to Rwanda.[32]

Pretoria was not alone in playing the role of proxy for the great powers in its own extended periphery. Simultaneously, similar concerns were raised about another new democracy with a centre-left regime, Brazil, which took leadership of the armed occupation of Haiti, just four months after the US-supported overthrow of the previous government.[33] The Congress-led government in New Delhi, likewise, has come under criticism for its close military ties to Washington. From Brazil to South Africa to India, the dangers of growing regional political hegemony, in the context of military alliance with the US, are amplified when we consider some of Pretoria's *global* opportunities.

PRETORIA'S WORLD LEADERSHIP?

Once the South African government showed its willingness to put self-interest above principles, the international political power centres invested increasing trust in Mandela, Mbeki, Manuel and Erwin, giving them insider access to many international elite fora. As global-establishment institutions came under attack, they sometimes attempted to reinvent themselves with a dose of New South African legitimacy; witness Mandela's 1998 caressing of the IMF during the East Asian crisis, and of Clinton during the Lewinsky sex scandal. Indeed, Pretoria's lead politicians were allowed, during the late 1990s, to preside over the UN Security Council, the board of governors of the IMF and Bank, the United Nations Conference on Trade and Development, the Commonwealth, the World Commission on Dams and many other important global and continental bodies. Simultaneously taking Third World leadership, Pretoria also headed the Non-Aligned Movement, the Organization of African Unity and the Southern African Development Community.

But this was just the warm-up period. During a frenetic four years beginning in September 2001, Mbeki and his colleagues hosted, led, or played instrumental roles at the following major international events: the World Conference Against Racism in Durban (September 2001); the launch of NEPAD in Abuja, Nigeria (October 2001); the Doha, Qatar, ministerial summit of the World Trade Organization (November 2001); the UN's Financing for Development conference in Monterrey, Mexico (March 2002); G8 summits in Kananaskis, Canada (June 2002), Evian, France (June 2003), Sea Island, Georgia (June 2004) and Gleneagles, Scotland (July 2005); the African Union launch in Durban (July 2002); the World Summit on Sustainable Development (WSSD) in Johannesburg (August–September 2002); the Davos World Economic Forum (January 2003 and occasionally thereafter); George W. Bush's first trip to Africa (July 2003); the Cancun WTO ministerial (September 2003); World Bank/IMF annual meetings in Dubai (September 2003) and Washington (September 2004 and 2005); the UN Millennium Development Summit (September 2005); and the Hong Kong WTO ministerial (December 2005).

Virtually nothing was actually accomplished through the 2001–5 opportunities:

- at the UN racism conference, Mbeki colluded with the EU to reject the demand of NGOs and African leaders for slavery/colonialism/ apartheid reparations;
- NEPAD provided merely a home-grown version of the Washington Consensus;
- at Doha, trade minister Alec Erwin split the African delegation so as to prevent a repeat of the denial of consensus that had foiled the Seattle ministerial in December 1999;
- at Monterrey, Manuel was summit co-leader (along with former IMF managing director Michel Camdessus and disgraced Mexican ex-president Ernesto Zedillo), and legitimized all ongoing IMF/ Bank strategies;
- from Kananaskis, Mbeki departed with only an additional $1 billion commitment for Africa (aside from funds already pledged at Monterrey), and none of the subsequent G8 summits – Evian, Sea Island and Gleneagles – represented genuine progress;
- the African Union supported both NEPAD and the Zimbabwean regime of president Robert Mugabe, hence further delegitimizing the self-defensive political project of Africa's elite;
- at the Johannesburg WSSD, Mbeki undermined UN democratic procedure, facilitated the privatization of nature, and did nothing to address the plight of the world's poor majority;
- in Davos, global elites ignored Africa, in 2003 and subsequently;
- for hosting a leg of Bush's Africa trip, Mbeki merely became the US's 'pointsman' on Zimbabwe, and he avoided any conflict over Iraq's recolonization;
- in Cancún, the collapse of trade negotiations – again, catalysed by a walkout by Africans – left Erwin 'disappointed';
- at World Bank and IMF annual meetings during 2001–5, with Manuel leading the Development Committee, there was no Bretton Woods democratization, new debt relief or post-Washington policy reform; and
- the UN Millennium Review Summit provided Mbeki with grounds for heartbreak, leaving him to reflect that, 'We should not be surprised when these billions do not acclaim us as heroes and heroines.'[34]

Elsewhere I have recounted these consistent defeats for African interests, with attention to South Africa's own complicity.[35] Further failures can be reasonably anticipated in 2006 when Pretoria hosts the

Progressive Governance Summit (with very unprogressive leaders like Tony Blair and Meles Zenawi) and the G77 group of Third World countries. Notwithstanding periodic 'talk left' gripes such as Mbeki's in New York, Pretoria's failures left it slotted into place as a subimperial partner of Washington and the EU. Although such a relationship dates to the apartheid and colonial eras, the ongoing conquest of Africa – in political, military and ideological terms – and the reproduction of neoliberalism together require a coherent new strategy: NEPAD.

STAKING CLAIMS THROUGH NEPAD

The origins of the NEPAD plan are revealing. Mbeki had embarked upon a late 1990s' 'African Renaissance' branding exercise, which he endowed with poignant poetics but not much else. The contentless form was somewhat remedied in a Powerpoint skeleton unveiled in 2000 during Mbeki's meetings with Clinton in May, the Okinawa G8 meeting in July, the UN Millennium Summit in September, and a subsequent European Union gathering in Portugal. The skeleton was fleshed out in November 2000 with the assistance of several econo-mists and was immediately ratified during a special South African visit by World Bank president James Wolfensohn 'at an undisclosed location,' due to fears of the disruptive protests which had soured a Johannes-burg trip by IMF managing director Horst Koehler a few months earlier. By this stage, Mbeki managed to sign on as partners two additional rulers from the crucial North and West of the continent: Algeria's Abdelaziz Bouteflika and Nigeria's Olusegun Obasanjo. Both suffered regular mass protests and various civil, military, religious and ethnic disturbances at home.

By early 2001, in Davos, Mbeki made clear whose interests NEPAD would serve: 'It is significant that in a sense the first formal briefing on the progress in developing this programme is taking place at the World Economic Forum meeting. The success of its implementation would require the buy-in from members of this exciting and vibrant forum!'[36] International capital would benefit from large infrastructure construct-ion opportunities on the public–private partnership model, privatized state services, ongoing structural adjustment, intensified rule of inter-national property law and various of NEPAD's sectoral plans, all coordinated from a South African office staffed with neoliberals and open to economic and geopolitical gatekeeping.

Once Mbeki's plan was merged with an infrastructure-project initiative offered by the neoliberal Senegalese president, Abdoulaye Wade, it won endorsement at the last meeting of the Organization of African Unity, in June 2001. (In 2002, the OAU transformed into the African Union, with NEPAD serving as the official development plan of the latter.) Then, as 300,000 protesters gathered outside the July 2001 Genoa G8 summit, Mbeki and other African leaders provided the G8 with a modicum of cover.

In the wake of the World Conference Against Racism, the actual NEPAD document was publicly launched in Abuja, Nigeria, by African heads of state on 23 October 2001. In February 2002, global elites celebrated NEPAD in sites ranging from the World Economic Forum meeting in New York City to the summit of self-described 'progressive' national leaders (but including Blair) who gathered in Stockholm to forge a global Third Way. Elite eyes were turning to the world's 'scar' (Blair's description of Africa), hoping that NEPAD would serve as a large enough Band-Aid, for, as *Institutional Investor* magazine reported, the G8's 'misleadingly named' Africa Action Plan represented merely 'grudging' support from the main donors with 'only an additional $1 billion for debt relief. [The G8] failed altogether to reduce their domestic agricultural subsidies (which hurt African farm exports) and – most disappointing of all to the Africans – neglected to provide any further aid to the continent.'[37] Mbeki had requested $64 billion in new aid, loans and investments each year, but South Africa's *Sunday Times* remarked that 'the leaders of the world's richest nations refused to play ball'.[38] So, on the one hand, within weeks NEPAD was endorsed by the inaugural African Union summit, by the WSSD as the chapter on Africa, and by the UN's heads of state summit in New York. Yet, on the other hand, pro-NEPAD lip-service could not substitute for the 'new constitutionalism' (to borrow Gill's phrase) that would translate into long-term, non-retractable leverage over the continent.

The main reason for doubt about Mbeki's commitment to disciplinary neoliberalism and the rule of law was his repeated defence of the main violator of liberal norms, Robert Mugabe.[39] Both Mbeki and Obasanjo termed Zimbabwe's March 2002 presidential election 'legitimate', and Mbeki repeatedly opposed punishment of the Mugabe regime by the Commonwealth and UN Human Rights Commission (although finally in 2003 then Commonwealth host Obasanjo agreed that Zimbabwe should be suspended, at which point Mugabe simply quit the organization). NEPAD secretariat's Dave Malcomson, responsible for international liaison and coordination, once admitted to a reporter, 'Wherever we go, Zimbabwe is thrown at us as the reason why NEPAD's a joke.'[40]

Just prior to the 2003 G8 meeting in Evian, France, *Institutional Investor* magazine captured the tone: 'Like other far-reaching African initiatives made over the years, this one promptly rolled off the track and into the ditch.'[41] More than 100,000 activists protested against G8 policies in nearby Geneva and Lausanne. To Mbeki's consternation, African activists joined them, in part because NEPAD had recently been described as 'philosophically spot-on' by the White House's main Africa official.[42] Moreover, just prior to the Evian summit, former IMF managing director Michel Camdessus, subsequently France's personal G8 representative to Africa, explained NEPAD's attraction in the following way: 'The African heads of state came to us with the conception that globalization was not a curse for them, as some had said, but rather the opposite, from which something positive could be derived.... You can't believe how much of a difference this [home-grown pro-globalization attitude] makes.'[43]

Given this background, the African left has expressed deep scepticism over NEPAD's main strategies. A succinct critique emerged from a conference of the Council for Development and Social Science Research in Africa (CODESRIA) and Third World Network-Africa in April 2002. According to the meeting's resolution:

> The most fundamental flaws of NEPAD, which reproduce the central elements of the World Bank's *Can Africa Claim the Twenty-first Century?* and the UN Economic Commission for Africa's *Compact for African Recovery*, include:
>
> (a) the neoliberal economic policy framework at the heart of the plan, and which repeats the structural adjustment policy packages of the preceding two decades and overlooks the disastrous effects of those policies;
>
> (b) the fact that in spite of its proclaimed recognition of the central role of the African people to the plan, the African people have not played any part in the conception, design and formulation of NEPAD;
>
> (c) notwithstanding its stated concerns for social and gender equity, it adopts the social and economic measures that have contributed to the marginalization of women;

(d) that in spite of claims of African origins, its main targets are foreign donors, particularly in the G8;

(e) its vision of democracy is defined by the needs of creating a functional market;

(f) it under-emphasizes the external conditions fundamental to Africa's developmental crisis, and thereby does not promote any meaningful measure to manage and restrict the effects of this environment on Africa development efforts. On the contrary, the engagement that it seeks with institutions and processes like the World Bank, the IMF, the WTO, the United States Africa Growth and Opportunity Act, and the Cotonou Agreement will further lock Africa's economies disadvantageously into this environment;

(g) the means for mobilization of resources will further the disintegration of African economies that we have witnessed at the hands of structural adjustment and WTO rules.[44]

Given NEPAD's purely destructive role in Zimbabwe, Mbeki and Obasanjo apparently did not even take good governance seriously, beyond platitudes designed for G8 governments. Those governments need NEPAD, as Camdessus's comment indicates, partly because it reinforces their capacity to manipulate African countries through the aid mechanism; NEPAD helps sell their own taxpayers on the myth that Africa is 'reforming'.

There was, nevertheless, hope that the good-governance rhetoric in the NEPAD base document might do some good: 'With NEPAD, Africa undertakes to respect the global standards of democracy ... core components include ... fair, open, free and democratic elections periodically organized to enable the populace choose their leaders freely.'[45] South Africa under Mbeki's rule permits free and fair elections (after all, the ANC wins easily, with 70 per cent of the vote in the 2004 elections, in the absence of a credible alternative), but Obasanjo does not, judging by an April 2003 'victory' that strained democratic credibility,[46] notwithstanding Mbeki's strong endorsement.[47]

JOHANNESBURG BUSINESS INTERESTS

What of the subimperial part of the equation? To be sure, there were many naive observers who expected, as Manuel Castells put it, that

the end of apartheid in South Africa, and the potential linkage between a democratic, black majority-ruled South Africa and African countries, at least those in eastern/southern Africa, allows us to examine the hypothesis of the incorporation of Africa into global capitalism under new, more favourable conditions via the South African connection.[48]

In reality, the most important new factor in that incorporation is the exploitative role of Johannesburg business.[49] For example, in 2002, the UN Security Council accused a dozen South African companies of illegally 'looting' the DRC during late 1990s turmoil that left an estimated three million citizens dead, a problem that went unpunished by Pretoria.[50] Other South African companies had collaborated with the corrupt dictator Mobutu Sese Seko in looting then-Zaire.

But such roles did not stop officials from Pretoria, Kinshasa and the IMF from arranging, in mid-2002, what the South African Cabinet described as 'a bridge loan to the DRC of Special Drawing Rights (SDR) 75 million (about R760 million). This will help clear the DRC's overdue obligations with the IMF and allow that country to draw resources under the IMF Poverty Reduction and Growth Facility.' What this represented was a shocking display of financial power, with the earlier generation of IMF loans to Mobutu now codified by South Africa, which under apartheid had maintained a strong alliance with the then Zaire. Moreover, IMF staff would be allowed back into Kinshasa with their own new loans, and with neoliberal conditionalities (disguised by 'poverty reduction' rhetoric) again applied to the old victims of Mobuto's fierce rule. In the same statement, the South African Cabinet recorded its payment to the World Bank of R83 million for replenishment of its African loan fund, to 'benefit our private sector, which would be eligible to bid for contracts financed from these resources'.[51] Within eighteen months, Mbeki forged what Pretoria claimed was a $10 billion deal with Kabila for trade and investment, and gained access to $4 billion worth of World Bank tenders for South African companies.

The relationship between Pretoria, Johannesburg-based capital, Kinshasa and the IMF was merely an extreme case of a typical situation, in which state power is required to lubricate otherwise difficult markets. South African capital was already advancing rapidly into the region during the late 1990s, supported by special exchange control exemptions. By 2001, a researcher of the SA Institute of International Affairs warned that then Trade Minister Alec Erwin's self-serving trade strategy 'might signify to the Africa group of countries that South Africa, a prominent leader of the continent, does not have their best

interests at heart'.[52] In 2003, a colleague issued a technical report on
trade which conceded that African governments viewed Erwin 'with
some degree of suspicion' because of his promotion of the WTO, which
in Seattle and Cancún put Erwin in direct opposition to the bulk of the
lowest-income countries, whose beleaguered trade ministers were
responsible for derailing both summits.[53]

On the one hand, officials in Pretoria regularly claimed to be
advancing regional projects in part so as to steer the investment path
of (and also regulate) Johannesburg capital, with NEPAD the main
example. Capital was not so malleable, however, and the (pro-NEPAD)
Business Day newspaper admitted in mid-2004 that 'The private
sector's reluctance to get involved threatens to derail NEPAD's
ambitions.'[54] Hence the prospect that Johannesburg-based corporations will be 'new imperialists' was of 'great concern', according to
Pretoria's then Public Enterprises Minister Jeff Radebe in early 2004:
'There are strong perceptions that many South African companies
working elsewhere in Africa come across as arrogant, disrespectful,
aloof and careless in their attitude towards local business communities,
work seekers and even governments.'[55]

But Radebe could also have been describing his Cabinet colleagues
Erwin and Mbeki. In August 2003, the *Sunday Times* remarked on
Southern African Development Community delegates' sentiments at a
Dar es Salaam regional summit: 'Pretoria was "too defensive and
protective" in trade negotiations [and] is being accused of offering too
much support for domestic production "such as duty rebates on
exports" which is killing off other economies in the region.'[56] More
generally, the same paper reported from the AU meeting in Maputo
the previous month, Mbeki is

> viewed by other African leaders as too powerful, and they privately accuse
> him of wanting to impose his will on others. In the corridors they call him
> the George Bush of Africa, leading the most powerful nation in the neigh-
> bourhood and using his financial and military muscle to further his own
> agenda.[57]

Indeed, the pumping up of Pretoria's post-apartheid military
muscle has been rather revealing. Thanks especially to former international banker Terry Crawford-Brown of Economists Allied for Arms
Reduction, much more is known about how the French, German and
British governments (and even Swedish trade unions) corrupted African

National Congress leaders through a multibillion-dollar arms deal.[58]

Perhaps, then, it is no surprise to find – as we turn to resistance in the last chapter – that some of the most exciting anti-imperial initiatives being advanced in contemporary Africa are emanating from the most proletarianized and arguably organized country, South Africa. Critique and practical opposition to neoliberalism in South Africa are stronger than in any other African country, with the possible exception of Ghana.[59] Indeed, in 2005 the long-standing Campaign Against Privatization in Ghana sent staff to South Africa's major cities to meet water activists, as Johannesburg's Rand Water won a commercialization joint venture concession for Accra's water arranged by the World Bank. Rand moved into Accra under the rhetorical cover of NEPAD and the Millennium Development Goals, sparking strong critical reactions from the Anti-Privatization Forum in Johannesburg.

The question for us, in conclusion, is whether those South African activists – and their comrades up-continent and across the world – are achieving an appropriate mix of local, regional anti-subimperial, and global justice struggles, and whether their analysis, strategies, tactics and allies are feasible and sufficiently militant to be really effective?

NOTES

1 South African Press Association (SAPA), 29 January 2003.

2 *Business Day*, 20 February 2003.

3 Mbeki, T. (2002), 'Address by President Mbeki at the Welcome Ceremony of the WSSD', Johannesburg, 25 August.

4 *Straits Times*, 3 September 2003.

5 Bond, P. (2004), *Talk Left, Walk Right: South Africa's Frustrated Global Reforms*, Pietermaritzburg, University of KwaZulu-Natal Press.

6 Clarno, A. (2003), 'Denel and the South African Government: Profiting from the War on Iraq', *Khanya Journal*, 3, March.

7 *Business Day*, 11 July 2003.

8 Anti-War Coalition press statement, 1 July 2003.

9 *Mail and Guardian*, 24 May 2004.

10 Gill, S. (2003), *Power and Resistance in the New World Order*, Basingstoke, Palgrave Macmillan.

11 Panitch, L. and S. Gindin (2003), 'Global Capitalism and American Empire,' in L. Panitch and C. Leys, *Socialist Register 2004*, London, Merlin Press and New York, Monthly Review Press.

12 Biel, R. (2003), 'Imperialism and International Governance: the Case of US Policy towards Africa', *Review of African Political Economy*, 95, p. 87.

13 Martin, B. (2004), 'Beyond Bush: the Future of Popular Movements and US Africa Policy', *Review of African Political Economy*, 102, pp. 585–7.

14 Notes from David Wiley's presentation to the Association of Concerned African Scholars, African Studies Association, Washington, 19 November 2005.

15 Plaut, M. (2004), 'US to Increase African Military Presence', <http://www.bbc.co.uk>, 23 March.

16 <http://www.allAfrica.com>, 2 May 2003.

17 *Ghana News*, 11 June 2003.

18 Taylor, I. (2003), 'Conflict in Central Africa: Clandestine Networks and Regional/Global Configurations', *Review of African Political Economy*, 95, p. 49.

19 Training for African soldiers will be undertaken at the Kofi Annan Centre in Ghana, along with a centre in Kenya and three others still to be chosen. Other training candidate countries include Mali, Mauritania, Chad and Niger. The African Contingency Operations Training Assistance Programme aims to place soldiers into many conflict-ridden settings, under the rubric of the UN, but with direct Pentagon control. The major dilemma, here, appears to be the very high level of HIV-positive members of the armed forces in key countries. Hence both Namibian and South African defence ministers recently banned HIV-positive soldiers from active duty, to the great consternation of human rights advocates (the decision was reversed in Namibia). See Elbe, S. (2003), *Strategic Implications of HIV/AIDS*, Adelphi Paper 357, International Institute for Strategic Studies, Oxford, Oxford University Press, pp. 23–44.

20 *Vancouver Sun*, 11 May 2004.

21 Martin, 'Beyond Bush', pp. 590–1.

22 South African Press Association (SAPA), 2 July 2003. Other African countries where US war criminals are safe from ICC prosecutions thanks to military-aid blackmail are the DRC, Gabon, The Gambia, Ghana, Kenya, Mauritius, Sierra Leone and Zambia.

23 For India, see Chibber, V. (2004), 'Reviving the Developmental State?', in L. Panitch and C. Leys (eds), *The Empire Reloaded: Socialist Register 2005*, London, Merlin Press and New York, Monthly Review Press. For a critique of Brazilian neoliberalism, see Morais, L. and A. Saad-Filho (2004), 'Lula and the Continuity of Neoliberalism in Brazil: Strategic Choice, Economic Imperative or Political Schizophrenia?', unpublished manuscript, available from <as59@soas.ac.uk>.

24 Africa Policy Advisory Panel (2004), 'Rising US Stakes in Africa', Washington, Center for Strategic and International Studies, May, Executive Summary.

25 South African Press Association (SAPA) (2003), 'Mandela Criticises Apartheid Lawsuits', 25 August.

26 Loney, M. (1975), *Rhodesia: White Racism and Imperial Response*, Harmondsworth, Penguin, pp. 31–2.

27 Phimister, I. (1992), 'Unscrambling the Scramble: Africa's Partition Reconsidered', paper presented to the African Studies Institute, University of

the Witwatersrand, Johannesburg, 17 August.

28 Schmidt, M. (2004), 'US Offers to Train and Equip Battalions', *ThisDay*, 19 July.

29 South African Press Association (2004), 'Denel to Benefit from US Defence Trade', 21 July.

30 Batchelor, P. and S. Willett (1998), *Disarmament and Defence Industrial Adjustment in South Africa*, Oxford, Oxford University Press; Crawford-Browne, T. (2004), 'The Arms Deal Scandal', *Review of African Political Economy*, 31.

31 Black, D. (2004), 'Democracy, Development, Security and South Africa's "Arms Deal"', in P. Nel and J. van der Westhuizen (eds), *Democratizing Foreign Policy? Lessons from South Africa*, Lanham, MD, Lexington Books.

32 Majavu, M. (2004), 'Interview with Ernest Wamba dia Wamba', <http://www.zmag.org>, 22 June.

33 Emir Sader (2004), 'What is Brazil Doing in Haiti?', Interhemispheric Resource Center, <http://www.americaspolicy.org/commentary/2004/0406brazil.html>, 29 June.

34 Mbeki, T. (2005), 'Address of the President of South Africa at the United Nations Millennium Review Summit Meeting', New York, 15 September.

35 Bond, P. (2005), *Elite Transition: from Apartheid to Neoliberalism in South Africa*, Pietermaritzburg, University of KwaZulu-Natal Press; Bond, P. (ed.) (2005), *Fanon's Warning: a Civil Society Reader on the New Partnership for Africa's Development*, Trenton, Africa World Press and Durban, University of KwaZulu-Natal Centre for Civil Society; Bond, P. (2004), *Talk Left, Walk Right: South Africa's Frustrated Global Reforms*, Pietermaritzburg, University of KwaZulu-Natal Press; Bond, P. (2003), *Against Global Apartheid: South Africa Meets the World Bank, IMF and International Finance*, London, Zed Books and Cape Town, University of Cape Town Press; and Bond, P. (2002), *Unsustainable South Africa: Environment, Development and Social Protest*, London, Merlin Press and Pietermaritzburg, University of KwaZulu-Natal Press.

36 *Business Day*, 5 February 2001. Community activist Trevor Ngwane replied in the same issue of *Business Day*: 'This sounds suspiciously like June 1996, when the Growth, Employment and Redistribution policy was launched prior to public debate, to parliamentary enquiry, to consultations with the people affected. And the exclusive club of Davos fatcats who use Third World leaders like Mbeki as figleafs will probably give the new programme exactly the same support they have given GEAR: currency speculation, capital flight, refusal to invest, free-trade deals filled with last-minute Northern protectionism, and pressure on our government not to provide desperately-needed cheap drugs to ward off HIV/AIDS.' For other critiques, see Bond, *Fanon's Warning*; Adedeji, A. (2002), 'From the Lagos Plan of Action to the New Partnership for Africa's Development, and from the Final Act of Lagos to the Constitutive Act: Whither Africa?', keynote address prepared for the African Forum for Envisioning Africa, Nairobi, 26–29 April; Adesina, J. (2002), 'Development and the

Challenge of Poverty: NEPAD, Post-Washington Consensus and Beyond', paper presented to the CODESRIA/TWN Conference on Africa and the Challenge of the Twenty-first Century, Accra, 23–26 April; Nabudere, D. (2002), 'NEPAD: Historical Background and Its Prospects', in P. Anyang'Nyong'o, *et al.* (eds), *NEPAD: a New Path?*, Nairobi, Heinrich Böll Foundation; and Olukoshi, A. (2002), 'Governing the African Political Space for Sustainable Development: a Reflection on NEPAD', paper prepared for the African Forum for Envisioning Africa, Nairobi, 26–29 April.

37 Gopinath, D. (2003), 'Doubt of Africa,' *Institutional Investor*, May.

38 *Sunday Times*, 30 June 2002; *Business Day*, 28 June 2002.

39 There exists enormous confusion over Mbeki's role in Zimbabwe, which is addressed in Bond, P. and M. Manyanya (2003), *Zimbabwe's Plunge: Exhausted Nationalism, Neoliberalism and the Search for Social Justice*, London, Merlin Press, Pietermaritzburg, University of KwaZulu-Natal Press and Harare, Weaver Press. For an extremely important critique of Mugabe from an Afro-feminist standpoint, see Campbell, H. (2003), *Reclaiming Zimbabwe: the Exhaustion of the Patriarchal Model of Liberation*, David Philip, Cape Town.

40 *Business Day*, 28 March 2003.

41 Gopinath, 'Doubt of Africa'.

42 Gopinath, 'Doubt of Africa.' A few months later, Walter Kansteiner resigned as Assistant Secretary of State for Africa, but the sentiment remained.

43 <http://www.g7.utoronto.ca/ summit/2003evian/ briefing_apr030601.html>.

44 Council for Development and Social Science Research in Africa, Dakar and Third World Network-Africa (2002), 'Declaration on Africa's Development Challenges,' resolution adopted at the 'Joint Conference on Africa's Development Challenges in the Millennium', Accra, 23–26 April, p. 4.

45 *The New Partnership for Africa's Development*, <http://www.nepad.org>, paragraph 79.

46 During the April 2003 presidential poll, in Obasanjo's home state of Ogun, the President won 1,360,170 votes against his main opponent's 680. The number of votes cast in a simultaneous race in the same geographical area was just 747,296. Obasanjo's explanation, by way of denigrating European Union electoral observers, was that 'certain communities in this country make up their minds to act as one in political matters.... They probably don't have that kind of culture in most European countries.' International observers found 'serious irregularities throughout the country and fraud in at least 11 of 36 states'. (*Mail and Guardian*, 26 April 2003.)

47 Mbeki's weekly ANC internet *ANC Today* letter proclaimed, 'Nigeria has just completed a series of elections, culminating in the re-election of President Olusegun Obasanjo into his second and last term. Naturally, we have already sent our congratulations to him.' Mbeki registered, but then dismissed, the obvious: 'It is clear that there were instances of irregularities in some parts of the country. However, it also seems clear that by and large the elections were

well conducted.' <http://www.anc.org.za>, 25 April 2003.

48 Castells, M. (1998), *The Information Age, Vol III: End of Millennium*, Oxford, Blackwell Publishers, p. 88.

49 Daniel, J., V. Naidoo and S. Naidu (2003), 'The South Africans Have Arrived: Post-Apartheid Corporate Expansion into Africa', in J. Daniel, A. Habib and R. Southall (eds), *State of the Nation: South Africa 2003–04*, Pretoria, Human Sciences Research Council.

50 United Nations Panel of Experts on the Illegal Exploitation of Natural Resources and Other Forms of Wealth of the Democratic Republic of the Congo (2002), 'Final Report', New York, 8 October.

51 South African Government Communications and Information Service (2002), 'Statement on Cabinet Meeting', Pretoria, 26 June.

52 *Mail and Guardian*, 16 November 2001.

53 *Business Day*, 2 June 2003.

54 Rose, R. (2004), 'Companies "Shirking" their NEPAD Obligations', *Business Day*, 24 May.

55 SAPA (2004), 'SA's "Imperialist" Image in Africa', 30 March.

56 *Sunday Times*, 24 August 2003.

57 *Sunday Times*, 13 July 2003.

58 Brown, T. (2005), 'The Arms Deal', unpublished paper, Durban, Diakonia.

59 See, for example, Saul, J. (2005), *The Next Liberation Struggle*, Toronto, Between the Lines Press, London, Merlin Press, New York, Monthly Review Press and Pietermaritzburg, University of KwaZulu-Natal Press; Gumede, W. (2005), *Thabo Mbeki and the Struggle for the Soul of the ANC*, Cape Town, Zebra Press; Barchiesi, F. and T. Bramble (eds) (2003), *Rethinking the Labour Movement in the 'New South Africa'*, London, Macmillan; Kimani, S. (ed.) (2003), *The Right to Dissent: Freedom of Expression, Assembly and Demonstration in the New South Africa*, Johannesburg, Freedom of Expression Institute; Alexander, N. (2002), *An Ordinary Country*, Pietermaritzburg, University of Natal Press; Jacobs, S. and R. Calland (eds) (2002), *Thabo Mbeki's World*, London, Zed Books and Pietermaritzburg, University of KwaZulu-Natal Press; Hart, G. (2002), *Disabling Globalization*, Pietermaritzburg, University of KwaZulu-Natal Press and Berkeley, University of California Press; Desai, A. (2002), *We are the Poors*, New York, Monthly Review Press; Bell, T. and D. Ntsebeza (2001), *Unfinished Business*, Cape Town, RedWorks; Adams, S. (2001), *Comrade Minister*, New York, Nova Science Publishers; and Marais, H. (2000), *South Africa: Limits to Change*, London, Zed Books and Cape Town, University of Cape Town Press.

7

Civil Society Resistance
Two views

Just as there are two opposing views regarding sources of Africa's poverty – one top-down, paternalistic and co-optive, the other bottom-up, movement-oriented and radical – so there are two parallel views of how to fight poverty, and these have come into sharp contrast even within 'civil society'. In this final chapter we contrast the mainstream efforts – the Global Call to Action Against Poverty (GCAP), Make Poverty History and Live 8 campaigning so evident at the Gleneagles G8 events of mid-2005 – with more radical grassroots initiatives.

Irrespective of their occasional internecine disputes, the mainstream civil society efforts all suffered from the direction of their gaze – to the powerful – and from their simultaneous diminution of the organic anti-poverty, pro-justice struggles that will genuinely make history. The problem is simple: *that gaze to the powerful takes for granted that the G8, the WTO, Bretton Woods institutions and Third World state elites are the solution, not the main part of the problem.* The radical groups do not suffer from such a delusion, but have their own internal crises to overcome.

We start with the critique of NGO efforts, especially concern that the Millennium Development Goals may continue to remain a distraction for progressive campaigners, North and South. We then move to consideration of how, instead, an alternative set of social struggles based on a critique of corporate and financial power – and potentially some accompanying economic policy shifts – could ultimately end the looting of Africa.

As was reported, the credibility of Bob Geldof's Live 8 consciousness-raising concert was questioned when, with a three-million record sales minimum requirement, only one act in the originally scheduled line-up (Youssou N'Dour) turned out to be from Africa. At the same time, Make Poverty History was unveiled in the British press as a front for Gordon Brown's office via the Oxfam/Treasury/World Bank revolving door.[1] At the end of 2005, writers like Stuart Hodkinson, Noreena Hertz and Maxine Frith analysed the fatal flaws of Make Poverty History. According to Frith, the problem was that celebrities 'hijacked' the campaign.[2] For Hertz, 'We achieved next to nothing' because 'the campaign's design allowed it to accept inappropriate markers for success that were never real proxies for justice, empowerment or accountability. And also because its demands were never in fact audacious enough.'[3] Hodkinson was even more critical:

> By being too dependent on lobbying, celebrities and the media, by failing to give ownership of the campaign to southern hemisphere social movements, by watering down the demands agreed by grassroots movements at the World Social Forum, and by legitimizing the G8 summit, the campaign was doomed from the start. Ten out of 10 on aid, eight out of 10 on debt? More like G8, Africa nil.[4]

South African leftists amplified these concerns, based on flaws in the Johannesburg-based GCAP, known primarily for advocating white headband fashion.[5] Tellingly, the group's first newsletter, issued on 14 June 2005, was a 3,600-word report-back on campaigning across the world that ignored organic anti-poverty activism in the Global South (labour strikes, popular mobilizations for AIDS treatment and other health services, reconnections of water/electricity, land and housing occupations, anti-GMO and pro-food security campaigns, women's organizing, municipal budget campaigns, student and youth movements, community resistance to displacements caused by dam construction and the like, anti-debt and reparations movements, environmental justice struggles, immigrants' rights campaigns, political movements to take state power, etcetera). Two decades of unrest went unnoticed: 1980s–90s IMF riots, high-profile indigenous people's protests after Zapatismo in 1994, global justice activism since Seattle in 1999, the Social Forum movement since 2001, anti-war demos since 2001, autonomist protests and the Latin American left's revival. Instead, GCAP and similar efforts dedicated their efforts to UN Millennium Development Goals advocacy.

A MAJOR DISTRACTION GIMMICK

Attention paid to Africa may have been at its height in July 2005 because of global civil society campaigning like Make Poverty History and the GCAP. However, more typical was a low point just over two months later, during discussions in New York about the Millennium Development Goals (MDGs). United Nations aspirations for halving poverty by 2015 were generated five years earlier within an agency beset with contradictions, simultaneously moving to embrace the Washington Consensus with its pro-corporate Global Compact, endorsement of 'Type 2' Public-Private Partnership privatization strategies, and growing collaboration with the World Bank. To activate the MDGs, United Nations General Assembly resolution 55/2 set seven targets:

- reduce the proportion of people living in extreme poverty by half between 1990 and 2015;
- enrol all children of school age in primary schools by 2015;
- make progress toward gender equality and empowering women by eliminating gender disparities in enrolment in primary and secondary education by 2005;
- reduce infant and child mortality ratios by two-thirds between 1990 and 2015;
- reduce maternal mortality ratios by three-quarters between 1990 and 2015;
- provide access for all who need reproductive health services by 2015; and
- implement national strategies for sustainable development by 2005, to reverse the loss of environmental resources by 2015.

Yet the MDG process and the concrete strategies for achieving these objectives – including privatization of basic services such as water and electricity – do more harm than good, according to many traditional critics in civil society and academia, as well as some in the United Nations itself.

To be sure, there may be some benefits associated with globally constituted, universal objectives. As Peggy Antrobus of Development Alternatives with Women for a New Era (DAWN) puts it, 'Viewed within the context of "the new aid agenda", the MDGs provide a common framework agreed to by all governments with measurable targets and indicators of progress, around which governments, UN agencies, international financial institutions and civil society alike could rally.'[6] They permit at least notional accountability for donor agencies and states, which civil society activists are already pointing to as a guilt trip reminder.

However, speaking the language of many feminists and social justice activists, Antrobus is blunt:

> I do not believe in the MDGs. I think of them as a Major Distraction Gimmick. There is evidently widespread awareness of their limitation: their inadequate targets and indicators; their restriction to indicators that are quantifiable, when much of what is most important – such as Women's Equality and Empowerment – is not easily quantifiable; their omission of important Goals and Targets, such as Violence against Women and Sexual and Reproductive Rights;[7] their silence on the context and institutional environment in which they are to be met.... In fact, a major problem of the MDGs is their abstraction from the social, political and economic context in which they are to be implemented – the 'political economy' of the MDGs.

Central to MDG political economy is that the Bretton Woods institutions and the WTO – acting mainly for G8 governments and corporations – appear intent upon bringing ever more aspects of life under the rules of commodification, attributing market values to society and nature. Hence, as the UN itself admits, 'International Monetary Fund programme design has paid almost no systematic attention to the goals when considering a country's budget or macroeconomic framework.' A 2005 UN report complains that 'In the vast number of country programmes supported by the IMF since the adoption of the goals, there has been almost no discussion about whether the plans are consistent with achieving them.' The report documents how budget constraints prevent scaling up sectoral strategies for some of the MDGs, and that in some cases 'countries are advised not to even to consider such scaled-up plans' by the Bretton Woods institutions.[8]

UN Habitat's website also admits 'the common criticism of MDGs as a "top-down" process, which excludes Local Authority and other stakeholders' involvement.... There is, thus, an inherent danger that even if the targets are achieved, the inequalities within a nation across people and places would still persist.'[9] Minority Rights Group International agrees: 'There is a genuine risk that the strategies used to achieve the MDGs will be less beneficial for minority groups, might

increase inequalities and may harm some minority communities.'[10] That
risk was acknowledged in the UNDP's *Human Development Report
2003: Millennium Development Goals,* which conceded that 'Women,
rural inhabitants, ethnic minorities and other poor people are typically
progressing slower than national averages – or showing no progress –
even where countries as a whole are moving towards the Goals.'[11]

The MDGs themselves are sometimes ridiculed for their lack of
ambition. Kumi Naidoo of Civicus – responsible for energetic advocacy
of MDGs within GCAP – concedes that 'Those that use the MDG
framework do so on a strategic level and are pushing for goals beyond
the MDGs, i.e. Vietnam speaks of MDG Plus, and others speak of
"beyond MDGs".'[12] Civicus staff sometimes refer to the 'Minimalist
Development Goals', even though MDGs are the central focus of the
GCAP. The disappointing minimalism is evident in a 2003 article by
leading UNDP bureaucrats, who argued that the MDG commitments
to a 'global partnership' on aid, trade and debt

> find their current official commitments in the Monterrey Consensus on
> development finance, the Doha 'development' round on trade, and the
> Highly Indebted Poor Country (HIPC) initiative, respectively. Progress on
> global commitments for improved aid, fairer trade and steep debt relief will
> determine, to a large extent, the successful achievement of the first seven
> MDGs by 2015 in most if not all developing countries.[13]

If so, that official commitment worsens poverty rather than reduces it.
The UN bureaucrats do admit that while 'Monterrey, Doha and HIPC
hold great promise to make significant contributions to the achievement of the MDGs, however, progress thus far has been extremely
slow.' As Monterrey, Doha and HIPC all show, global elite commitments
on aid, trade and debt relief are, in short, so far short of progressive
change, that reaching the MDG targets is impossible.[14]

This was abundantly clear in September 2005, by the time of the
heads of state summit meant to celebrate progress on the MDGs. As
South African president Thabo Mbeki observed with uncharacteristic
pessimism, 'our approach to the challenge to commit and deploy the
necessary resources for the realization of the MDGs has been half-
hearted, timid and tepid'.[15] According to an apparently surprised
Vicente García-Delgado, the UN representative for Civicus,

> What took place at the UN during the few weeks leading to the Summit was
> a disgrace – an ugly diplomatic spectacle where a large majority of Member

States saw their carefully drafted outcome document blown up before their eyes, and where the entire process of delicate inter-governmental negotiations was held hostage to a small minority pulling in opposite directions.[16]

Nevertheless, García-Delgado claimed, GCAP 'actions have not been in vain. Without their participation and activism, the results of this Summit might have been much, much worse.' But, to be quite frank, weren't these efforts in vain given that no new resources or strategic changes emerged? Didn't the September 2005 fiasco demonstrate the need for the much deeper and also much more urgent work of expanding existing organic activist initiatives?

Perhaps once the dust has settled on the wretched deals done by the G8 to the applause of coopted NGOs, and once it is evident to all that the MDGs were a charade, the latest version of the Africa charity fad will be buried. Then the more durable activists will again be on the frontlines and front pages, whether through specific campaigns against state and corporate malfeasance (such as the war and occupation in Iraq), or other forms of progressive mobilization and democratic advocacy, or the construction of national Social Forums and internationally networked sectoral forums that deliver serious solidarity. Before turning to the prospects for a formal programme uniting these kinds of movements, two emblematic campaigning examples deserve consideration.

REPARATIONS FROM – AND CLOSURE OF – GLOBAL FINANCIAL INSTITUTIONS

From South Africa, the demand for reparations from apartheid's financiers is a crucial precedent for wider campaigns aimed at reversing the outflow of resources from Africa, just as the struggle against apartheid included successful grassroots-driven 'financial sanctions' against the old Pretoria regime that subsequently inspired a contemporaneous battle to close the World Bank and other international financial institutions. These are just two telling examples of African-initiated campaigns to restore the continent's capacities.

As noted in the previous chapter, activists from Jubilee South Africa and other church and apartheid-victims groups were frustrated by the failure of the September 2001 World Conference Against Racism – the single most appropriate international forum – to advance their agenda. The conference was so tightly controlled by Thabo Mbeki that a reparations endorsement, supported by the rulers of Nigeria and Zambia, amongst others, was simply not permitted in the final resolution.

The activists turned to the US courts, following the model set against Swiss and German bankers and corporations which violated human (and property) rights during the Nazi era. Civil cases for billions of dollars in damages were filed on behalf of apartheid victims against large multinational corporations which profited from South African investments and loans. In the most important case, Jubilee South Africa and the Khulumani Support Group, representing 32,000 South Africans (with 87 specific claimants seeding a larger class action), sued 23 financing, technology, transportation, oil, and arms corporations for their role in apartheid-era human rights abuses.[17] The fear engendered was so great that the Bush regime and corporate lobbies urgently pleaded with US courts, initially unsuccessfully, to nullify an interpretation of the Alien Tort Claims Act that made suits seeking apartheid reparations possible.[18]

South Africa's Justice Ministry and Mbeki himself had initially responded to the reparations campaign with 'neither support nor condemnation'. However, in the wake of the Truth and Reconciliation Commission's final report, which recommended a reparations payment by businesses which benefited from apartheid, he changed tack. As of April 2003, it was suddenly 'completely unacceptable that matters that are central to the future of our country should be adjudicated in foreign courts which bear no responsibility for the well-being of our country and the observance of the perspective contained in our constitution of the promotion of national reconciliation'. The President expressed 'the desire to involve all South Africans, including corporate citizens, in a cooperative and voluntary partnership' – obviously failing to recognize the numerous futile attempts in that direction by the Jubilee SA, the Apartheid Reparations Task Force and Cape Town's Anglican archbishop Njongonkulu Ndungane for several years prior to filing the lawsuits.

In July 2003, Mbeki and Justice Minister Penuell Maduna then explicitly defended the international bankers and corporations against reparations proceedings in the US courts, arguing in a nine-page brief that the judge must not discourage 'much-needed foreign investment and delay the achievement of the government's goals. Indeed, the litigation could have a destabilizing effect on the South African economy as investment is not only a driver of growth, but also of employment.' Pretoria's appeal to the court was apparently catalysed by a request from the then US secretary of state Colin Powell.[19]

Nevertheless, hopes were high when two Nobel laureates – former Archbishop Desmond Tutu and Columbia University economist Joseph Stiglitz – filed friend-of-the-court briefs supporting the activists and discounting Pretoria's arguments. In mid-2004, the US Supreme Court ruled that the Alien Tort Claims Act was indeed an appropriate vehicle for these lawsuits.

However, based in part upon Maduna's brief, a New York judge dismissed the reparations litigation in November 2004 (Jubilee and Khulumani appealed his judgment in late 2005). In June 2005, US courts rejected another lawsuit, by 'comfort women' victims of Japanese Second World War torture and rape, in part by citing Maduna's letter to the effect that reparations lawsuits could have adverse foreign policy implications. Jubilee then challenged Barclays Bank in a citizens' campaign during the London financier's purchase of the large South African bank ABSA. Maduna's replacement, Justice Minister Bridgette Mabandla, responded with another friends-of-the-court brief in October 2005, on behalf of Barclays, other banks, oil companies, arms merchants, auto firms and technology giants, prompting more demonstrations against Pretoria's collaboration with apartheid profiteers.

Two lessons from these experiences were simple: first, it was impossible to find allies in the fight for global justice amongst the nationalist leadership of South Africa, despite the Pretoria politicians' occasional anti-imperialist rhetoric; and second, court action was unreliable, and increased popular protest was needed. Firm alliances against financial power would have to be forged amongst Third World social movements themselves, along with solidarity from Northern supporters, unhindered by distractions from international NGOs and labour movements which typically sought mere reform, not abolition, of the international financial institutions (IFIs).

An excellent example of such campaigning occurred in September 2005, when Jubilee South Africa picketed eight international banks located in Sandton, including Barclays and Citibank, reporting that

> All of these banks either never left South Africa during sanctions or have returned post-1994; they are all doing business – making money hand over fist – as if they have no moral culpability or responsibility, supported by

anti-poor economic policy. These banks gave billions of dollars of loans to the apartheid government, renegotiated its debts and thus enabled it to spend even more on its military, and, in the case of Barclays, gave money directly to the South African Defence Force in 1976. All of these banks need to fully apologize to the South African people for the support they gave to the apartheid regime, and pay reparations to those who have suffered from its actions.[20]

The Washington-based Mobilization for Global Justice and a coalition of Swiss activists (Comtec, Déclaration de Berne, and Campagne pour l'Annulation des Dettes et pour les Réparations en Afrique Australe) joined Jubilee South Africa protesters in exemplary solidarity demonstrations. From Sandton to Washington, Citibank was the target, for, as the UN's Special Committee against Apartheid had observed in 1979, 'Citigroup has loaned nearly one-fifth of the $5 billion plus which has gone to bolster apartheid' and in subsequent years made yet more loans for segregated housing and for the rollover of apartheid debt during the 1985 financial crisis. In Berne, Credit Suisse and UBS were the subject of protest because from the early 1980s they replaced US and British banks as the main apartheid financiers.

There is no shortage of such opportunities, for African movements regularly voice anger against international finance. David Seddon and Leo Zeilig distinguish between a 'first wave' of popular struggles and 'IMF Riots' from the mid-1970s and through the 1980s that might be seen as a 'precursor to the contemporary phenomenon of the "anti-globalization movement"; others are more sceptical, seeing them as merely localized expressions of anger and outrage'. The second wave of popular protest during the 1990s was 'more explicitly political with more far-reaching aims and objectives', with 86 major protest movements in 30 countries evident in 1991 alone, and three dozen dictatorial regimes swept out of power in 1990–4 'by a combination of street demonstrations, mass strikes and other forms of protest'.[21]

Will a 'third wave' emerge, based upon 'new social movements', the World Social Forum phenomenon and more focused, militant African labour movements? There are grounds for pessimism, to be sure, but many moments of inspiration when issues move from localist demands and critiques merely of venal elites, to an awareness that the struggle is far more profound, and that merely replacing old with new rulers does not make much difference. An example was the February

2004 anti-IMF strike called by the Zambia Congress of Trade Unions, in which half a million workers participated. A large march descended upon parliament in Lusaka to reject a civil service wage freeze promoted by the IMF, as activists demanded instead a minimum wage and other budgetary concessions.[22]

In making these kinds of links and establishing coherent alternative programmes, intra-African activist connections are becoming stronger. In June 2004, a Cape Town meeting of Jubilee Africa members from Angola, Cameroon, Côte d'Ivoire, the DRC, Kenya, Mozambique, South Africa, Swaziland, Zambia, Tanzania and Zimbabwe, and partners from Brazil, Argentina and the Philippines working on a comprehensive Illegitimate Debt Audit 'expressed deep concern with South Africa's subimperialist role and its use of NEPAD to promote the neoliberal paradigm to further dominate the rest of the African continent politically, economically, culturally and militarily, serving the interests of transnational corporations'. The groups demanded:

- full unconditional cancellation of Africa's total debt;
- reparations for damage caused by debt devastation;
- an immediate halt to HIPC and PRSPs and the disguised structural adjustment programme through NEPAD and any other agreements that do not address the fundamental interests of the impoverished majority and the building of a sustainable and sovereign Africa; and
- a comprehensive audit to determine the full extent and real nature of Africa's illegitimate debt, the total payments made to date and the amount owed to Africa.[23]

This rhetoric is not uncommon. At the global scale a few weeks earlier, a new network of impressive mass-based social movements[24] and radical NGOs[25] called 'IFIs-Out!' emerged, with 'unifying principles' that included the following:

- We believe in dismantling the IFIs, since we believe them to be fundamentally incapable of transforming into just institutions.
- We believe in decommodification, in opposition to the neoliberal trend of privatizing all common property.
- We believe that IFIs reinforce patriarchy and the oppression of women.
- We believe that IFIs reinforce a racist system of global apartheid, including the oppression of indigenous communities.

- We believe in the free global movement of people.
- We believe in the deglobalization of capital.
- We believe in cross-territorial work, crossing national, regional, and continental boundaries, and boundaries between issues (such as women, agriculture, indigenous peoples, public health, etcetera).
- We believe in global South leadership.
- We believe in strengthening popular social movements.
- We believe in linking global struggles against IFIs with local struggles around land, food, water, etcetera ('global–local linkage').

Are there concrete ways to take these principles into battle against the IFIs? One anti-imperialist financial tactic based on the strategy of defunding the World Bank was introduced four years earlier: the World Bank Bonds Boycott. Launched by Jubilee South Africa, Brazil's Movement of Landless Workers, and numerous other Third World activist groups in April 2000, the Bonds Boycott poses this simple question that harks back to anti-apartheid disinvestment campaigning: is it ethical for socially conscious people to invest in the Bank by buying its bonds, responsible for 80 per cent of the institution's resources, hence drawing out dividends which represent the fruits of enormous suffering?

Within a few years, the world's largest pension fund, TIAA-CREF, had sold its bonds under activist pressure, and an impressive array of investment funds committed never to buy another Bank bond again.[26] In addition, preparations were under way for campaigns to oppose recapitalization of the IFIs. Another front was neoliberal knowledge reproduction via the IFIs, especially the World Bank's 'Knowledge Bank' role, which would also be subject to a campaign of intellectual delegitimation in coming years.

Whatever the tactics, the strategy and analysis deployed by the activists must continue to stress the relationship between market power and imperialism, the way Leon Trotsky and Rosa Luxemburg did a century ago, and the way so many African critics have done over the past half-century. Indeed, with Paul Wolfowitz running the Bank at least until 2009 – when potentially either the selection system might change (highly unlikely) or a Democratic president might appoint someone else with a slightly less obvious imperial orientation – these questions are being raised in a way that unifies global justice movements with the broader anti-imperialism/war struggle.

For example, in Washington on 24 September 2005, a mass march of at least 200,000 people demanding US withdrawal from Iraq wound its way to an intersection near Pennsylvania and 18th Streets, where the World Bank and IMF annual meetings were under way. As Soweto activist Virginia Setshedi told InterPress Service, 'It is not just about war. It is about how many people die around the world because of unfair policies and actions – a large part of which are economic. So it is not just the military injustice that we are facing. We need to connect the dots together.' Protest organisers attacked the policies of Bretton Woods institutions for placing 'corporate profits ahead of basic human needs worldwide. We will speak out against the corporate theft of Iraq's resources and the decimation of the Iraqi economy through privatization and "free trade".'[27] A mock wedding was held outside the Bank on 22 September, uniting the Pentagon with the Bank under Wolfowitz's leadership.

According to Reuters, protesters grieved for 'the rights of the poor in Louisiana displaced by Hurricane Katrina, the poor in Iraq who are being hurt by war and those that protesters say are forced into poverty by IMF policies'.[28] Centrifugally dispersed around the globe, the effects of neoliberalism are also centrifocally massed in the World Bank's host city, according to a vibrant local activist group, the Mobilization for Global Justice:

> These policies extend even into the US: as residents of Washington DC, we are the reluctant hosts of the World Bank, the IMF, and other institutions of empire. With our only public hospital closed, a deteriorating public school system, and a private baseball stadium being built with public funds, we see that the same policies of private gain at public expense imposed on borrowing countries by the World Bank and IMF are also at work in Washington. The World Bank and IMF make billions a year in profits, use services provided by the city, and sit on valuable property downtown, yet they pay no property taxes or corporate revenue taxes. This is an injustice in a city with a majority low-income population and is a cruel hypocrisy on the part of the institutions, which state 'poverty reduction' and 'economic development' as part of their goals.[29]

Tellingly, the same week as the big protests, two other indications of Bank resilience appeared: a somewhat farcical gathering with civil society organizations inside the Bank,[30] and the release of the 2006 *World Development Report: Equity and Development*, whose cover borrowed the leftist Mexican muralist Diego Rivera's incendiary

'Dream of a Sunday Afternoon in Alameda Park' (1947–8). That report, according to Sanjay Reddy, 'often relies on questionable indicators and analytical tools. For example, more secure property rights, as judged by foreign investors, are used as a proxy for the "quality of institutions".… Its intellectual basis is weak, its contents are not adequately complete and its prescriptions are often either questionable or of limited practical value.'[31]

Connecting dots between neoliberalism and militarism, African activists are contributing to resistance against financial imperialism, South African subimperialism, and the compradorization process. Their simultaneous, overlapping, interlinking efforts are bringing together some of the most advanced leftist mass movements across the world. What they are doing, through praxis, is updating the classical theories of imperialism – but without basing their arguments on the thesis (see, for example, Rudolf Hilferding's 1910 classic *Finanz Kapital*, which so influenced Vladimir Lenin's *Imperialism*)[32] of overwhelming *power* located in global financial institutions. They have, instead, begun to focus systematically upon the *vulnerability* of financial circuits of capital, and are taking advantage of opportunities to combine their attacks against these weaknesses of capital with critiques of the illegitimacy of the political form, US-led empire.

Although working on financial institutions is a top priority, these campaigners are not alone. Efforts to bridge global–local and Northern–African divides are being advanced in more areas than can be listed here: when Treatment Action advocates break the hold of pharmaceutical corporations on monopoly antiretroviral patents; when activists fight Monsanto's GM drive from the US to South Africa to several African countries; when blood-diamonds victims from Sierra Leone and Angola generate a partially successful global deal at Kimberley; when Kalahari Basarwa-San Bushmen raise publicity against forced removals, as the Botswana government clears the way for De Beers and World Bank investments; when Lesotho peasants object to displacement during construction of the continent's largest dam system (solely to quench Johannesburg's irrational and hedonistic thirst), along with Ugandans who are similarly threatened by the overly expensive, corruption-ridden Bujagali Dam; when a growing network of activists questions Liberia's long exploitation by Firestone Rubber; when Chadian and Cameroonian activists pressure the World Bank not to continue funding their repression and environmental degradation; when Oil Watch links Nigerian Delta and many other Gulf of Guinea communities; and when Ghanaian, South African and Dutch activists oppose water privatization.

How far they go in part depends upon how far valued allies in the advanced capitalist financial and corporate centres recognize the merits of their analysis, strategy and tactics – and offer the solidarity that African and other Third World activists can repay many times over, once Northern pressure is lifted from their countries' necks and they gain the space to win lasting, emancipatory objectives. But setting out campaigns on reparations, IFI closure, corporate malfeasance and an end to many other specific forms of looting is only part of an even bigger challenge for bottom-up construction: establishing a durable programmatic approach that the world's progressive movements can unite behind.

PROGRAMMES TO END THE LOOTING

Only a few years ago, it appeared that even post-colonial African civil society organizations which once had a more radical developmental agenda were largely civilized, tamed and channelled into serving each new incarnation of elite interest. In reaction to the excesses of exhausted, corrupt and repressive nationalist political parties, many of which were tossed from power in the early 1990s, there emerged a new generation of democratic movements, human rights advocates, NGOs, churches, youth and women's groups and a variety of civil society groups. Structural adjustment meant the loss of state welfare programmes, and in turn the need for civil societies to pick up the pieces. When, amidst the wreckage, alternative political parties emerged from the grassroots and shopfloors (most spectacularly in Zambia, perhaps), they too often fell into the trap of deepening the market's rule, at the expense of popular interests.

Today, a more critical approach is evident in Africa's social movement hotspots, especially South Africa. Some scholars might recognize these dynamics as more akin to Hungarian social scientist Karl Polanyi's view of society – as an active, countervailing force against market excesses (in *The Great Transformation,* 1944) – than to the pessimistic picture of civil society painted by Italian political theorist and activist Antonio Gramsci (in his 1930s *Prison Notebooks*). This dichotomous reading of civil society – as a stabilizing, conservative force (Gramsci), or instead as a 'new social movement' challenge to neoliberalism (Polanyi) – presents us with interesting problems.

Gramsci analysed the rise of fascism and the simultaneous failure of liberatory political movements in Italy and other Western societies, and explained that the hegemony of capitalism depended not merely upon repression, but also upon consent:

> When the State trembled, a sturdy structure of civil society was at once revealed. The State was only the outer ditch, behind which there stood a powerful system of fortresses and earthworks.... The massive structures of modern democracies, both as State organizations, and as complexes of associations in civil society, constitute for the art of politics as it were the 'trenches' and the permanent fortifications of the front in the war of position....[33]

Michael Burawoy interprets: 'Civil society smothers any attempt to seize state power directly, so that revolutionary activity involves the slow, patient work of reorganizing associations, trade unions, parties, schools, legal system, and so forth' – i.e., Gramsci's 'war of position', in contrast to a more insurrectionary 'war of movement'.[34] Polanyi's most powerful idea, meanwhile, was probably that of 'a double movement' in which 'the extension of the market organization in respect to genuine commodities was accompanied by its restriction', as society resisted excessive commodification.[35]

Some have suggested that a formal *programme* aimed at this sort of political coherence is the prerequisite. The World Social Forum's Africa Council was founded in 2004 and announced that its key challenges were ending 'the dictatorship of neoliberal policies and the policy geared towards the militarization of the management of the world Triad (Europe, United States and Japan), under the leadership of the American Empire'.

Specifically, how might progressives advance this agenda? In early 2005 at the World Social Forum (WSF) in Porto Alegre, 19 well-known movement intellectuals and activists gathered to produce a draft of 'Twelve proposals for another possible world' (abridged as follows):[36]

1 Cancel the external debt of Southern countries;
2 Implement international taxes on financial transactions (most notably the Tobin tax on speculative capital), on direct foreign investments, on consolidated profit from multinationals, on weapon

trade and on activities accompanied by large greenhouse effect gas emissions;

3 Progressively dismantle all forms of fiscal, juridical and banking paradises;

4 All inhabitants of this planet must have the right to be employed, to social protection and retirement/pension, respecting equal rights between men and women;

5 Promote all forms of equitable trade, reject all free-trade agreements and laws proposed by the World Trade Organization, and putting in motion mechanisms allowing a progressive upward equalization of social and environmental norms;

6 Guarantee the right of all countries to alimentary sovereignty and security by promoting peasant, rural agriculture;

7 Forbid all types of patenting of knowledge of living beings (human, animal or vegetal) as well as any privatization of common goods for humanity, particularly water;

8 Fight by means of public policies against all kinds of discrimination, sexism, xenophobia, antisemitism and racism. Fully recognize the political, cultural and economic rights (including the access to natural resources) of indigenous populations;

9 Take urgent steps to end the destruction of the environment and the threat of severe climate changes due to the greenhouse effect, resulting from the proliferation of individual transportation and the excessive use of non-renewable energy sources;

10 Demand the dismantling of all foreign military bases and the removal of troops on all countries, except when operating under explicit mandate of the United Nations, especially for Iraq and Palestine;

11 Guarantee the right to access information and the right to inform, for/by all citizens;

12 Reform and deeply democratize international institutions by making sure human, economic, social and cultural rights prevail.

Excellent ideas notwithstanding, it is fair to ask: did those who authored these proposals think them through as thoroughly as possible? Should critiques of their process – namely, launching a major manifesto into the WSF without proper consultation (and with extreme gender imbalance) – be joined by concern that, for whatever reasons, the authors are perhaps not sufficiently close to the issues?

But these are minor concerns in relation to the more important question: does the WSF represent an appropriate *process* for arriving at programmatic and practical strategic unity? Trevor Ngwane of the Soweto Electricity Crisis Committee offers these reservations:

> The WSF governing structures – its international council and secretariat – are unwittingly allowing the marginalization and eclipse of social movements by their hands-off, laissez-faire approach to the organization of events and activities in the WSF space…. The WSF 2007 in Africa cannot afford to be a talkshop. We should consider a specific concrete campaign and outcome which will benefit the African masses practically.[37]

FROM SPACE TO NETWORK TO STATE?

Whatever its shortcomings, Porto Alegre has served as an unprecedented 'space' for these sorts of debates. Likewise, at a key Addis Ababa meeting in 2003, the African Social Forum described itself as 'a pluralist and diversified, non-confessional, non-governmental and non-partisan space, which links, in a decentralized way and in networks, entities and movements engaged in concrete actions, from the local to the international level, for the construction of another Africa and another world'.[38]

But beyond serving as a sort of left-wing trade fair in ideas and experiences, it is probably overdue that the WSF and its affiliates democratically develop programmatic points of convergence. It is crucial for any such programme of global justice to emerge from real social struggles. And, unfortunately, it is likely that the ideological diversity encompassed within the WSF will prove a serious barrier to addressing problems of the sort raised in the 'Twelve proposals', especially over whether we should 'fix' or 'nix' embryonic global-state institutions.

Instead, I think real progress in these directions will be found in transnational sectoral forums, of which there are many examples, some of which are already generating the global-scale analysis, demands, strategies, tactics and alliances to which the 19 authors should have made reference. Serious activists are increasingly crossing borders, races, classes and political traditions to find a unity of purpose in sector after sector: land (Via Campesino), healthcare (International Peoples Health Council), free schooling (Global Campaign for Education), water (the People's World Water Forum), energy/climate change (the Durban Declaration), debt (Jubilee South), democratic development finance (IFIs-Out! and World Bank Bonds Boycott), trade (Our World is Not for Sale) and so on.

Of course, it is not at all easy to interlock the already overlapping grassroots and shopfloor justice campaigns into a coherent political approach. South Africans now campaigning for an overall programme of 'decommodification' and socio-economic rights know this, thanks to the various movements' political splits (mainly over the merits of alignment to the corruption-ridden, neoliberal ruling party of Thabo Mbeki). To be sure, there is broad unity in the South Africans' objectives – free anti-retroviral medicines to fight AIDS; at least 50 litres of free water and 1 kilowatt hour of free electricity for each individual every day; extensive land reform; prohibitions on service disconnections and evictions; free education; renationalized telecommunications; the right to employment; and even a monthly 'basic income grant' – but hard work lies ahead to connect the concrete struggles.

Would having a more rigorous set of *national* social forums – affiliated to the WSF but with federalist autonomy – permit the development of a universal programme of action? Probably not, for in South Africa and elsewhere, there are far too many divisions between the key organizations representing oppressed peoples to forge the necessary unity for a workable national forum. (However, in Zimbabwe, Kenya, Nigeria, Ghana, and Malawi, the Social Forum has already become the venue for a national regroupment of the left forces, in the best spirit of coalition building and programmatic work.)

The problems with the WSF model to date are in part rooted in the initiative's 2001 origins: amongst elite social democrats who, activist critics regularly point out, mirrored the Davos World Economic Forum with a top-down call for an expensive gathering at a symbolic site. At the 2003 Porto Alegre WSF, organizers were accused of systematically sidelining more radical forces such as Indymedia, the youth network Intergalactica and the ZNet network. Asked anarchist writer Andrej Grubacic after the 2003 WSF, 'Do we really want to create a movement that will resemble a cocktail party in the lounge of the Plaza São Rafael Hotel in Porto Alegre? Do we want a movement dominated by middle-aged bureaucrats wearing Palestinian scarves?...'[39] (This isn't a matter of insufficient grassroots participation; it is about the accountability, vision and militancy of the leading players.)

Interpreting the radical political potential of the WSF given such beginnings is one of the most interesting dilemmas for the global justice movements. WSF organizers are now more than a bit embarrassed that their Workers Party comrades performed so ably in the service of Brazilian neoliberalism, subimperialism (in Haiti for instance) and imperialism (at the Hong Kong WTO summit). As one reflection of its failure to deliver meaningful change, the Workers Party lost elections and hence state power in the very city and province which became synonymous with the WSF, Porto Alegre.

Regardless of the venue, what is surely the main accomplishment of the WSF is the construction of dialogical spaces. These spaces might ultimately support ideological, analytical, strategic and even tactical convergence between far-flung movements which span the globe. Indeed, the Social Forum network is potentially a means by which the 'globalization of people' can become real, a genuine counterpoint to the 'globalization of capital'.

In the process, Michael Hardt and Antonio Negri insist that their new category, 'the *multitude*' of oppressed people (as distinct from the 'masses'), might also 'be conceived as a network: an open expansive network in which all differences can be expressed freely and equally, a network that provides the means of encounter so that we can work and live in common'. Again, ideally, the network form provides 'the model for an absolutely democratic organization that corresponds to the dominant forms of economic and social production, and is also the most powerful weapon against the ruling power structure'. According to Hardt and Negri, the challenge is 'to communicate and act in common while remaining internally different'. Whereas previously, dissenters were divided along sectoral, geographical and other lines, 'today network movements are able to address all of [the grievances] simultaneously'. Drawing upon Ashwin Desai's pathbreaking book about South African urban social movements, *We Are the Poors,* Hardt and Negri note both the remarkable non-racialism through which Africans and people of Indian descent struggle in unison, and the global vision through which these movements 'target neoliberal globalization as the source of their poverty'.[40] But in targeting neoliberalism in this manner, dangers certainly arise, according to Desai and Richard Pithouse, from the political current promoted by Hardt and Negri, amongst others: 'Autonomism's fetish of spontaneity means that it lacks any meaningful capacity for posing, let alone answering, the important questions about democratic structure, practice and leadership within movements.'⁴¹

Moreover, returning to the broader question of whether a coherent political and programmatic strategy can emerge from the various strands of African, Third World and indeed global justice activities, the other crucial flaw of autonomism is its disdain for the state. So on the one hand, it should be clear that any genuine programme of liberation will have to emanate from grounded mass democratic struggles and the networks which bring these together (probably first in sectors and then later in African Social Forum and World Social Forum venues).

On the other hand, the activists are continually confronted by globally imposed national-scale initiatives by elites, and are often compelled to reply with an 'alternative' national strategy. What are they to do, given how far the left is from power in every African country? In contrast, Latin America is a more hospitable site for posing and answering these questions, from semi-liberated sites – Cuba, Venezuela and perhaps Bolivia – to terrains where centre-left governments (Brazil, Argentina, Uruguay) are rejecting the IMF and privatization under pressure from social and labour movements.

It is not at all unusual in Africa for activists to refer to the admittedly rancid and repressive national state apparatus as a potential saviour. This is not naivety, but instead reflects the concrete sense of so many movements, that their states – once democratized – are ultimately the only real site of countervailing power against market excesses. And given the weaknesses in recent global-elite and African-elite policy proposals aimed at reversing the continent's socio-economic collapse, these activists are continually pressed to develop new policy options that are more amenable to society and nature.

To reiterate, it is unquestionable that such options wll have to emerge from the bottom up, through activism and critiques that emanate from Africans themselves. Although it is presumptuous to predict anything in the sphere of civil society dynamics, it *may be* that some or all of the options below would emerge as the policy menu for these progressive forces:

• with regard to aid, the simple refusal of tied aid and phantom aid might be accompanied by an international 'naming and shaming' exercise, which some campaigners have already embarked upon;

- under the slogan 'Don't Owe Won't Pay', the obvious policy implication of overindebtedness is systemic Third World default, a policy successfully carried out in earlier periods *en masse*, but also hinted at by Argentina's contemporary example;
- as for uneven private sector capital flows in Africa, there are also well-tested strategies – such as prescribed assets – that can force the domestic reinvestment of pension and insurance funds as well as other large institutional investment reserves;
- for controlling capital flight, it will be crucial to address offshore tax havens through national-scale regulation and even prohibition of financial transfers from these sites, as part of a more general re-establishment of exchange controls to limit currency convertibility, and through revitalized state financial regulation;
- for trade relations, an inward-oriented development strategy is preferable (entailing infant industries and judicious tariff and quota policies), given the decay of prices for non-petroleum exports, which in turn represents a treadmill to rising physical output and declining revenues;
- regarding migration, a balance is required between increasing freedom of movement and increasing incentives to maintain residence after local tertiary and professional training, with internationalism a central value;
- foreign direct investment should also, in future, be carefully measured so as to include natural resource depletion and many other costs (such as transfer pricing and profit/dividend outflows), not simply benefits – and then permission refused if these calculations are not favourable, a tactic that was successful in South Korea's initial post-war industrialization drive;
- fiscal austerity, monetarism, privatization, liberalization and other macroeconomic policies should be firmly resisted, given their maldistributive impacts, while civil society intensifies budget oversight;
- politically, the deep democratization of all African societies will be required to rid the ruling circuits of corrupt comprador elements, which in turn implies more attention not only to contesting aspects of state power and capital accumulation (as so many civil society groups are doing), but also ultimately to *taking* power through progressive political parties;
- a dramatic change in the national balance of forces across Africa, following the transitions under way in Latin America, is in turn the

prerequisite for gaining sufficient political weight to begin installing vital global-scale measures (such as Tobin taxes, greenhouse gas mitigation, and reparations for ecological debt); and

* while a progressive change in government is a long way away for most countries, in the meantime it is feasible to amplify existing activist initiatives aimed at controlling the outflow of African resources, and ensuring that the redistributive strategies are catalysed and owned at the level of households, grassroots communities and shopfloors.

Again, the matter of agency is critical. In the aftermath of struggles against colonialism, Walter Rodney was one of the leading admirers of

> the vital activity of the broad African masses, including the sacrifice of life and limb. In brief, it is enough to say that the African people as a collective had upset the plans of the colonialists, and had surged forward to freedom. Such a position may seem to be a mere revival of a certain rosy and romantic view of African independence which was popular in the early 1960s, but, on the contrary, it is fully cognisant of the shabby reality of neocolonial Africa.[42]

To replace shabby neoliberal projects like the New Partnership for Africa's Development with a bottom-up programmatic strategy that can confront the looting of Africa requires the rapid development of mass democratic movements across the continent, suffused with values of liberty, equality (including between the sexes) and solidarity. In addition, the intellectual plays a crucial role. The possibility of a revived African left intent on halting and reversing the looting of the continent depends upon the nurture of Africa's independent-minded nationalists, feminists, critical political economists and anti-imperialists, who are already helping to shape the strategies of progressive movements.[43]

Perhaps Fanon put it best, in his discussion of intellectuals in liberated zones of Algeria, *circa* 1961:

> One of the greatest services that the Algerian revolution will have rendered to the intellectuals of Algeria will be to have placed them in contact with the people, to have allowed them to see the extreme, ineffable poverty of the people, at the same time allowing them to watch the awakening of the people's intelligence and the onward progress of their consciousness.... Today, the people's tribunals are functioning at every level, and local planning commissions are organizing the division of large-scale holdings,

and working out the Algeria of tomorrow. An isolated individual may obstinately refuse to understand a problem, but the group or the village understands with disconcerting rapidity. It is true that if care is taken to use only a language that is understood by graduates in law and economics, you can easily prove that the masses have to be managed from above. But if you speak the language of everyday, if you are not obsessed by the perverse desire to spread confusion and to rid yourself of the people, then you will realize that the masses are quick to seize every shade of meaning and to learn all the tricks of the trade.[44]

In an Africa with no such revolutionary opportunities at present, one responsibility of applied intellectuals is surely, in the same humble spirit, to help develop issues and identify sites of interrelationship between sectors, spaces and scales of radical politics. An April 2002 conference of two such committed organizations – the Council for Development and Social Research in Africa and Third World Network-Africa – called upon 'scholars and activist intellectuals within Africa and in the diaspora, to join forces with social groups whose interests and needs are central to the development of Africa'.[45] This is a good mandate: in Africa, everywhere, very urgently indeed.

CONCLUSION: FROM LOOTING TO LIBERATION

The looting of Africa dates back many centuries, to the point at which value transfers began via appropriation of slave labour, antiquities, precious metals and raw materials. Unfair terms of trade were soon amplified by colonial and neocolonial relations. These processes often amounted to a kind of 'primitive accumulation', by which capital of Northern countries grew by virtue of looting Africa.

But, as this book demonstrates, this was not a once-off set of problems, solved by the 1950s-90s independence struggles. In recent decades, wealth extraction through imperialist relations has intensified, and some of the same kinds of primitive looting tactics are now once again evident. Moreover, key causes of Africa's underdevelopment since the early 1980s can also be identified within the framework of *neoliberal* (free market) policies adopted nearly universally across the continent and indeed the world, in part thanks to the emergence of local allies of the North within African states.

This book has considered arguments emerging from the neoliberal camp, and the most obvious rebuttals. The mainstream impression –

for example, Tony Blair's Commission for Africa – is mistaken when it cites what appears to be a vast inflow of aid, for 'phantom aid' should be taken into consideration. Instead of a sustainable level of debt service payments, as claimed by those supporting the elites' limited debt relief schemes, Africa's net financial accounts went negative during the 1990s. And although remittances from the African diaspora now fund a limited amount of capital accumulation, capital flight is far greater. At more than US$10 billion/year since the early 1970s, collectively, the citizens of Nigeria, Côte d'Ivoire, the DRC, Angola and Zambia have been especially vulnerable to the overseas draining of their national wealth. In addition to the lifting of exchange controls, a major factor during the late 1990s was financial deregulation. In South Africa, for example, financial liberalization included the relisting of the primary share-issuing residence of the largest South African firms: from Johannesburg to London.

Likewise, trade liberalization has cost sub-Saharan Africa $272 billion since the early 1980s, according to Christian Aid. Trade is especially difficult to rely upon for growth, given that agricultural subsidies accruing to Northern farmers rose from the late 1980s to 2004 by 15 per cent, to $279 billion, mainly benefiting large agro-corporate producers. Flows of people – a veritable brain drain – have also been formidable, but the value of wealth lost to the process is incalculable, given that more than 15 per cent of Africa's best-educated professionals now live outside the continent.

Non-financial investment flows are driven less by policy – although liberalization has also been important – and more by accumulation opportunities. Foreign direct investment to sub-Saharan Africa began rising in the late 1990s after two decades of stagnation. But the vast bulk of investments were accounted for in two major processes: South African capital's changed domicile, and resurgent oil investments (especially in Angola and Nigeria).

In the latter cases, a report by the World Bank (*Where Is the Wealth of Nations?*) acknowledges stagnant and net negative 'genuine savings' in countries with high resource dependence and low capital accumulation. These include Nigeria, Zambia, Mauritania, Gabon, Congo, Algeria and South Africa. Worst of all, Gabon's people lost $2,241 each in 2000 due to oil company depletion of the country's tangible wealth, followed by the Republic of the Congo (–$727), Nigeria (–$210), Cameroon (–$152), Mauritania (–$147) and Côte d'Ivoire (–$100). A

few countries do benefit under this broader definition (the Seychelles,
Botswana and Namibia). But the vast majority of African countries saw
their wealth depleted. Even industrialized South Africa saw its *per
capita* wealth drop by $2 in 2000 and the genuine savings rate was
reduced to just 6.9 per cent of national income once a variety of other
factors associated with natural resource depletion are included.

Moreover, much of Africa – including South Africa – has been
victimized by privatization-related foreign investment. Transparency
International blames part of the 'disappointment in many African
countries' upon corruption. Other forms of corruption occur through
tax fraud and transfer pricing.

The ecological debt that the North owes the South, especially Africa,
is also vast. Joan Martinez-Alier and UN climate change commissioner
Jyoti Parikh estimate that a total annual subsidy of $75 billion is
provided by the Third World to polluting countries merely in the form
of the 'carbon sink' function.

Reflecting another form of non-market exploitation, women are the
main victims of neoliberalism, whether in productive circuits of capital
(increasingly subject to sweatshop conditions) or in the sphere of
reproduction, where much primitive accumulation occurs through
unequal gender power relations. This is especially evident in the case
of migrant labour flows, largely because rural women have roles in
childrearing, healthcare and the care of elders that maintain an
artificially inexpensive supply of labour.

In identifying policies that might reverse these flows, we had to
enquire whether African countries have gone 'off track', as the IMF
argues unconvincingly in explaining the continent's residual failures.
Instead, as warned by critics such as Fanon and Cabral, a post-
independence cadreship of petit-bourgeois leaders were 'on track' in a
different way: in their loyalty to Northern objectives. During the
1980s–90s, 'comprador' politicians were joined by the establishment
of a formal neoliberal 'technocratic' corps within ministries of finance,
central banks and agencies, with oversight mandates for privatization
and commercialization.

At a time when the World Bank has also begun to highlight the idea
of 'leadership' in Africa, vehicles such as the NEPAD Africa Peer
Review Mechanism, for example, will be given higher status than
African social movements yet contemplate. And it is the government in
Pretoria that plays the most active 'subimperial' role on the continent,

with not only NEPAD to its credit, but a range of other attempts to relegitimize neoliberalism and US-dominated geopolitics.

All of these problems mean that progressive African activists may now be in a position to build upon their fellow citizenries' basic scepticism towards ruling elites. The challenge will be to establish not only alternative conceptions of their problems, but also a different approach to public policy and politics.

Those conceptions are not limited to a set of policy reforms (though such can be provided whenever necessary, drawing upon real experiences in history and across the contemporary world). Most importantly, this chapter has argued, the solution to the looting of Africa is to be found in the self-activity of progressive Africans themselves, in their campaigns and declarations, their struggles – sometimes victorious but still mainly frustrated – and their hunger for an Africa finally able to throw off the chains of an exploitative world economy and a power elite who treat the continent without respect.

NOTES

1 Quarmby, K. (2005), 'Is Oxfam Failing Africa?', *New Statesman*, 30 May.

2 Frith, M. (2005), 'Celebrities "Hijacked" Poverty Campaign, say Furious Charities', *Independent*, 27 December.

3 Hertz, N. (2005), 'We Achieved Next to Nothing', *New Statesman*, 12 December.

4 Hodkinson, S. (2005), 'G8, Africa Nil', *Red Pepper* and *Counterpunch*, 27 October.

5 GCAP's website is <http://www.whiteband.org>. Critiques of GCAP and Make Poverty History are found in two mid-2005 articles by myself, Dennis Brutus and Virginia Setshedi: 'Are Mainstream NGOs Failing Africa?', in *ZNet Commentary* (21 June 2005), *Global Dialogue* (August 2005); and 'When Wearing White Is Not Chic, and Collaboration Not Cool', in *Pambazuka, Counterpunch*, and *Foreign Policy in Focus* (17 June 2005).

6 Antrobus, P. (2003), 'Presentation to Working Group on the MDGs and Gender Equality', UNDP Caribbean Regional Millennium Development Goals Conference, Barbados, 7 July. Citations below are from this paper.

7 Antrobus argues: 'The deliberate exclusion of this fundamental indicator of women's human rights and empowerment from the MDGs symbolizes both the lack of sincerity on the part of the majority of those who voted on them, and the struggle that lies ahead for anyone who seriously seeks equality, equity and empowerment for women.'

8 Waruru, W. (2005), 'IMF, World Bank Come Under Heavy Criticism', *East*

African Standard (Nairobi), 18 January.

9   UN Habitat, 'Urban Management Programme', website <http://hq.unhabitat.org/cdrom/ump/CD/about.html>, accessed 7 July 2005.

10 Minority Rights Group International (2005), 'The Millennium Development Goals: Helping or Harming Minorities?' Presentation to UN Commission on Human Rights Sub-Commission on Promotion and Protection of Human Rights, Working Group on Minorities, New York, 30 May.

11 United Nations Development Programme (2003), *Human Development Report 2003. Millennium Development Goals: a Compact among Nations to End Human Poverty*, New York, p. 3.

12 Naidoo, K. (2005), 'Civil Society Gears up for a Major Global Campaign against Poverty', statement by Civicus Secretary General and Chief Executive Officer, Johannesburg, 21 January.

13 Vandemoortele, J., K. Malhotra and J. Lim (2003), 'Is MDG 8 on Track as a Global Deal for Human Development?', United Nations Development Programme Bureau for Development Policy, Socio-economic Development Group, New York, June.

14 Bond, P. (2004), *Talk Left, Walk Right: South Africa's Frustrated Global Reforms*, Pietermaritzburg, University of KwaZulu-Natal Press.

15 Mbeki, T. (2005), 'The UN Millennium Review – Time Running Out!', Address of the President of South Africa at the United Nations Millennium Review Summit Meeting, New York, 15 September, p. 3.

16 García-Delgado, V. (2005), 'The Big Letdown: UN Summit Shortchanges the Poor', Civicus statement, New York, 16 September.

17 The companies included IBM, General Motors, Exxon Mobil, JP Morgan Chase, Citigroup, Caltex Petroleum Corporation, Ford Motor Company and the Fluor Corporation.

18 In June 2004, the Supreme Court confirmed the applicability of the Act to such cases, although it also warned courts to bear in mind US foreign policy objectives.

19 For details see Bond, *Talk Left, Walk Right*, Chapter 3.

20 Jubilee South Africa (2005), 'Strike Against Corporate Greed!', Johannesburg, 23 September.

21 Seddon, D. and L. Zeilig (2005), 'Class and Protest in Africa: New Waves', *Review of African Political Economy*, 103, pp. 16–22.

22 SouthScan (2004), 'Massive Strike Against Austerity Plan,' 24 February. For background to the failed privatizations on the Zambian copperbelt and formidable popular resistance to national bank privatization, as well as the exhaustion of neonationalist official politics, see Larmer, M. (2005), 'Reaction and Resistance to Neoliberalism in Zambia', *Review of African Political Economy*, 103.

23 <http://www.aidc.org.za>

24 Social movement attendees at the founding conference (25–26 April 2004) included Association of Communities Organizing for Reform Now, US; CEIBA, Guatemala; Citizens Network for Essential Services, US; CODDEFFAGOLF,

Honduras; COPINH, Honduras; Council of Canadians; Freedom from Debt Coalition, Philippines; Jubilee South, Philippines; Jubilee South Africa; MPNKP, Haiti; Narmada Bachao Andolan, India; Halifax Initiative Coalition, Canada; and Soweto Electricity Crisis Committee, South Africa.

25 These included Center for Economic and Policy Research, US; Center for Economic Justice, US; CEJ Southern Africa, South Africa; CIEPAC, Mexico; Development Gap/SAPRIN, US; Focus on the Global South, Thailand/India; Institute for Global Networking, Information and Studies, Norway; Public Citizen, US; and Rocky Mountain Peace and Justice Center, US.

26 <http://www.worldbankboycott.org>. Organizations that have endorsed the boycott included major religious orders (the Conference of Major Superiors of Men, Pax Christi USA, the Unitarian Universalist General Assembly, and dozens of others); the most important social responsibility funds (Calvert Group, Global Greengrants Fund, Ben and Jerry's Foundation, and Trillium Assets Management); the University of New Mexico endowment fund; US cities (including San Francisco, Milwaukee, Boulder and Cambridge); and major trade union pension/investment funds (e.g., Teamsters, Postal Workers, Service Employees International, American Federation of Government Employees, Long-shoremen, Communication Workers of America, United Electrical Workers).

27 Shirin (2005), 'Thousands Rally Against "Economic Apartheid"', InterPress Services, Washington, 24 September.

28 Lambert, L. (2005), 'Thousands in US Protest Iraq War, Globalization', Reuters, 25 September.

29 Mobilization for Global Justice (2005), 'Block the Bank! Fight the Fund! Reclaim Our Communities! Confront Economic Violence and Corporate Capitalism during the World Bank and IMF Annual Meetings', Washington, 21 July.

30 According to a transcript, the meeting's chair, Civicus board president Aruna Rao, opened the meeting by joking – revealingly? – about the mock Bank/Pentagon wedding ('We hope that despite the recent marriage you will be open to a liaison with Civil Society Organizations') and closing with praise for Wolfowitz's 'openness to dialogue with civil society organizations on a range of issues. So I will go back to how I started. I think this liaison, despite the marriage, is something that can continue.' An alternative approach for progressive civil society groups, in contrast, is to frankly acknowledge the marriage of neoliberalism and militarism and break off any further liaisons. The meeting also included outgoing Development Committee chair Trevor Manuel's blame-the-victim critique of his constituents who suffer from both TB and persistent unemployment (<http://www.imf.org/external/np/tr/2005/tr050 922a.htm>).

31 Reddy, S. (2005), 'The World Development Report 2006: a Brief Review', unpublished paper, Columbia University, New York.

32 For more on the historic dispute over financial power, see Bond, P. (2004), 'Bankrupt Africa: Imperialism, Subimperialism and Financial Politics',

Historical Materialism, 12, 4.

33 Gramsci, A. (1971), *Selections from the Prison Notebooks*, New York: International Publishers, pp. 238, 243.

34 Burawoy, M. (2003), 'For a Sociological Marxism: the Complementary Convergence of Antonio Gramsci and Karl Polanyi', *Politics and Society*, 31, 2.

35 Polanyi, K. (1957), *The Great Transformation: the Political and Economic Origins of Our Time*, Boston, Beacon, p. 76.

36 The signatories – 18 men and, regrettably, just one woman – were Aminata Traoré, Adolfo Pérez Esquivel, Eduardo Galeano, José Saramago, François Houtart, Boaventura de Sousa Santos, Armand Mattelart, Roberto Savio, Riccardo Petrella, Ignacio Ramonet, Bernard Cassen, Samir Amin, Atilio Boron, Samuel Ruiz Garcia, Tariq Ali, Frei Betto, Emir Sader, Walden Bello and Immanuel Wallerstein. In a comradely critique, published at <http://www.zmag.org/sustainers/content/2005-02/22bond.cfm> on 22 February 2005 ('Discussing the Porto Alegre Manifesto'), I offer minor friendly amendments.

37 Ngwane, T. (2005), 'WSF 2007 in Africa Must Build a Mass Movement against Capitalism', unpublished paper, 7 February, Johannesburg.

38 <http://www.africansocialforum.org/english/charter.htm>.

39 Grubacic, A. (2003), 'Life After Social Forums: New Radicalism and the Questions of Attitude towards Social Forums', <http://www.nadir.org/nadir/initiativ/agp/free/wsf/life-after-sf.htm>. See also the deservedly influential writings of Naomi Klein, e.g., (2003), 'The Hijacking of the World Social Forum', <http://www.nologo.org>, 30 January.

40 Hardt, M. and A. Negri (2004), *Multitude*, New York, Penguin, pp. xii, xiii, 88, 135.

41 Desai, A. and R. Pithouse (2004), 'Sanction All Revolts: a Reply to Rebecca Pointer', *Journal of Asian and African Studies*, 39, 4, p. 300.

42 Rodney, W. (1972), *How Europe Underdeveloped Africa*, Dar es Salaam, Tanzania Publishing House and London, Bogle L'Ouverture Publications; <http://www.marxists.org/subject/africa/rodney-walter/how-europe/>.

43 Of course, conditions are not easy in most sites of African intellectual work, with many academics surviving on less than US$100 a month pay. Even in once proud universities like Dar es Salaam and Makerere, former progressive intellectuals are prone to taking jobs or consultancies with multilateral agencies, donors, corporations and wealthy Northern NGOs, instead of devoting time and energies to unremunerated, risky work on behalf of civil societies.

44 Fanon, F. (1963), *The Wretched of the Earth*, New York, Grove Press, p. 189.

45 Council for Development and Social Science Research in Africa, Dakar and Third World Network-Africa (2002), 'Declaration on Africa's Development Challenges', adopted at the Joint Conference on Africa's Development Challenges in the Millennium, Accra, 23–26 April.

Index

165